24 0522905 5

PHL

KT-579-502

94060000300623

REFERENCE ONLY
DO NOT REMOVE

Business Information
at Work

WITHDRAWN

Michael Lowe

INFORMATION MANAGEMENT

0 4 OCT 2000

R658:016 LOW

Published by Aslib/IMI

ISBN 0 85142 403 1

© Michael Lowe 1999

Except as otherwise permitted under the Copyright, Designs and Patents Act 1988, this publication may only be reproduced, stored or transmitted in any form or by any means, with the prior permission in writing of the publisher. Enquiries concerning reproduction outside these terms should be sent to Aslib at the address below.

The author asserts his moral right to be identified as such in accordance with the terms of the Copyright, Designs and Patents Act 1988.

Information Management International (IMI) is a trading name of Aslib.

Aslib/IMI provides consultancy and information services, professional development training, conferences, specialist recruitment, Internet products, and publishes primary and secondary journals, conference proceedings, directories and monographs.

Aslib, The Association for Information Management, founded in 1924, is a world class corporate membership organisation with over 2000 members in some 70 countries. Aslib actively promotes best practice in the management of information resources. It lobbies on all aspects of the management of, and legislation concerning, information at local, national and international levels.

Further information is available from:

Aslib/IMI
Staple Hall
Stone House Court
London EC3A 7PB
Tel: +44 (0) 20 7903 0000
Fax: +44 (0) 20 7903 0011
Email: *aslib@aslib.co.uk*
WWW: *http://www.aslib.co.uk/*

THE BRITISH MUSEUM

THE PAUL HAMLYN LIBRARY

028.7 LOW

About the Author

With a background as a lending and a reference librarian, Michael Lowe now teaches in the Department of Information and Library Studies at the University of Wales Aberystwyth, where he has created a course on business information. He currently also teaches information retrieval, and coordinates first year undergraduate studies and the department's online services. He has monitored the development of business and business information sources in former communist countries with interest, having worked as a consultant in Poland, Hungary and Russia, among other countries, and constantly records developments in worldwide sources available to British businesses, with a special interest in the revolution brought about by online services and the Internet. His previous publications include a bibliography of sources of business information, and reports and articles on the state of business information sources and services in countries around the world.

Contents

List of Figures

List of Tables

Permissions

Diagram of corporate structure of Voyager Investments [BVI] Limited on page 24 reprinted by permission of Jordans Ltd.

Web site of The Groves Hotel, Aberystwyth on page 29 reprinted by permission of The Groves Hotel.

'Data sources: the ultimate business universe' from Dun & Bradstreet on page 33 reprinted by permission of Dun & Bradstreet Reference Services.

Annual periodical prices from *Library Association Record* on page 99 copyright Library Association; reprinted by permission. Acknowlegement is also made to Blackwells for allowing us to reprint their data reproduced in this survey.

Example of statistics of business relevance from *Social Trends* 28 p. 102; Office of National Statistics © 1998; reprinted by permission.

Map of the City of London on page 145 taken from a Slaughter and May brochure and reprinted with their permission.

Yahoo! UK and Ireland Finance opening page on page 161 © Yahoo! Inc. 1999; reprinted by permission of Yahoo! Inc.

Headline from *Construction News* 22.10.98 on page 188 copyright *Construction News* and reprinted with their permission

Worldsearch-Wireline search using Infosort categories p. 264

Contents page from Profound Quicksearch on page 272 copyright Dialog Corporation; reprinted with their permission.

Dow Jones Interactive home page on page 274 copyright Dow Jones Interactive; reprinted with their permission.

Norfolk and Waveney Business Link Home page on page 301 reprinted by permission of Norfolk and Waveney Enterprise Partnership.

Preface

In many ways business information is as old as business itself; sought on the same subjects for the same reasons as it always was. In other ways, especially the wealth of it, and in the form of delivery, it has changed beyond recognition in recent years. This book is offered as a bridge in the gulf between the business decision maker and the new world of information waiting to be discovered. Businesses continue to grow less capital and infrastructure intensive, and more people intensive, and therefore knowledge intensive. The globalisation of both markets and communication, the expansion of 'Ecommerce', the increase in competition, and tightening of margins; all demand systematic exploitation of the corporate resource which is information. Experts assert that it is information management which will be the main strategic weapon of the first decade of the 21st century.

There is no time like the present for a manager to take business information seriously, and for boardrooms to implement convictions on the value of information, knowledge, and its scientific management. Proliferation of PCs, graphic user interfaces and the Internet are making the information or knowledge society a reality; internal and external information resources have become accessible, flexible and credible in the eyes of senior management. They are embracing terms like *intranets, data mining, push technology, intelligent agents* and *disintermediation,* for concepts which are not all quite so new. The suppliers of information are enthusiastically using the same knowledge imperative and IT revolution to reach more end-users more fruitfully than ever before, repackaging their products to attract any user with a networked PC, laptop or mobile phone. Much of the information industry is already concentrating on managing all the information now assaulting the decision maker, and avoiding the consequences of information overload.

The book is aimed at any user or potential user of business information, whether more a searcher, or more a consumer of the results. It aims to do something which is all too rare: to relate together the points of view of information providers, information professionals and business people. Building the bridge between business' need and potential information, requires a considered view of this magic triangle of components. The book is theoretical in that it analyses and categorises relevant elements of businesses and external information, and practical to the extent that it relates real information needs to specific types and named examples of information sources and services.

Business information is defined here as it has come to be understood by a large industry and profession: as information on those factors outside and largely beyond the control of the business which have a direct commercial significance. It is information on what has been called the external, or macro, or marketing environment, to distinguish it from a business' equally significant internal environment. Any factor in the external environment can be the subject of business information; but not everything *about* a factor has the direct commercial effect which distinguishes it as business information. External factors and the business information sources which report on them, fall naturally into 'domains'; it is common to refer to the major divisions of business information as 'company information'; 'market information'; 'City' or 'financial information'; 'product information'; and 'country' or 'geopolitical information'. The terms 'news information' and 'industry information' describe major exceptions to the above domain or subject approach. Of course these groupings are not mutually exclusive, and do not always coincide with either the information need of the decision maker, or the scope of a source; alternative classifications and terms exist.

Left out of this approach are the clearly important external influences of technology, legislation, economics and so on; the reason is that like management and other essential professional skills, these domains less often exert a commercial effect. Thus for most purposes a business person can use the dedicated technical, legal and other information infrastructure. We shall also find sources covering these subjects for commercial purposes, under headings above such as 'country information' and 'industry information'. In the effort to build the bridge between available information and its incorporation in business decisions, chapters 2 to 7 correspond to the business information divisions identified above. Each has the same three roles: to consider the business person's problems and information needs in relation to the subject; to examine the relevant primary information which exists; and to characterise and evaluate the available sources. Current significant examples of sources are named and illustrated where appropriate, with an awareness of the fact that details are likely to change very quickly. Examples are cited as being potentially worth pursuing, but not as recommendations.

One of the book's objectives is to lead the user to appropriate sources for each of the many subjects and purposes discussed, nevertheless this is by no means an exhaustive guide to business information sources. Sources of further information are given at the end of each chapter, and systematic guides to sources are given in the 'Identification and Selection of Sources' section of the final chapter. The versions of sources, and the routes to them which are referred to, are not necessarily the only ones; similarly, where the name of an online host is given in connection with a database, that is not necessarily the only or best host. Sufficient information is given to trace the many sources discussed or listed, despite the fact that details such as URLs and publication dates are liable to frequent change. The author has no commercial interest in any information products or services; coverage is only influenced by what has been said, written, discovered from guides to sources, products and product literature seen.

Chapter 1 considers the relationship between a business and the external factors which affect it; and introduces the types of information and source through which it can sense those which affect it commercially. Chapter 8 complements the others by providing an overview of the means of systematically exploiting so much information, including the role of information intermediaries, the Internet, and of online hosts. Where appropriate in chapters, needs and sources are seen from the point of view of the UK business person; which of course does not exclude coverage of Europe, the USA or the rest of the world.

1

Business Information at Work

The Role of Information in *Scientific* Management

Management becomes ever more objective, professional, scientific and knowledge-based, and ever less based on subjectivity or chance. We assume that this has resulted from a combination of increased motivation to make money, increased accountability, and not least the development of enabling methods, including information and communications technology. All of which stems from and leads to increased competition, and even more scientific management.

And yet making business decisions is by no means a precise science. Deciding which product to develop, which distributor to use, which currency or shares to invest in, involves a gamble, a leap into the unknown. No amount of research on the past and present behaviour of the factors involved will predict a future outcome with any certainty, because the factors are often many, complex, and interact in unpredictable ways to result in an even more uncertain future outcome. However, far from spinning a coin in such circumstances, like a canny racing punter, the business decision maker gathers the established facts, assembles data on the influencing factors, processes the whole through an actual or mental computer model, and *then* gambles. As so often in business, the combination of quantitative and qualitative, hard and soft information, skill and experience only reduces uncertainty, lowers the risk and shortens the odds. Nevertheless, judicious use of that information so often proves to be the most important variable between two decisions and two competitors, leading to an all important margin equating to success or failure, profit and loss.

Perhaps because to a scientific manager the contribution of hard or soft information is obvious; perhaps because the new electronic information media have high credibility, successful businesses and business people are indeed very systematic about information. We find *communications audits* and *information audits* preceding valuations of *corporate knowledge*, the latter even appearing on some firms' balance sheets. We find integrated management of information gathering and purchasing, of information flows in, out, and around; and of dissemination and storage. The term *knowledge management* (as opposed to *information management*) has been adopted by many to emphasise the financial value of the corporate resource of information in minds, filing cabinets and databases, and to acknowledge that to be truly effective, data has to be converted into information, and information into knowledge. As well as creating and gathering information, its sharing and exploitation must be effected by a combination of systems, technology, organisational and personal culture.

The Business in its Environment

Business information was defined in the preface as information on the external factors which directly affect commercial decisions or performance. So almost by definition, any business needs such information, and so does any other organisation or individual that this could apply to. It is obvious that a car maker in a free market economy lives or dies according to its performance in the market, but not so obvious that a university loses income and staff if others attract more students; or that the value of an individual's savings is affected by the government's policy on inflation.

The external factors affecting a business' performance, and therefore its decisions, are potentially many; they interact with each other as well as in some cases directly with the business itself. They can be envisaged rather like an ominous sky: a dividing and coalescing mass of threats and opportunities hovering over any organisation and activity subject to competition or market forces. To succeed, it is of course necessary to get the internal house in order at the same time, attuning its strategies and its operations to fit the external

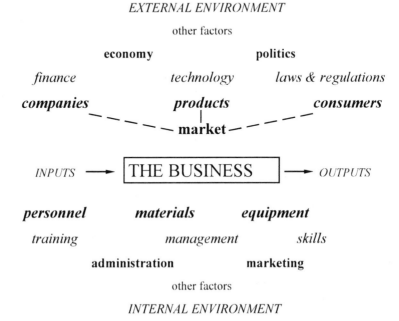

Figure 1. The business in its environment

environment. Monitoring the internal environment using a *management in-formation system* has to be complemented by constant monitoring or scanning, as well as, when necessary, answering specific questions about the external environment. The latter involves business or commercial information, but the system does not have a generally accepted separate name. In an organisation where information is well managed and integrated, relevant information on both environments is brought together for use at the points where decisions are made. It has already been said that a business depends on input from outside on many professional, technical and managerial matters; however, the least controllable factor, the one needing most careful watching because of its commercial significance, is its position in relation to the commercial external environment.

A business does not sense the commercial environment through touch or smell, nor simply through the disappearance through its doors of goods and services. The only realistic interface with the outside world is data, humanly or automatically recorded as words or numbers. When communicated it has information value, and when added in the right context to a recipient's existing knowledge, it can solve problems, or at least inform decision making. The role of this book is to consider what businesses need to know about that environment, in order best to position themselves in it, and to help in finding and using the information which can provide the answers.

Strategic Decision Making

Among all the operations of a business, it is decision making and planning of a strategic nature which makes the greatest demands for information on the external environment. It requires ongoing monitoring for developments which would change the position of the business in relation to its market or other environments, and ad hoc research for particular purposes. In neither case is it easy to predict what information will be relevant, or to recognise it when found. Such research may be time intensive, involve a wide range of source material, producing much data, which may do no more than confirm what was suspected, or marginally reduce uncertainty. Which is not to say that it would not save or gain millions of pounds, or make the difference between boom or bust!

Checking for relevant environmental factors in strategic decision making is no different from a surgeon checking for a heart condition before major surgery. Just as the patient's death might result from a failure to use medical information, it should equally be considered neglectful to ignore the available information in managing a stock market flotation, a takeover bid, a new product line, or just a business' continuing market position. Given the number of complex variables affecting future business outcomes, it is necessary to be aware of factors beyond those immediately responsible for an effect. A currency speculator looks far beyond past and present prices in order to best guess future prices, probably to consider company performance in the country; market trends and the social and economic factors which will affect consumers; the economic outlook, and the way political and other factors might affect that; and of course the comparative performance of other currencies which might affect the first.

Models of the external commercial environment usually show immediate and less immediate (or *indirect*) layers of identifiable factors (or *domains*, or *environments*). In reality the immediacy of the effect of a domain depends on the particular business, its particular circumstances, and the aspect of it being considered. Nevertheless, it is reasonable to place other businesses in the immediate environment, as well as products and services, and private consumers. Any business, by definition, is most dependent on and affected by competitors, suppliers, customers and products – including their interaction in 'the market', so almost everything about those aspects of the environment is of interest. Some models describe the factors which directly affect a business or are directly affected by it as the 'task environment', and include regulatory bodies among its domains. A business relates directly to its task environment, and can have some influence or even control over it. In these models the 'general' or outer environment is considered beyond the influence of a business, and more often impacts on a business via the task environment.

All models demonstrate that businesses are less often and less directly affected by certain identifiable areas of their external environment, and it is harder to predict which aspects of the rest of this wide world have significance for any given business or business decision within it. Thus the rest of the external environment is regarded as business' indirect, outer or general external environment. Significant areas are separately identified: such as money, the economy, politics, technology, laws and regulations. Because domains other than the first are so wide, and their significance for business so unpredictable, business people are not best served by the detailed documentation associated with each, but need sources which monitor, collate and analyse from the business point of view. Many of these do exist, either related to specific domains above, or for the diverse topics they do not include, related to specific countries. Relevant chapters of this book similarly concern themselves with the business-oriented sources, rather than the specialist economic, legal, scientific and other literatures.

Rather than as separate entities in an outer layer affecting an inner layer, as below, it is as well to envisage external commercial factors in a network structure, where each potentially interacts with every other as well as potentially directly with a business. The diagram is intended to show that the environment does not just impinge on a business through the exposure of its products to the market, but also through inputs, such as raw materials, money, and human resources; and through internal operations, for example the effect of laws on employee welfare or the use of chemicals in consumer products.

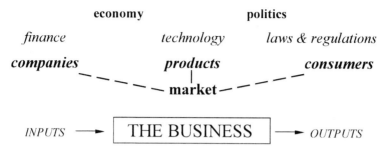

Figure 2. External commercial factors in a network structure

Operational and Tactical Decision Making

Observers have related different organisational functions to different levels of need and demand for business information. Decisions of operational and tactical levels are less often dependent on or affected by external factors than internal ones. When they require information on external factors, the need is simpler, and comparatively easy to satisfy with a definite factual answer. In fact it is debatable whether a question like 'Who is the sales director of Company X?' involves business information as we have defined it – it is certainly about business, but does not directly affect commercial decisions or performance. Like local planning regulations and tax legislation, for operational purposes such information just has to be acted on.

Business Information Demand and Use Variables

It follows from the earlier definition that every firm, organisation and individual doing business needs business information, and consciously, formally or not, gets it. It is salutary to consider how need for information the external environment may vary from business to business, or person to person – this is need perceived by an observer, and not the same thing as demand. It follows that if greater need for intelligence on the external environment attaches to the strategic management function, then absolute need should be related to the proportion of strategic work necessary in a particular organisation.

Indeed, there are permanent reasons for an unstable relationship between a business and its market, and temporary reasons, all of which have been found to equate to heightened need to scan the environment. The predominant permanent variable determining the level of business information need is the line of business, the product or service. Some business activities are inherently vulnerable, insecure and risky – where the degree of success or failure depends greatly on unpredictable future outcomes. Financial investment is an obvious example, compared with, say, catering at the other extreme; investment success is almost completely dependent on the outcome of many and complex, therefore unpredictable, factors. Unlike the food industry, investors yield no tangible product with an inherent value whatever the vagaries of the market place; all their efforts are directed at reducing the uncertainty of the many and complex factors which determine success or failure – a process which is entirely dependent on information. Industries with a similar reason for exceptionally high demand for external information include financial services in general, insurance and actuaries. Due mainly to their strategic consultancy role, where the product again stands or falls according to hard-to-predict future outcomes, management consultants and consulting accountants demonstrate a very high business information need and demand. Coming somewhere between the caterer and the stock broker are players in markets which are unpredictable because of volatility of technology, and even fashion. This is true of pharmaceuticals, information technology and the fashion industry itself; though it must be said that it can be even harder to reduce risk in rock bands, soccer teams and cult toys than in the stock market.

A second notable permanent variable is organisation type. Some businesses have to be more scientific in their monitoring for external threats and opportunities, because they are either financially vulnerable, and/or highly accountable. In particular, PLCs have high expectations of professionalism and efficiency placed upon them by current and potential shareholders. Although some are near-monopolies, the privatised UK public utilities make a far higher demand for business information than they did as public sector organisations; their aim has to be growth in size as well as in share price. Hence the conclusion that organisational vulnerability makes for competitiveness in both internal and external spheres of operation. The limited financial liability afforded to owners of registered private companies, and responsibility limited to two or more owners, combined often with a product whose future market position is thought predictable, probably explains the surprisingly low use of external information by in particular small manufacturing firms. It probably helps explain the high failure rate of small enterprises also.

Less permanent characteristics of businesses known to affect business information need and demand include the degree of competitiveness of the market, resulting from factors including degree of concentration, convergence and market maturity; and related changes such as new players, new products and new trade areas or agreements. Other more temporary organisational factors include structural changes like mergers, takeovers, public flotation and re-engineering, leading to voluntary or forced repositioning in relation to the market, and a short-term need for information on the unknown.

Variability in Demand and Use

The fact that there is a gap between need and demand for business information, is a matter of concern for producers, intermediaries and potential users alike. Research shows time and time again that too many business people look no further than internal information sources as a basis for commercial decisions. A survey commissioned by the Library Association in 1996 did confirm a coincidence between the 'line of business' variable described above, and prominence of an information policy within a firm (Jenny Baxter, 'The Trade in Information', *Library Association Record*, 99 (1), pp. 28-29). However, the overwhelming impression was of the low profile of systematic information or knowledge management in up to one half of the 994 companies. Again, permanent and temporary reasons can be identified, relating to factors like business size, wealth, training and past experiences of employees; and whether the management functions associated with high levels of external information need are differentiated within the organisation – such as managing director, marketing manager, market analyst, information manager. The designation of an information manager or information unit leads to increased information usage, even to increased demands on external services, and if the research reported in the next section is to be believed, is associated with successful businesses.

Problems and Advantages in Exploiting Information

Unfortunately the very nature of documentary information can be a deterrent to the busy, pragmatic business person, more at home with more tangible commodities, and using the evidence of their own eyes, ears, and personal contacts. Recent studies discussed and cited in the final chapter, quantify the problems presented to managers by the volume and complexity of information sources. Information is strange and problematic in that it is not diminished by being used, effort is required to unlock it from data, and its value depends so much on time and context. It is often expected to be free, and yet it can also be very expensive. Although knowledge is gaining recognition as the most valuable resource, we rarely attempt to cost the results of the use or lack of information, or the value of corporate information or knowledge. It is not surprising so many people tacitly subscribe to the adage that information gathering is rather like hand washing: desirable but not strictly necessary. 'Many of Europe's family-run firms are operating in the dark . . .' was the opening statement of a report in the *Sunday Times* of a survey carried out by Grant Thornton (*Sunday Times Business*, 13th September 1998, pp. 3-14). Fewer than a third of family businesses in Europe were monitoring early-warning signals such as the declining credit-status of debtors and outstanding orders.

Unfortunately the effects of the use or non-use of information is difficult to detect directly, and even harder to quantify in financial terms. Business information publishers and information managers do sometimes attempt to do so; tangible benefits gained by business users of public libraries were reported in the The Library Association's Business Survey of 1997 (*Library Association Record*, 99(12), p. 665; extract given under 'Public Libraries' in the 'Information Services' section of the 'Accessing Business Information' chapter). The book *Great Information Disasters* (edited by F. Horton and D. Lewis, Aslib, 1991) drew attention to more dramatic incidences of information deficiency. Research has attempted to equate information usage with success or failure in business, and not surprisingly found that success coincides with effective information policy, gathering and usage. The data below were reported by PricewaterhouseCoopers in a 1996 issue of their *Trendsetter Barometer*, based on interviews with 400 CEOs of the fastest-growing US companies:

Competitor information is:		
	Not important	14%
	Somewhat important	37%
	Very important	31%
	Of critical importance	18%
	Critical/Very important	49%

Ironically, equally outstanding in this data is the fact that over half of the leading companies rank competitor information as no more than 'somewhat important'. However it was calculated that **'Companies that value information as a competitive tool grew 200% faster, showed 80% higher revenues and 33% higher productivity than the others surveyed.'**

Despite the demonstrable advantages, acquiring information is sufficiently complex to explain why someone like a hairdresser, who is owner, manager, hair stylist, marketing manager and everything else, neglects it. The subject, source and physical medium of useful information is often hard to predict, compounded by the fact that it may not be up to date, or reliable, or make any measurable difference to a business outcome anyway, even if it exists. Systematic information acquisition is especially daunting if the person has little experience of information retrieval, the related technology or of intermediary services, and if their only past experience was not a positive one!

The following chapters exist to show that business information is too good to miss, and to reduce the mysteries associated with acquiring it. At least they should inspire the confidence to have a meaningful dialogue with an informational professional.

The Business Information Industry

A well-established and financially-viable business information industry exists today, the centre of gravity of which is source producers – otherwise known as publishers, content providers or information providers. Also significant are source distributors; and intermediaries between sources and ultimate users of a different kind – commercial providers of information services. In fact the volume and probably the value of *subsidised* intermediary services is high compared with private sector information brokers. At the turn of the millennium the industry is being shaken by the wholesale switch to the Internet as the delivery medium, with its immediate accessibility to businesses and individuals worldwide. New players are threatening to eclipse established quality content providers, as is the devaluation of content by the widespread availability of free information. Commercial success now depends more on the value added to the data, by for instance 'push technology' and 'intelligent agent' software. As Martin White of TFPL said, in a paper to the UKOLUG Conference, Manchester, 1998, 'content is not king, the edge is in bundling and branding'.

The diagram below models the transmission of business information from its creation to its consumption, showing the main areas of value-adding activity.

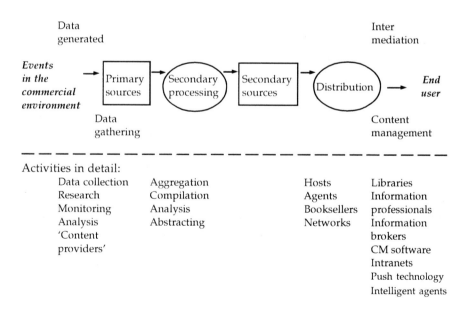

*Figure 3. The transmission of business information from its creation to
its consumption*

In 1998, Martin White of business information consultants TFPL broke down the business information market in terms of commercial significance, as in the left column below. Counting the entries in each section as a proportion of all databases, in the 1999 edition of Online/CD-ROM Business Sourcebook, yields the breakdown on the right (CD-ROMs comprised over 30% of all the database). Though not directly comparable, the figures show striking differences between volume and value in the industry:

By commercial value		By number of databases	
Real time financial	30%	Economics and finance	12%
Credit	16%	Company directories	19%
Company	14%	Company financial data	8%
Market	10%	Market data	8%
News	8%	Business and financial news	18%
Product	5%	Industries	14%
Other	17%	Legislation and regulations	5%
		Other	25%

Table 1. Breakdown of the business information market
by commercial value and number of databases

In business information, every distribution medium is used and has its role, with the emphasis very much on the electronic. In general, the CD-ROM format continues to be important for less time-sensitive data, while use of the Internet has vastly expanded as an online distribution channel aimed at end-users. Searching for business information usually involves searching a field-structured database, sometimes via hosts' command-driven search software, but much more likely in systems aimed at end-users, point and click graphic user interfaces. More direct use is made of publishers' online, on-disk or printed products, than indirect use via the online hosts which offer up to several hundred databases in a complementary range.

There are still many small specialist players, but convergence and concentration is progressive, acquisitions of smaller players constantly happening for defensive reasons. A few large corporate groups now compete for the high volume though not yet demonstrably lucrative mainstream business. In the English speaking Western world, the financial media giant Pearson, and an American equivalent Knight Ridder, had bought into parallel ranges of information providers, and the most used online business database hosts. Just as the Internet was though to be causing a switch away from mediated use of databases via hosts, to end-user access direct from providers, MAID has rapidly expanded from a market information provider and host, first to try to match the generalist business hosts, then buy the parallel Dialog and DataStar hosts from Knight Ridder to create the single Dialog Corporation. While all this goes on, the 'Big money news gatherers' as they have been called, including Reuters in the UK and Bloomberg in the USA, continue a more lucrative business centred on the distribution of real-time information from the world's financial markets.

Characteristics of Sources

The information products themselves centre on many, often overlapping sources of information on what this book has called the immediate external commercial environment; that is: other companies, products, and consumers, mainly because these are components of the all-important market. There are fewer information sources on all the other environmental factors which may be relevant to a business; those that exist tend to complement existing specialist literature by orienting their treatment of subjects like technology, law, economics and politics to the needs of the strategic business decision maker. Partly for the providers' commercial reasons, the majority of business information products are secondary sources: that is, they add value, from a business person's point of view, for predictable business intelligence purposes, to primary information which first appeared in another form.

Effects of the Commercial Imperative

The existence of what on the face of it looks like a wealth of relevant information is due largely to its commercial value, leading to overlapping sources of the most commonly used and needed types, and lack of coverage of minority interest types. While most publishers or providers are businesses, charging what the market is willing to pay, the role of the public sector is vital in the collection of less commercially valuable primary information, and in assisting access to sources which for reasons of cost and/or ignorance would otherwise be underexploited.

Essential Qualities of Sources

From the user's point of view of information sources, it is essential that:

- a necessary topic is covered;
- information is accurate and reliable;
- information is up to date;
- information is in the form needed, or can be so manipulated;
- cost, format and availability make its use feasible.

None of these is necessarily affected by changes in the corporate structure of the providers; however, recent developments in information technology offer real advances in the last three of these, especially in terms of widening accessibility. Since most of the sources are in digital format, anyone with Internet access is today a potential user of the world's business information resources.

Problems of Sources

Problems inherent in exploiting information in business decision making, have already been discussed; different problems are associated with the actual sources which carry the information. There is the bibliographical problem of identifying the source which matches all the parameters of the information need – which are not only the right subject and the appropriate treatment, but also format, authority, cost, speed of access, language, and so on. Related to this, those quality criteria must be evaluated for the candidate sources, and when using them, the information contained. Among business information sources, high cost is often a factor, whether buying outright or paying as you go for online or 'metered' CD-ROM sources, necessitating both careful selection and efficient use. A typical range of bases for charging, and costs is given in the 'Online Hosts' section of the final chapter, and in the appendix. Accuracy, reliability and currency all vary between providers, sources, and the records within them, not only in subjective, predictive information like forecasts or credit ratings, but even in what should be established facts, such as company accounts figures. Business people, or information professionals on their behalf, have to rely on their knowledge of the source and its producer, combined with cross-checking, using a primary and non-documentary source if necessary. Any source has to be considered in satisfying business information needs, which often means going beyond published documents, and asking organisations or persons.

Further Sources

Ian Owens and Tom Wilson. *Information and Business Performance: A Study of Information Systems and Services in High Performing Companies.* Bowker-Saur, 1996.

Allan Taylor and Stephen Farrell. *Information Management for Business.* Aslib, 1994. Explores the role of internal and external information in business management.

2

Company Information

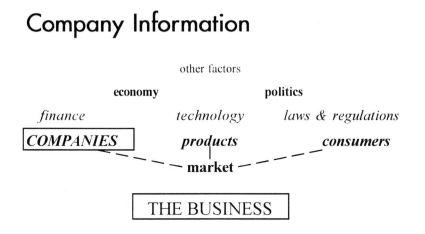

Different Relationships, Different Information Needs

Other enterprises are inescapable factors in any business' external environment. Most obviously they can be competitors, and therefore part of the market, not only competing with their outputs but even for inputs including employee skills, raw materials and components. Other firms might instead be actual or potential customers in the market, or suppliers and therefore creditors. Alternatively a second firm may not have a market relationship to the first, but may be significant as a collaborator, or a member of the same corporate group. Companies may also be important to each other because one is investing in or borrowing from the other, or one has takeover ambitions involving the other.

Operational, Tactical and Strategic Purposes

For all these reasons, information about businesses themselves – what is generally called *company information* – constitutes a large part of business information. It follows that the motivation for finding out about a business, and the information needed, varies greatly. In one case it may be for a routine operational purpose: to discover the address of a supplier; in another for a tactical purpose: to select the most relevant supplier; in a third case, for a strategic purpose: to decide which firm to try to buy up in order to guarantee the supply of an essential component. Similar information may be used differently for different purposes. For operational purposes it may provide a definite answer; for strategic purposes it may only be one factor to reduce the risk in a decision. It is not just businesses which need to know such things about companies, but also private individuals: as employees, citizens, and investors. Though made here in relation to company information, these points about usage apply to business information in general.

Figure 4. Business-to-business relationships

In a flyer for their broad scope *Juniper* online services, ICC crystallised the different needs for company information as:

> 'Credit assessment, risk analysis, pre-sales vetting, competitor analysis, prospect targetting, performance benchmarking, research on directors.'

Implications of the Needs for the Information Required

The implication of such pressing and wide ranging needs is for a great range and depth of information on firms. Indeed, there has long been a plethora of offerings, from the simple factual to the complex and predictive – which is of course not to say that needs can ever be satisfied in any and every parameter. Many familiar business information providers made their names in company information, even if they have since succumbed to the trend to diversify, or been taken over by larger firms with even wider portfolios. ICC (originally Inter Company Comparisons), and Jordan's in the UK, and Dun & Bradstreet and Disclosure in the U.S.A. continue to be known essentially for generalist company information.

Today each of these large company information providers claims to satisfy the whole range of user needs. They have reached this position either through developing specialisms to keep abreast of user expectations, or by taking over or entering into partnership with specialists. This has been done particularly recently to enhance their credit reference products, and to broaden geographical range. The following excerpts illustrate how Infocheck Equifax's *Global Scan* achieves breadth (also branded as *International Reports Service*):

> 'Global Scan links you to the local information providers throughout the world . . . Using the latest gateway and telecommunications technology, reports are instantly available on over 9 million public and private companies.' (From a company flyer.)

> 'Accounts information provided by Companies House; County Court judgements information from the Registry Trust; press information from numerous sources including the Financial Times and Reuters.' (From an article in *Information World Review*, December 1996, p. 63.)

ICC, Infocheck Equifax or Dun & Bradstreet aim to meet the range of needs in two ways: by offering users access to their 'comprehensive' database of company records, and by offering tailored and selective spin-off sources from the database. In the first option, the user's desired view is achieved by means of the search and output software. In the second, separately purchasable products include printed company financial details for separate industries, and CD-ROMs of large companies' details for marketing purposes.

As will become apparent, many niche sources of company information are still available, as well as the primary sources on which the mainstream sources are based. They are essential for information on certain aspects of certain firms, and for the level of detail and currency which may be needed. In practice, obtaining the necessary information on a company can involve a variety of printed and electronic formats, personal and organisational contacts, and primary and secondary sources.

Primary Sources

To gain a critical appreciation of the sources, it is necessary to know the origins of the primary sources, and how the information in them ends up as the secondary sources which we more often use. Information about companies is made public in three major ways:

- disclosure under company law;
- voluntary disclosure;
- disclosure by third parties.

We can obtain the raw and immediate results of each in a variety of primary sources; however, for most purposes we prefer to pay for value added by the publishers of secondary sources.

Sources of primary company information – Xs indicate comparative volume of information and sources

	Disclosure by law	Voluntary disclosure	Third party disclosure
Sole Traders and Partnerships	None	X	X
Private Companies	XXX	X	X
Public Limited Companies	XXXX	XXX	XX

Statutory Disclosure

Legal disclosure can ensure at least a basic level of data on most of the firms we deal with or are concerned about, namely registered private and public companies. States encourage people to create businesses, and people to do business with them, by granting owners limited liability in return for fulfilling certain disclosure and operating requirements. An introduction to the official European Business Register system (below) included the following statements:

> 'Official and reliable company information is critical if you want to effectively conduct safe business transactions. . . . By making information on European companies easily available and more affordable for all potential users, the EBR will contribute to making the European Community a truly competitive market. . . . This in turn improves policy making in such areas as the prevention of fraud and the infiltration of organised crime, as well as abuses of the freedom of movement.'

In the UK, owners registering as a public or private *limited company* are only financially liable up to the amount of their individual stake in the capital. Useful information depends on a country specifying that sufficient is disclosed as part of the company registration process, enforcing that in terms of currency and accuracy, and making it available for public consumption. As in the UK under the Companies Acts 1985, 1989 and amendments, initial and regular data on name, constitution, ownership, and accounts must normally be disclosed.

Like Companies House in the UK, a central national agency is often responsible for the registration process, including both information collection and dissemination. Companies House (see below) achieves a compliance rate of about 90%. Doing business internationally and even within the EU is frustrated by considerable variability in countries' registration and disclosure requirements, compliance rates, and information collection and dissemination methods. Within Europe, France is an example of decentralised registration and disclosure, based on chambers of commerce. It is particularly difficult to obtain information on a German company, and Switzerland is a case where minimal detail has to be disclosed. Unfortunately, harmonisation within the EU may be achieved by accepting a lower level of company accounting standards and of legal disclosure than hitherto enjoyed in Britain by the public and the publishers of secondary sources. In the USA all public companies have to disclose much information via the national Securities and Exchange Commission; however, dislosure by private limited companies depends on individual states' legislation.

The following summary of world financial statements filing requirements is based on a list appearing in Experian's product literature, in 1997; the nomenclature of different legal types of company is often also given. Even assuming good compliance where there are filing requirements, it is clearly difficult to obtain reliable information on a considerable proportion of the world's companies:

Country	Details
Albania	No financial statements
Algeria	SA, public limited companies required to file
Andorra	See Spain
Angola	SA, public limited companies required to file
Argentina	SA, public limited companies required to file
Armenia	No financial statements
Australia	Ltd, public limited companies required to file Pty, some companies file
Austria	AG, public limited companies required to file
Azerbaijan	No financial statements
Bahamas	No financial statements
Bahrain	No financial statements
Balearic Islands	See Spain
Bangladesh	No financial statements
Belgium	SA or NV, public limited companies required to file. SPRL or BVBA, private limited companies required to file
Benin	No financial statements
Byelorussia	No financial statements
Bolivia	No financial statements
Botswana	No financial statements
Brazil	Public limited companies required to file

Country	Details
Bulgaria	No financial statements
Burma	No financial statements
Cameroon	No financial statements
Canada	Public companies required to file
Canary Islands	See Spain
Cape Verde	No financial statements
Cayman Islands	No financial statements
Central African Republic	No financial statements
Chad	No financial statements
Chile	SA, public limited companies required to file
China	No financial statements
Columbia	No financial statements
Costa Rica	No financial statements
Croatia	No financial statements
Cuba	No financial statements
Cyprus	No financial statements
Czech Republic	AS, joint stock company required to file
Denmark	AS and ApS, public and private limited companies required to file
Djibouti	No financial statements
Dominican Republic	SA, public limited companies required to file
Egypt	No financial statements
El Salvador	No financial statements
Equador	SA, Public limited companies required to file
Equatorial Guinea	No financial statements
Estonia	No financial statements
Ethiopia	No financial statements
Falkland Islands	No financial statements
Fiji	No financial statements
Finland	OY, limited companies required to file
France	SA and SARL, public and private limited companies required to file
Gabon	No financial statements
Gambia	No financial statements
Georgia	No financial statements

Germany	AG corporations required to file
Ghana	Public and private limited companies required to file
Gibraltar	No financial statements
Greece	AE and SA, public and private limited companies requiredto file
Guatemala	No financial statements
Guinea Bissau	No financial statements
Honduras	No financial statements
Hong Kong	Public limited companies required to file
Hungary	No financial statements
Iceland	AS, public limited companies required to file
India	Public limited companies required to file
Indonesia	PN, state companies required to file
Iran	No financial statements
Iraq	No financial statements
Ireland	PLC and Ltd, public and private limited companies required to file
Isle of Man	No financial statements
Israel	Public limited companies required to file
Italy	SPA and SRL, public and private limited companies required to file
Ivory Coast	SA and SARL, public and private limited companies required to file
Japan	KK, public corporations required to file
Jordan	No financial statements
Kazakhstan	No financial statements
Kenya	No financial statements
Kyrgyzstan	No financial statements
Korea	CH, Public corporations required to file
Kuwait	No financial statements
Latvia	No financial statements
Lebanon	No financial statements
LeewardIslands	No financial statements
Lesotho	No financial statements
Liberia	No financial statements
Libya	No financial statements
Liechenstein	No financial statements
Lithuania	No financial statements

Country	Details
Luxembourg	No financial statements
Madagascar	No financial statements
Maiawi	No financial statements
Malaysia	BHD and SDN public and private limited companies required to file
Maldives	No financial statements
Mali	No financial statements
Malta	Public limited companies required to file
Mauritania	No financial statements
Mauritius	No financial statements
Mexico	SA, public limited companies required to file
Moidavia	No financial statements
Monaco	SA and SARL, public and private limited companies required to file
Morocco	SA and SARL, public and private limited companies required to file
Mozambique	No financial statements
Namibia	No financial statements
Nepal	No financial statements
Netherlands Antilles	No financial statements
Netherlands	NV, public limited companies required to file
New Zealand	Public limited companies required to file
Nicaragua	No financial statements
Niger	No financial statements
Nigeria	PLC, public limited companies required to file
Norway	AS, limited companies required to file
Oman	No financial statements
Pakistan	No financial statements
Panama	No financial statements
Papua New Guinea	No financial statements
Paraguay	No financial statements
Peru	SA, public limited companies required to file
Philippines	No financial statements
Poland	No financial statements

Portugal	SA and Ltda, public and private limited companies required to file
Qatar	No financial statements
Romania	SA, joint stock companies required to file
Rwanda	No financial statements
Russia	No financial statements
Saudi Arabia	No financial statements
Senegal	No financial statements
Seychelies	No financial statements
Sierra Leone	No financial statements
Singapore	Limited companies required to file
Somalia	No financial statements
South Africa	No financial statements
Spain	SA, public limited companies required to file
Sri Lanka	No financial statements
St Helena	No financial statements
Sudan	No financial statements
Sweden	AS, limited companies required to file
Switzerland	GMBH and SARL, limited companies quoted on the stock exchange required to file
Swaziland	No financial statements
Syria	All companies required to file
Taiwan	No financial statements
Tajikistan	No financial statements
Tanzania	No financial statements
Thailand	No financial statements
Togo	No financial statements
Tunisia	SA and SARL, public and private limited companies required to file
Turkey	No financial statements
Turkmenistan	No financial statements
USA	Public companies required to file (private companies also in certain states only)
Uganda	No financial statements
Ukraine	No financial statements
United Arab Emirates	No financial statements
Uruguay	No financial statements

Country	Details
Uzbekistan	No financial statements
Venezuela	SA, public limited companies required to file
Virgin Islands	No financial statements
West Indies	In all islands, public and private limited companies are required to file, but the information can be difficult to obtain
Yemen	No financial statements
Yugoslavia (Former)	No financial statements
Zaire	SA or NV, public limited companies required to file. SPRL or BVBA, private limited companies required to file
Zambia	No financial statements
Zimbabwe	Public and private limited companies required to file

All this means that legal status has significance, not least because it determines the amount and type of information we can discover as of right. The table below shows British firm types, and an indication of disclosure requirements.

- *Sole traders* – a status common to keepers of small shops, carpenters, window cleaners etc., are defined as businesses owned by one person, who has unlimited financial liability.

- *Partnerships*, such as of vets, accountants or solicitors, are similar to sole traders, except that the partners share the liability.

- The majority of larger traders opt to be *private limited companies*, where at least two specific owners have liability up to the amount of their share.

- Non-profit-making organisations often register as *companies limited by guarantee*, where liability is limited to the amount guaranteed.

- *Public limited companies* must have a share capital of at least £50,000, with wide and tradeable shares in ownership, often achieved by a *listing* or *quotation* on a stock exchange. Foreign businesses must register according to the regulations for *oversea* companies, only if they have a place of business in the UK.

Disclosure Requirements of the Main Legal Types of UK Firm

Type	Note	Outline of disclosure requirements
Sole Traders and Partnerships	Numerically the largest category	None
Private Companies ('Ltd.')	Approx. 1 million	On incorporation: name, address/es, 'Memorandum & live companies articles of association', director/s', & company ('Ltd.') secretary's details.
		Annually (within 10 months of end of accounts period)
		'Annual return' showing any changes to above; balance sheet & profit & loss account, incl. notes and reports (reduced if *small* or *medium-sized* turnover)
		At other times: Changes to directors and other items;
		Company's or creditors' applications concerning winding up or related matters
Public Companies ('PLC')	Approx. 14,000; approx. 2,000 quoted on London stock exchange	Similar to private companies; balance sheet & profit & loss account within 7 months of accounting date

An example of company accounts, and help in interpreting them, is given in the section of this chapter entitled 'Sources of Company Financial Information'.

Complicating Factors: Parent and Subsidiary Companies; Consolidated Accounts

As well as the problem of locating compatible data for *foreign* enterprises, the above UK table shows that there is variation in both details to be filed and when they are due, depending on both legal type and size. Although expert search agents can be employed, such complications are still apparent as variable quality data in company diectories or databases. Searching is also complicated by a proliferation of names associated with

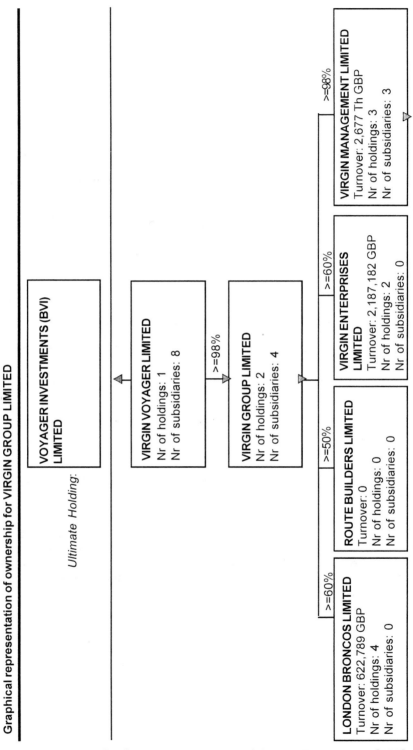

Figure 5. Example of a corporate structure (Voyager Investments [BVI] Limited)

companies, some of which turn out to be brand names and others subsidiaries or holding companies which may be little more than nominal entities. A *subsidiary* is a company controlled by another; that is, where the equity is at least 51% owned by the other, or where the board of directors is controlled by it, equity being capital which carries with it the right of participation. Subsidiaries are therefore either *wholly owned* or *partially owned*. If less than 51% of a company's equity is owned by another, it may be considered an *associate*, but independent. The controlling company is said to be the *parent*, and if that company is in turn controlled by another, at the top of the tree is the *ultimate parent*. Parent companies can be referred to as *holding companies*, especially where its only business is controlling subsidiaries, where the operations take place. Since UK companies law requires in most circumstances *consolidated accounts* to be filed for the 'group' formed by parent and subsidiaries, it is difficult to ascertain financial details for any one of them.

Companies House

Companies House is the government agency responsible for the whole process of registering and ensuring the compliance of companies under the Companies Acts. Its headquarters in Cardiff grants and renews company status to applicants meeting the specified organisational, trading, accounting and disclosure requirements. A unique registered number is allocated from the end of the sequence on 'incorporation', and dates set for initial and subsequent submission of documents. All the statutorily submitted documents are available for unrestricted access by any member of the public. Events such as incorporation, notices of meetings of creditors, and winding up, are also published by Companies House in the official London and Edinburgh *Gazettes*.

Other than ensuring that documents are available, Companies House has a limited role in value-added information sources or services. It offers a directory of currently registered and recently dissolved companies, which can be consulted in its public search rooms, amongst other services on the dial-up online service Companies House Direct , or as the monthly updated *Companies House Directory* CD-ROM. It is obvious from the data and search facilities shown below, that this is more than a catalogue of Companies House records, and can be used for instance to select marketing targets, including as a source of machine-readable name and address data.

Companies House Directory: information (CD-ROM version)

Company name
Registered company number
Registered office address
Accounting reference date
Date of latest annual return filed

Date of latest accounts filed
Accounts type
Date of incorporation
Company type
Company status
Trade classification–SIC(92)
Mortgage indicator
Postcode

Search facilities include
Searching on any number or word
Phrase searches
Date ranges
Search on items containing certain values
Phonetic searching of company name
Wildcard searches
Combined search criteria within and between fields

Currently the only other major products are databases of directors names and details, of mortgage information, and two million companies on the *Change of Name and Dissolved Index* CD-ROM. These are created by extracting this data from appropriate parts of the submitted documents; there are also plans for a database of issued capital and shareholder information. Companies House direct is the platform for all the database and search ordering services, soon to include online viewing or delivery of accounts images.

The databases can be consulted in all Companies House offices, and 'searches' for inexpensive copies of document sets ordered. The *Companies House Monitor* service allows the pre-ordering of selected documents from selected companies, so that copies are despatched whenever they are submitted. Documents can be delivered to users in hardcopy, microform, or via fax or courier. Microform copies of all documents can be inspected at the Cardiff headquarters, or the London and Edinburgh main offices. Reduced level services are available from satellite offices in Leeds, Manchester and Glasgow. This leaves much scope for information professionals and for commercial information providers to compile, selectively extract, compare, calculate, alert, and add even more value to this UK data, and to deal with the complexities of foreign equivalents. Companies House facilitates commercial providers in doing so, by selling them bulk machine-readable copies of the raw data. However, developments in the digitisation of company documents, the Internet, and the European Business Register project, are radically reducing the role of the intermediary in delivery of disclosed documents.

European Business Register

EBR is an EU funded project to network the member states' company registration authorities, so that any company record is accessible to anyone at any time, via the Internet (*http://www.ebr.org*). Initially (from the end of 1998) standardised 'company profile' data (as below) will be available from 'national business registers', with additional services such as electronic full-text or image delivery, dependent on the national register.

The EBR Company Profile

(Available in the local language for registered companies in Austria, Belgium, Denmark, Finland, France, Greece, Italy, Norway, Portugal, Spain, Sweden and United Kingdom.)

Company name	Company description
Company number	Status (active, dissolved etc.)
Address	Activity code
Country of registration	Activity description
Telephone number	Currency code (the currency used in record)
Registration date	Currency unit (if figures not given as currency)
Registration authority	Last share capital
Legal structure	Last annual account date

In an earlier section of the chapter, it was shown how needs for information arise from the variety of possible relationships between the enquirer and the business which is the subject of the enquiry. The following table shows how those different relationships and different levels of decision making result in the questions typically asked. 'Information needed' ranges from the simple and factual through to the complex.

Potential Usage of Different Types of Company Information

Information needed	*Likely management purpose*		
Discover company's:	Operational	Tactical	Strategic
Registration & statutory data		X	
Legal status (registered type; current, dormant, or dissolved)		X	
Basic details (name, addresses, registered number etc.)	X	X	
Ownership details (parent, subsidiary, group structure issued capital; shareholdings)		X	X
Products, services	X	X	X
Financial details (breakdown of income, assets & expenditure; profits)		X	X
Personnel (e.g. Managing Director, head of sales, purchasing)	X	X	X

[Other specific facts] (e.g. details of plant, employees, professional advisors, policy and record on charitable giving)	X	X	
Operating methods (Ethics; advertising; management style & structure; salaries)		X	X

Discover company's:	Operational	Tactical	Strategic
Share or bond performance			X
Credit worthiness; risk assessment	X		X
Plans (Product development; market strategies; acquisition intentions; structural change)			X
Future financial performance			X

Voluntary Disclosure

The earlier table, *Sources of primary company information,* shows that in the absence of any compulsion to register, voluntary disclosure is the vital source of information on UK sole traders and partnerships. It may be a comparatively haphazard source, and may do little more than reveal the existence of a certain kind of small enterprise at a certain address, but it may well be that nothing more is available in a public source. For registered private and public companies, the bigger businesses and the ones which affect more people more of the time, voluntarily disclosed information tops up the two other forms of disclosure. Though not an independent or predictable source of information on them, it can provide the extra detail and currency lacking in the basic level of detail required by Companies House by a generous submission date.

For most sole traders and partnerships, it is usually possible to find their name, activity and contact details, given out for promotional purposes. However, much more, albeit not independent, information on many is given on their own web sites, traceable via the general Internet search tools and the electronic directories and gateways discussed in the section below, 'Sources of Basic Company Information . . .'.

While web pages are highly searchable, printed press advertisements are almost useless as a systematic information source. However, sole traders and partnerships also volunteer information for telephone directories, local trades directories, national professional directories and web-based directories, also treated in 'Sources of Basic Company Information . . .' below. A comparatively small but growing proportion of sole traders and partnerships volunteer information to company information, especially credit information, providers. In response to a clients' request for information on such a

Figure 6. Example of small business' web site – The Groves Hotel, Aberystwyth

firm, Infocheck Equifax, for example, invites it to volunteer financial and other information. In their 'Non Limited Report', Infocheck supplement information from third parties with various details gained by telephoning and interviewing the firm, the names and addresses of the principals, details of the history and activities of the business, and even audited or unaudited accounts. For example, Infocheck's standard 'Credit Decisions Non Limited Business Report' includes:

- Business name and non-limited number
- Date established
- Businesses trading address
- Telephone number
- Fax number
- Business activity
- Partners/proprietors bankers details and bankers address
- Number of Employees
- VAT Registration Code CCJ/gazette records
- A recommended monthly credit limit
- Credit summary

Similar details can be found in similar sources for the many small private companies; though for these, directory publishers can use statutorily disclosed data to achieve more comprehensive coverage. Most PLCs, and limited companies up to the size and prominence of Richard Branson's Virgin Group, release even more information in the form of glossy annual reports and accounts and other brochures, house journals, interim reports and accounts, press releases, interviews, and elaborate web sites – which have the advantage of being instantly accessible to everyone. One of the surprises of the 1998 Annual Business Information Resources Survey was that business information services now use company web sites far more than they use any web-based provider of company financial data – the most sought category of business information (Gerry Smith, 'Annual Business Information Resources Survey, 1998' in *Business Information Review* 15(1) March 1998, pp. 5-21).

PLCs are the most prolific disseminators of what is usually selectively positive information, mainly intended for current and potential shareholders. In Britain the *Financial Times* is a systematic source not only of the information leaked, fed or otherwise voluntarily disclosed, but also of analysis of it. Under 'The week ahead' in its Companies section, the *Financial Times* regularly gives 'expected' figures from the annual or interim (6 months) results due to be announced by major companies on specific days in the following week. That is complemented by fuller tables giving headline profit and share dividend figures from the previous week's interims, and listing results due the following week.

It requires much time and effort to manage such diverse primary sources for systematic access; indeed, that is another role for both information managers and secondary company information sources.

Third Party Information

Through various relationships they have with each other, businesses and other organisations are in a position to release very significant information, which would not be disclosed voluntarily or under company law.

Transactions and relationships, and information arising:

Business' transaction or relationship	Third party's knowledge
Buying	Payment record: size, speed, reliability
Selling	Capacity, quality, speed
Banking	Financial status, credit worthiness
Use of auditor	As above
Appearance in law courts	Transgressions, financial status, bankruptcy
Membership of stock or other exchanges	Detailed financial and operating data

Dealings with industry regulatory bodies	As above; details from enquiries and judgements
Compulsory notification of e.g. emissions	E.g. chemicals and industrial processes used
Government commissions e.g. monopolies	Details from enquiries and judgements

Of course bankers and accountants need the client's permission to disclose information. However, in most other cases above, valuable information is either made public directly by the third party, or sold on to any willing publisher. The Environment Agency, for instance, has a legal duty to maintain public registers of chemical and other polluting emissions, which are thought to be inspected as much for 'legal industrial espionage', as for concern for the environment; the unfortunate result being that companies' reports are often too vague to be of use to anyone. Details of payments by business or individuals, especially if they involve credit, are an example of data sold by companies to information providers. Businesses' appearances before County Courts are monitored by The Registry Trust Ltd, who collate the data for purchase by interested publishers. These records are an important basis of secondary sources such as credit reference databases, and risk alerting services (covered later).

Disclosure by companies to highly regulated markets such as the London Stock Exchange, or to the USA's Securities and Exchange Commission (SEC) is another example of important information getting into the public domain through a third party. The SEC's electronic document filing system EDGAR (Electronic Data Gathering and Retrieval), and the London Stock Exchange's electronic *Regulatory News Service*, ensures for example that data released under the London Stock Exchange's Continuing Obligations of Listing, and Alternative Investment Market rules, are made available simultaneously to all who could be affected.

> 'RNS is the medium by which companies announce price sensitive information to the markets, and includes news of all official and regulatory announcements such as financial results, board changes, rights issues, dividend information, share holdings and merger and acquisition details.'

The above exerpt from the description of Profound's services confirms that the service is bought by online hosts and secondary business information providers; hosts including Profound resell it in the full and unabridged form, as does FT Profile where data is added three times daily, that is within three to nine hours of its release. (By contrast, EDGAR data is free to all, including via the web.) The specific coverage of the London Stock Exchange's *Regulatory News Service* is stated as:

- Reports and accounts
- Directors' dealings; disclosure shareholdings
- Board changes
- Shareholders' circulars
- Prospectuses; listing particulars
- Eurobond prospectuses
- Interim; preliminary figures
- Press notices
- Miscellaneous information provided by the companies (rights issues, offers, acquisitions, etc., sterling commercial paper details)
- Plus: all other price-sensitive company information officially released by the exchange

Secondary Sources

The previous section showed how information about individual businesses first finds its way into the public domain. Where those diverse primary sources can be consulted, they can provide the most detailed, cheap and timely information available. However, they have serious disadvantages for many purposes, in that the information is not appropriately cumulated, analysed or presented for the majority of users' information retrieval and operational needs. That is why the most common port of call for information on companies is the vast array of secondary sources: sources which package or add value in one or more of these ways:

Value-adding role of secondary sources

- Identifying & using diverse sources
- Selecting & abstracting for subject or purpose
- Cumulating information by subject or purpose
- Standardising data and its presentation
- Collecting and tabulating data
- Making calculations
- Analysing from diverse data
- Arranging data for access
- Cataloguing, indexing, organising for retrieval

An exerpt from Dun & Bradstreet's own product literature, the diagram 'Data sources – the ultimate business universe', shows the inputs to the *D&B UK Marketing* database. It illustrates the first of the above value adding functions:

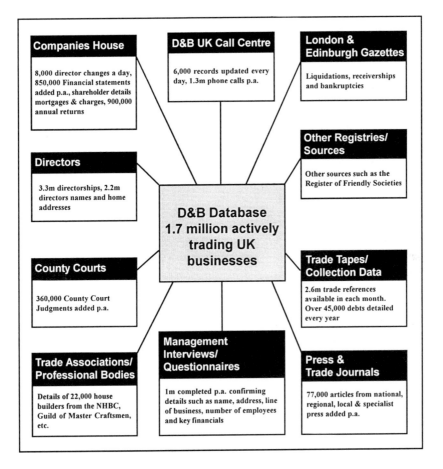

Figure 7. 'Data sources: the ultimate business universe'
from Dun & Bradstreet

Scope of Secondary Company Information Sources

The result is commercially produced and marketed information products, which are more readily incorporated into most business decisions than the equivalent primary sources. Most secondary company sources specialise, in terms of type of firm covered, aspect of the firms covered, information medium covered, or user need or group intended for. Thus most sources can be identified with one or more of the specific categories below:

Coverage

FIRMS, e.g.:
Legal type

Size

Geographical area

Activity/industry

SUBJECT, e.g. COMPANY'S:
Personnel

Finances

Ownership/corporate structure

Merger & acquisition activity

Products & services offered

Share or bond details/values

Credit status

Stability, exposure to risks

INFORMATION SOURCE/MEDIUM, e.g.:
Brokers & analysts reports

News media

Disclosed documents

USER NEED, e.g.:
General, quick reference

Marketing, selling to companies

Sourcing, buying from companies

Investing in companies

Creditors & customers

Economists

Charities' needs

The following sections introduce identifiable types of secondary company information source, giving examples of what they contain, showing their role and how they are used. Since sources usually combine several of the above criteria, each of the following sections deals with sources grouped according to one the subdivisions of the three main criteria above. Thus every kind of source is covered, though some could be considered under any of several criteria. Note that the main treatment of companies' stocks and shares is in the 'Financial Information' chapter. The objective is to show what each source type contains, give examples, show what its role is, and how it may be used.

How secondary company information source types match information need types (generalisation)

Information needed	Comprehensive d'bases	Document suppliers	Directories	Financial details	Credit assessment	Company news	Broker research	Other special
Discover company's:								
Registration and statutory data		X						
Legal status (registered type; current, dormant, or dissolved)		X	X			X		
Basic details (name, addresses, registered number)	X		X					
Ownership details (parent, subsidiary, group structure, issued capital, Mshareholdings)	X					X		X
Products, services	X		X			X		X
Financial details (income, assets expenditure, profits; data &/ or analysis)	X	X		X	X			
Personnel (e.g.details of MD, directors, head of sales)	X		X			X		X
Other specific facts (e.g. details of plant, employees, prof., advisors, policy and record on charitable giving)	X		X			X		X
Operating methods (Ethics; advertising; management style & structure; salaries)				X		X		X
Share or bond performance (current & future)				X	X	X	X	X
Discover company's: Credit worthiness; risk assessment	X			X	X		X	X
Plans (Product development; market strategies; acquisit. intentions; struct. change)						X	X	
Future performance				X	X		X	

The company information sources industry is converging towards 'comprehensive' super-sources of the type indicated by the first column above, and away from the specialist types indicated by the other columns. Several British and American players offer virtual or actual databases which aim in one source to meet most users' needs for wide coverage of businesses, and range of information about them. For the larger and more sought companies, they cover in at least basic detail many of the specialisms in the columns, for a range of countries. These one-stop company information sources were created through a combination of electronic and corporate links between information providers, and development by the established providers·of the coverage demanded by users. The launching of *Onesource*, Disclosure's *Global Access*, Infocheck's *Global Scan*, Dun & Bradstreet's online *Globalseek* access to *D&B Worldbase*, and Profound's *Worldsearch* with 'full financial reports on 4.5 million companies worldwide', coincided with the increasingly international nature of business in the 1990s. An exerpt from Infocheck's description of *Global Scan* indicates the aims and wide geographical coverage of such a service:

> 'Global Scan gives an account holder:
>
> Access to over 200 countries on-line providing credit and financial information on over 9 million companies. Custom report ordering service which allows the customer to order a report on any company in the world. Infocheck-Equifax has thousands of contacts around the world that are experienced in Company Investigations and report production.'

With *D&B Worldbase* Dun & Bradstreet matches Infocheck in the number of countries, but raises the number of businesses included:

> 'The world's largest single source of business records and corporate linkage. Features varying levels of business information on more than 40 million businesses in over 200 countries.'

As the table above can only partially show, specialised primary and secondary sources are nevertheless still essential for coverage of the widest range of companies, in terms of size, type and geographical area; and the widest range of types of information, types of presentation; as well as for alternative views, and specialist knowledge.

Searching for Specific Companies or Their Stocks

For the sake of brevity, and to avoid ambiguity in company names, company databases and databases of stock market prices usually employ at least one system of unique numbers or other codes for companies. The code or symbol often has to be known to retrieve share price and related data, though a convenient look-up facility is sometimes available. These are the commonly used vocabularies:

CUSIP e.g. 392690 QT 3 (issuer 6 characters, issue 2 characters, plus check digit)

For North American securities and financial instruments. CUSIP Service Bureau Mission Statement – from their CUSIP web site – *http://www.cusip.com/* (see also CINS below):

> 'The CUSIP Service Bureau, operated by Standard & Poor's for the American Bankers Association, exists for the primary purpose of uniquely identifying issuers and issues of securities and financial instruments within a standard framework, and disseminating this data to the financial marketplace via various media CUSIP numbers and standardized descriptions are used by virtually all sectors of the financial industry, and are critical for the accurate and efficient clearance and settlement of securities as well as back-office processing.'

CINS (CUSIP International Numbering System) e.g. A12345 12 9 (similar construction to CUSIP, preceded by country code)

For North American trading in foreign securities:

> 'This number was developed in 1988 by the CUSIP Agency (Standard & Poor's), the American Bankers Association (ABA) and TELEKURS, N.A. in response to the North American securities industry's need for a 9-digit identifier of international securities. CINS numbers appear in the International Securities Identification Directory (ISID), which is co-produced for the ABA by Standard & Poor's and TELEKURS, N.A. The ISID product contains over 260,000 securities, including the CINS number, ISIN codes, as well as cross-references to all major international numbering systems. This product has been designed to minimize the impact on back-office systems and operations, while facilitating cross-border communications among global custodians, depositories, banks, securities organizations, and exchanges.'

ISIN e.g. NL0000009454 (a Netherlands stock)

International Security Identification Number, for the common stock of a company. Sometimes necessary for the retrieval of share price and related information. Devised by ISO as an international standard to facilitate global transactions, intended to eventually replace other international coding systems. The code contains a country identifier, and the code issued to the stock by the national exchange authority (e.g. UK – SEDOL code, Germany – DWKN, USA – CUSIP, Switzerland VALOREN). See also the reference to ISIN in the CINS entry above.

Ticker e.g. MSFT (Microsoft Corporation)

Symbols for UK, USA and other countries' listed companies' names. The Ticker symbol must often be input to retrieve from certain databases of financial markets information.

Reuters Company Codes e.g. BCI (Blue Circle Industries PLC)

Used in Textline news database as a 'controlled vocabulary' way of indexing and searching company names. On some hosts, codes may be found in a separate Textline Company Lookup database.

Duns Numbers e.g. 21-862-2660 (Boots PLC)

Identifiers used for the unambiguous specification of companies in Dun & Bradstreet's databases and other publications.

SEDOL e.g. 00767640 (J. Sainsbury PLC)

'Stock Exchange Daily Official List' – codes assigned to stocks traded in on the London Stock Exchange.

The Dialog *Company Name Finder* 'search aid database' does not overcome the problem of variant company names, but does at a stroke trace all the records in all that hosts' databases which include the name the searcher inputs, in their company name fields. The systems reports the number of records found in each database; and offers to retrieve the records by automatically executing searches in the chosen databases.

'Comprehensive' Company Information Databases

ICC, Jordans, Infocheck Equifax, Dun & Bradstreet, and Disclosure are well known as UK and USA based company information providers. Their scope is only bettered by the big online hosts, which use the output of several of these together with specialist providers to build an even more 'global' and 'comprehensive' portfolio. The output of ICC and others is centred on electronic products, usually with a central database accessible online in dial-up or web formats direct from the publisher, with selective and specialised products available online via a number of other hosts, and on the company's and others' CD-ROM products. ICC and other long established providers continue a range of selective and specialised printed publications, which are becoming less prominent in comparison with the electronic alternatives. Demands arising from increasing globalisation, for equivalent data on any business in the world, are met by a combination of widening the central database, networking with foreign providers' databases and contracting agents around the world to search for and transmit copies of deposited data or documents.

Specialised and Complementary Services

Most providers also undertake company searches on behalf of clients for information which may or may not be available from the products, and email or mail the results in hard copy. Many use BIGNet (Business Information Group Network) to route requests electronically to network members in the USA and most European countries. Akin to the smaller RM Group, Jordans provides a wide range of company support in the UK, combining information from its *Jordanwatch* database, with services such as company status and document searches, company formations, local authority and land registry searches, and the printing of business stationery. Their range of ad hoc information services is shown in the left column below. Dun & Bradstreet also offers more than its company databases for many countries, and spin-off products in a variety of physical formats. As well as a debt collecting service, D&B offers software to link its databases with the client's customer database, to enhance and analyse it for marketing purposes:

Jordans	Dun & Bradstreet
Register of new companies	*File matching*
Clients receive brief details	Client's customer database matched
of new companies, monthly	against D&B's to identify common
	records, for:
New Company Information Service	*Data audit; file cleaning; enhancement*
Fully researched records for new	Client's customer database corrected
companies, weekly	updated & added to from D&B records
Nameguard	*Profiling and analysis with D&B Logic*
Clients' names/words are	PC software linked to D&B database
monitored for similar registrations;	allows profiling and analysis of cus-
matches notified monthly	tomer base
	GIS mapping
	Geographical analysis of customers
	Global linkage
	Links customers to corporate family

Via the *Jewel* Windows-based direct online access to *Jordanwatch*, users can select from 16 separately priced elements of company records, such as given on the left below. Via for instance the host Dow Jones Interactive, users choose from eight report formats, including those given on the right below:

Jordanwatch via *Jewel*		Via Dow Jones Interactive	
Registered name and address	£2.00		
Business activity	£1.50	Business Information Report	$69.95
Balance sheet	£2.50	Credit Scoring Repor	$42.95
Holding/subsidiary data	£2.50	Family Tree Summary Report	$64.95
Financial ratios/trends	£2.50	Duns Financial Profile	$109.95
Credit score and rating	£6.00	History and Operations	$39.95

ICC's range of products and means of distribution is fairly typical of company information specialists, and is given here as an example:

Example: ICC's Company Information Products

ICC was formed in 1969 (as Inter Company Comparisons), and in 1995 achieved the international standard ISO9002 for data compilation and analysis quality. The following is not a full list of ICC's products, does not include their ad hoc international services, and is subject to change.

At the core: *ICC Corporate Database*, otherwise explained as:

> '. . . four major databases – from which we have built an unrivalled range of business products: Directory and Financial Database, Image Bank, Directors Database, Shareholders Database.'(ICC web site, 1998 – *http://www.icc.co.uk/*)

> 'Data is taken daily from numerous sources including Companies House, London and Edinburgh Gazette and Registry Trust. Certain data items are keyed in, the others delivered by electronic data feed. The compiled database is then analysed . . .' (*ICC Bulletin*, 1997).

The result is 3 million-plus live & dissolved UK companies; each company's financial analysis includes '150 individual accounts and ratios fields, supplemented by growth rates and industry comparisons'. Company records also include details of directorships, shareholders, credit status; with an updated bank of 34 million images representing every statutory document filed at Companies House, the DTI and the Information Protection Registry. The ICC information products below typically include a choice of 10 predefined financial, credit and risk report formats; and software to search, create graphics, manipulate and export data.

Full database

- Online via ICC
  Juniper:
  VT100 and Windows format
  Plum:
  Web format
- Bulk data delivery to purchaser's own system:
  Damson
- Gateways from other providers:
  ICC Gateway via FT Profile

Selective products

- Document supply:

  Juniper XD:

  Image copies of filed documents – online or mail-order

- CD-ROMs in the *Index* series:

  Credit Index:

  'Corporate, financial & risk information on all 1.3 million live companies'

  Company Index:

  'Key financial data on all 1.3 million live companies'

- Other ICC CD-ROMS

  ROM:BUS: The Business Ratio Plus CD-ROM:

  To compare the financial performance of companies within their industry sectors

- ICC data on other providers' CD-ROMs

  UK Company Factfinder:. . . (Dialog Corporation):

  Equivalent of *ICC British Company Financial Datasheets*, below

- Online via hosts

  ICC Full Company Reports and Accounts via FT Profile:

  Companies quoted on London stock exchange

  ICC British Company Annual Reports via DataStar & Dialog:

  Companies quoted on London stock exchange

  ICC British Company Directory via DataStar & Dialog:

  All UK registered companies

  ICC British Company Financial Datasheets via DataStar & Dialog:

  Over 150,000 public and private companies

  UK Quoted Company Intelligence suite on OneSource:

  ICC provides the full text of annual and interim reports

Scope Factors – Size of Database; Detail of Records

These large company information providers can pass on to users the advantages of scale, in the range of countries and companies covered, and level of detail provided. Nevertheless, while developments such as availability of electronic data from Companies House mean that coverage of all UK registered companies is feasible, coverage and detail in fact usually diminish in relation to size of company, and/or expected importance to users. The force driving the provider is user demand; so considerable financial and other detail is available for quoted companies and larger companies in general, while for most other businesses not much more than brief details and credit status may be in the database. The table above indicated the scope of such databases in relation to company information needs; the record below illustrates actual content. This version of an Infocheck Equifax sample 'Full report' for a limited company is typical of databases designed for day to day company information needs, with an emphasis on financial reliability for risk management purposes. As is apparent from the later subsection, 'Quoted Companies; Financial Services Companies', databases of financial information on public limited companies have less credit information and more on strategies and share performance. The sections of the Infocheck record illustrate its scope:

- Company Identification
- Company Capitalisation
- Financial Analysis
- Auditors
- Extended Company Ratio Analysis
- Infocheck Analyst Report
- Gazette or Detrimental Information
- Credit Profile
- Industry Comparison
- Report of Company Directors/Officers
- Directors Details

Figure 8. Sample Infocheck Limited Company Full Report

```
Company  Identification

Company  Name          :  ABCDE  COMPANY  LTD

Company  Number        :  00000001 Date  of  Incorp:12/12/1996
                                    Annual  Return  Date:  01/05/1997
Credit  Limit          :  40,000.00

Company  Type          :  Private  Company

Legal  Status          :  Liquidator  Appointed

Legal  Status  Date    :  01/01/1997

Company  Secretary     :  Mr   D SMITH,

Registered  Office     :  ABCDE  HOUSE
                          NEW  STREET
                          ANYTOWN

Post  Code             :  A1  2BC

Trading  Adress        :  ABCDE  HOUSE
                          NEW  STREET
                          ANYTOWN
                          A1  2BC
```

```
Trading  Phone  No.          :  0181  000  000
Fax  Number                  :  0181  001  001


Names  of  Directors    :  Mrs    G  SMITH,


Supplementary  Director  Details


Company  Secretary          :  BR  Lancaster
Committee  of  management:  JW  Pugh  (Chairman),  M  Blanford,  R
Colwill,  JL  Lampitt,  WL  Price,  DR  Weaver,  RC  Beldam,  AR  Good,
RW  Green,  T  Lopas,  M  Howard,  H  Smith


Business  Activities    :
DEALERS  IN  ELECTRICAL  AUDIO  AND  VISUAL  APPLIANCES


US  SIC  Codes              :  3629  ELECTRICAL  AND  INDUSTRIAL
                                    APPLIANCES  NEC
                              5731  RADIO    TELEVISION  AND  ELECTRONIC
                                    STORES
Previous  Names
Name
Date
N/A
Company  Capitalisation


Share  Currency         :  #


Nominal  Capital        :     100,000


Divided  Into           :     100,000  ord      Shares  of  1.00  each


Issued  at  date  of  Report  :  100,000  ord


Names  of  Principal  Shareholders  :  ABCDE  (UK)  LTD      99,999


Immediate  Holding  Company  :  Not  Available


Ultimate  Holding  Company    :  01000001  Basic  Data  Test


Up  to  10  UK  Subsidiaries    :  00000001  ABCDE  COMPANY  LTD


Charges/Debentures  Registered


Bankers  are                :
Sort  Code        :


Financial  Analysis


Account  Type     :  Not  Available
Scale             :  Thousands


Profit  &  Loss  Extracts
```

No. of Months:	12	12	12	12
Period Ending:	31/12/95	31/12/94	31/12/93	31/12/92
Consolidated:	No	No	No	No

Turnover	3886.99	3019.92	2938.87	2039.56
Interest Paid	3.97	25.86	35.01	9.89
Exports	556.90	428.15	423.48	103.81
Dividends	45.00	0.00	N/K	0.11
Directors Fees	147.49	104.56	99.98	83.92
Wages	1890.32	1473.90	1329.30	880.08
Profit Before Tax	156.98	28.15	23.48	-10.81
Profit After Tax	112.74	21.11	17.61	-10.81

Balance Sheet Extracts

No. of Months:	12	12	12	12
Period Ending:	31/12/95	31/12/94	31/12/93	31/12/92
Tangible Fixed Assets	213.73	172.16	145.52	118.69
Intangible Assets	0.00	0.00	0.00	N/K
Investments	8.08	0.21	0.00	N/K
Total Fixed Assets	221.87	172.37	145.52	118.69
Stock	147.99	124.40	175.84	262.83
Trade Debtors	206.70	147.37	192.26	157.75
Cash & Equivalent	163.22	99.61	89.56	76.95
Inter Company Balances	256.38	86.56	165.01	126.98
Total Current Assets	974.29	871.53	848.05	721.28
Total Assets	1196.10	1043.90	993.57	839.97
Trade Creditors	329.95	322.14	355.30	300.57
Overdrafts	122.63	119.06	105.99	139.45
ShortTerm Loans	32.18	26.01	29.58	36.03
Inter Company Balances	123.85	99.55	101.23	87.66
Total Current Liabilities	702.61	731.70	720.42	605.53
Net Current Assets	271.68	139.83	127.63	115.75
Long Term Borrowings	85.15	56.12	77.89	17.21
Other L.T. Liabilities	168.86	173.57	140.90	216.35
Total L.T. Liabilities	254.01	229.69	218.79	233.56
Paid Up Equity	100.00	10.00	10.00	10.00
Reserves	139.48	72.51	44.36	-9.12
Shareholders Funds	239.48	82.51	54.36	0.88
Credit Limit	40.00	20.00	10.00	0.00
Number of Employees	126	101	103	59

Auditors

Auditors are   :   N/A

Town   :

Auditors Renumeration :   12500

Auditors Comment on the latest Balance Sheet :

The accounts give a true and fair view.

Auditors Qualified Accounts ? no

Extended Company Ratio Analysis

Figures Stated in   Thousands

Key Ratios

No. of Months:	12	12	12	12
Period Ending:	31/12/95	31/12/94	31/12/93	31/12/92
Profit Margin	4.04	0.93	0.80	-0.53
Profit/Capital Employed	65.55	34.12	43.19	-1228.41
Profit/Assets	13.12	2.70	2.36	-1.29
Current Debt	2.93	8.87	13.25	688.10
Total Debt	3.99	11.65	17.28	953.51
Long Term Debt	0.51	0.74	0.80	1.00
Current Ratio	1.39	1.19	1.18	1.19
Liquidity Ratio	1.18	1.02	0.93	0.76
Stock/Turnover	26.27	24.28	16.71	7.76
Collection Period	19.41	17.81	23.88	28.23
Creditors Days	30.98	38.94	44.13	53.79
Gearing (%)	32.04	123.11	227.92	13152.27
Interest Coverage	21.26	122.50	198.81	-91.49
Credit Gearing	16.70	24.24	18.40	
Indicator Ratio	12.35	7.95	4.08	

Infocheck Analyst Report

The Company's latest filed accounts are for the year ended
31.12.95. During the period the company increased its issued
share capital from #10000 to #100000.
Turnover has increased from #3.02M to #3.89M over the past
year. Pre-tax profit has increased from #28147 to #156976.
Profit is stated after deduction of directors remuneration of
#147492.
Proposed and paid dividends total #45000. Investments listed
under fixed assets are #8080.
Liquidity has improved over the past year from net current
assets of #140035 to net current assets of #271682. Bank and
cash figures total #163219. Work in progress is valued at
#103560.
#132531 (net) is due from other group companies on their
current accounts.
There is an overdraft of #122630. There are bank loans of
#117331 of which #32180 is current.
There are long term loans from group companies of #100000.
Provisions for liabilities and charges total #68857. The
company's total reserves stand at #139419 of which #127419 is
due to the profit and loss account balance.
Capital reserves amount to #2000. On the basis of these
accounts: We would suggest setting a credit limit on monthly

terms of #40000. The company appears to be of sufficient financial stability to undertake contracts to a value of #1.0M.

Having reviewed and analysed the latest information available:
We would suggest setting a credit limit on monthly terms of 40,000

Gazette or Detrimental Information

LA   Liquidator Appointed
            Published London Gazette   dated 01/01/1997
            On 01/01/1997 the company went into creditors
                  Liquidation. The Liquidator is 1 of 1;.

Credit Profile

CCJ's Registered: None. Records held since Jan 91
Gazette Information:

    Liquidator Appointed   01/01/1997

Payment Profiles:
    Creditor Days:
        Sector Average   :   38.95 Days
        ABCDE COMPANY LTD   :   30.98   Days

    Liquidity Ratio:
        Sector Average   :   0.89
        ABCDE COMPANY LTD   :   1.18

Vital Signs:
        Turnover increased by   :   28.7 %
        Pre Tax Profit increased by :   457.7 %
        Gearing decreased by   :   74.0 %
        Working Capital increased by :   94.3 %

Monthly Trade Credit Limit   :   40,000

Industry Comparison

Industry Type   : 19 Electricals (excluding Radio & TV)
No. of companies   : 12924
Last Updated   : 01/05/1997

Industry Comparison /Average Scale	Latest M	Previous M	Previous M	Previous M
Turnover	7.31	8.09	7.98	8.67
Profit Before Tax	0.65	0.47	0.46	0.49
Debtors	0.97	1.01	1.07	1.23
Total Assets	5.46	5.65	6.16	6.76
Shareholders Funds	1.79	2.20	2.42	3.57
Profit Margin (%)	8.89	5.81	5.76	5.65
Liquidity Ratio	0.89	1.00	1.02	1.00
Collection Period	48.43	45.57	48.94	51.78

Stock/Turnover	9.25	10.11	9.50	8.94
Creditors Days	38.95	38.35	37.51	36.63
Solvency Ratio (%)	32.78	38.94	39.29	52.81
Gearing (%)	78.21	55.45	55.79	43.98

```
Report of Company Directors/Officers
Co Secretary:
Mr D SMITH
Nationality : BRITISH          Date Appointed:  20/05/97
Home Address:                  Date of Birth :  20/03/44
20 The Drive                   Occupation: Managing Director
Sevenoaks                      Co Sec & Director: N
Kent TN13 2AA                  Other Directorships:  N
Great Britain

Directors details
Director   :
Mrs G SMITH
Nationality : BRITISH          Date Appointed:  20/05/97
Home Address:                  Date of Birth :  10/03/43
20 The Drive                   Occupation:    Manager
Sevenoaks                      Other Directorships:  N
Kent TN13 2AA  Great Britain
```

On Infocheck Equifax's web interface (*http://www.infocheck.com.uk*), certain elements of the above data are hypertext linked to other databases – for instance, directors' names to the personal consumer credit database, and to facilities such as an alert if a director's name crops up in another context, or if new detrimental information is filed on the company.

Quality Factors

Value to the user is not only dependent on the range of businesses included, and the range of detail given about them, but also on the range and quality of the primary sources, the ease and power of search and output software, cost, accuracy in data input and analysis, and currency of data. These factors can only be assessed through detailed examination and comparison of the claims and reputations of the providers, the results of independent reviews and tests, and by awards to providers of quality standards such as ISO9002.

Commercial Sources of Disclosed Company Documents

Sometimes for legal reasons, sometimes to obtain the full detail including any graphics, or even sometimes to evaluate design and quality, people need to see an original company document. Documents such as those referred to in the 'Primary Sources' section above are available cheaply, and often electronically, direct from the companies or the authorities themselves. Nevertheless, information brokers and providers are happy to add a premium to supply copies of documents which they have acquired as primary sources for their main products. There are several advantages in obtaining documents through an intermediary, including company confidentiality. It can be fast and convenient, and it avoids the need to monitor for new filings, to deal with different agencies, handle different formats, and to place and pay for orders.

For large companies, users formerly chose between the selectively transcribed text of annual reports and accounts in commercial databases, a microform image copy from Companies House or the Stock Exchange, or the paper original via the company. For most smaller limited companies, only the Companies House service was available, including via intermediaries. Today most nations' principal information providers complement their database-centred services with a document supply service for the filed reports of all or most registered companies, in full-text, often with colour digitised images. Alternatively, many companies make their filed documents, and much else, available via their web site, which is often linked from the company's record on the information providers' web databases. Dun & Bradstreet and search engine provider Lycos have jointly created the *Companiesonline* web site (*http://www.companiesonline.com/*) as an easy way to locate a company's home page. Free Duns basic data on a company is linked both to a fuller Duns record, and to the company's home page. The web site of the British office services company March Communications or MARCHCom includes free access to the database *CAROL – Company Annual Reports Online*, comprising data taken from Companies House records (*http://www.carol.co.uk/*).

ICC's main database, as above, includes document images for all UK limited companies, as does Infocheck Equifax's, its images deliverable and printable via the web, or by fax. Perfect Information offers the electronic *Pioneer* pay-as-you-go company documents service, covering London Stock Exchange and Companies House filings, and equivalent documents for certain other countries. The headline 'Plucky little aRMadillo challenges online giants' (*Information World Review*, December 1997, p. 15) introduced RM Online's own web-based pay-as-you-go (£14 +VAT per set) UK companies document image service.

ICC's text only records for London quoted companies appear as FT Profile's ICC *Full Company Reports and Accounts*, and DataStar and Dialog's *ICC British Company Annual reports*. As its name may suggest, Disclosure's products centre on searchable and digitised image databases of documents which companies have filed; especially those made public through USA SEC's *EDGAR* electronic filing system, rejoicing in names like 'Williams Act Filings', '10Ks' and '10Qs'. Disclosure's data collection has expanded to include selected UK and worldwide companies, and partly through alliances with other providers, to include data from primary sources other than statutory disclosure. While scanned US and European PLCs are at the core of Disclosure's databases, there is also standardised data for selected companies worldwide. EDGAR images are on Disclosure's Global Access database, while hard copies of the documents of millions of other companies can be ordered via the database. Dialog's *EdgarPlus* file holds the filings in plain text form. Examples of many other sources of EDGAR filings are *Moody's EDGAR Report Online* service, and the real-time document delivery *Moody's EDGAR Edge (SEC) Product*, both operated by Financial Information Services (FIS).

Profound and FT Profile host London Stock Exchange's *Regulatory News Service*, through which disclosed company documents are available between three and nine hours after release. The hosts index and cumulate the data for efficient retrospective access.

Disclosure's *Laser D* pre-dates web-based document image databases, and is an alternative way of holding and searching companies' original annual reports and accounts in-house: required ones can be printed at high quality as and when needed.

The First Call Corporation urges public companies to disseminate their communications to American investors via its real-time *Corporate Release* service, where they appear alongside analysts comments:

> 'Transmit earnings announcements, management or strategic changes, new product announcements, mergers and divestitures – all to the decision-makers whose opinion can affect the price of your company's stock. Send unlimited, unedited full-text news – including extensive financials – as well as investor communications.
> For maximum visibility, corporate releases appear side-by-side with analyst notes.
> Reach more than 9,000 money managers at 2,000 major institutional investment firms as well as the research departments of 80 premier brokerage firms.' (From their web site – *http://www.firstcall.com/*)

Sources of Basic Company Details – Company Directories

The databases referred to above as 'comprehensive' are just as capable of answering simple, factual questions as are dedicated printed or electronic directories. The sample Infocheck Equifax record in the section above includes the elements of a typical directory entry, mostly gathered at the beginning. Indeed, the most succinct of the standard *reports* or output formats normally offered by the software automatically selects such data from the full record. A *Company briefing* format is currently offered via Financial Times Electronic Publishing's *FT.com* web site (*http://www.FT.com/*) as a free output format of the very detailed company records available. Like many directories, Company briefing includes a standardised financial snapshot plus the more predictable basic data. Some of ICC's separate products listed above, most obviously *ICC British Company Directory*, are directory level extracts from the original full records. For the user, it can be simpler and more economical to use a source whose detail and software is dedicated to a particular purpose.

For smaller limited companies, many information providers hold little more in their databases than directory level information, not deeming it economical to enter all the data held by registration offices. At this level of information, it is feasible to include the one million-plus live UK limited companies in an online or CD-ROM database. In its *Credit Decisions* CD-ROM, Infocheck Equifax additionally includes brief financial information, a credit profile, and the names of directors; as well as records for some 200,000 non-limited businesses. Where further information is desired on a business, the software connects to the full online database.

More traditional directories, many still available in printed format, are valuable for the information they obtain directly from the business itself. For limited companies this includes facts such as number of employees, trade names, name of marketing manager. For sole traders and partnerships, which may predominate in local directories, all of the information has to be obtained this way. These directories selectively cover a country, such as for the UK (ranked here by frequency of usage as found in the Annual Business Information Resources Survey, 1998 (*Business Information Review* 15(1), March 1988, pp. 5-21) *Kompass*, *Key British Enterprises*, *Kelly's Business Directory*, *The Company Guide* (Hemington Scott); or more comprehensively cover a locality, such as Thomsons directories; or an industry, such as *Directory of Chemical Products and Buyers Guide* (Hamlet Information Services for the Chemical Industry Association). *Europages* (printed, CD-ROM, or free web directory – *http://www.europages.com/*) recently included 150,000 companies 'selected by size and selling capacity to Europe'.

Directories of Companies' Web Sites

It has to be remembered that free directories of companies and gateways to company web sites such as The UK Web Directory (*http://www.ukdirectory.com/*) are closer to self-selecting means of advertising than to independent reference works. For a minimum of £250 *COUNTYWeb* (*http://www.countyweb.co.uk*) places a subscriber's 'business card' on one or more of their UK county web business directories, or on the national site.

Many printed company directories are essentially *trades directories*, where the information contained, the arrangement and indexing is targeted at buyers – whose needs are covered in more detail in the 'Product Information' chapter. The sample from a *Key British Enterprises* entry below, shows the mix of company and products/services information presented for different uses. Through separate indexes and/or sequences, printed trades directories typically allow selective views of data on a company, and searching by either company or product. Scant information is normally given on products in directories; although trade names are often given, and are searchable (further information in the 'Product Information' chapter). The printed *Kompass* also reproduces trade marks in its classified sequence and allows you to distinguish between manufacturers, suppliers, importers, distributors etc. when searching it. Of course, great retrieval and output advantages attach to the electronic versions which are available for almost all but some local business directories; not least the ability to simultaneously search all *Kompass* European editions, and to download the results of searches directly into mailshot or spreadsheet software. Mailing lists can be designed and purchased online from *www.mailing-labels.com*, a database of 3 million addresses and contact names contributed by major UK information providers. *Kompass* publisher Reed Information Services have even created a single worldwide database of 1.5 million companies from 62 countries, searchable via the Reedbase Online web site, or on various CD-ROM products. *Kelly's British Companies* CD-ROM has 80% more companies than the printed version, as well as trade names, multiple-criteria searching, and the ability to build an in-house contacts database. Dun & Bradstreet's *Marketing Database* (*http:// shared.dwsearch.com:7501/*) can be searched free for selected details of 2 million businesses worlwide. Kelly's also offers a free level of access to their UK company data, for anyone prepared to register (*http://www.kellys.co.uk/*).

Because of their near comprehensive coverage of businesses large and small, and their complementary classified approach, telephone directories are an important company information resource, especially if searchable on a national basis. Various commercial compilations of companies phone and fax numbers are available, not long ago TDS was offering its *Telepower Pro* CD-ROM of 2.4 million UK businesses for £40, and getting favourable reviews in comparison with BT's Phonedisc at £910 (including domestic numbers). The UK *Electronic Yellow Pages* (*EYP* – *http://www.eyp.co.uk/*) and the USA GTE's *BigBook Yellow Pages* (*http://www.bigbook.com/*) can be searched free of charge, by firm's name, product or service, and geographical area. Furthermore many of the directory entries are linked to firms' own web sites. In the *Annual Business Information Resources Survey*, 1998 (cited above), business libraries ranked *Yellow Pages* as the third most used UK hard copy company directory, and the most used company directory web site. The *555-1212* (*http://www.555-1212.com/*), and *Whowhere?* (*http://www.whowhere.lycos.com/*) sites currently provide good retrieval of both personal and business names and numbers. The *Globalyp* site (*http://www.globalyp.com/world.htm*) is a worldwide gateway to web-based, mostly business, telephone directories, and the 'Directories' page of Strathclyde University's *Business Information Sources on the Internet* is a gateway to all kinds of directory sites worldwide.

It should be remembered that other than the telephone directory or web search tool, the only systematic way of tracing information on a sole trader may be a local trades directory or databases. The former are often only produced in printed form, by commercial publishers, local authority departments, and organisations like chambers of commerce and enterprise agencies, the latter are often unpublished (see the Thames Valley Chamber of Commerce example of a local directory below). Thomsons series of local directories can also be searched free of charge on their *ThomWeb site* (*http://www.thomweb.co.uk/*):

> 'The ultimate search on the Net for over 2.2 million UK businesses. To search over 2.2 million UK business listings, type in the company name, location or business type (or any combination of these three), then click on the "Search" button.'

Professional partnerships are usually much larger than sole traders, so it is fortunate that considerable detail on them can usually be found in the appropriate national or international professional directory, such as: *Directory of European Information Brokers and Consultants*, 9th edn, 1997. Edited by Marshall Crawford and Vaughan Buchanan. Effective Technology Marketing, 1997.

Examples of Company Directories

Countries or Larger Regions

Key British Enterprises 1997. Dun & Bradstreet, 1997.

A considerable amount of data on the top 50,000 firms; separate indexes in the annual six volume set (plus updates) include directors' names, trade names and geographic area; also CD-ROM versions.

UK Companies. Reedbase (a division of Reed Information).

Financial, news, M & A & other data on 200,000 firms; CD-ROM or via Reedbase online.

Kompass Register of Business and Industry 1996. Reed Information, 1996. The CD-ROM version is *CD-Plus, volumes 1 & 2: Products & Services; Company Information*

'Company, product and financial information on 53,000 leading UK companies.'

Thomas Register

Long established North American directory, with printed, CD-ROM and online (e.g. via Profound) alternatives. Includes 56,000 US and Canadian 'Company profiles.'

Major Companies series. Graham & Whiteside.

Approximately 30 titles, each usually covering a world region or an industry sector in a region – e.g. *Major Companies of Africa, . . . Latin America; and Major Energy Companies of Europe*. 72,000 businesses worldwide; single CD-ROM or separately for each of seven regions.

The Companies Database on CD-ROM. ENKI Information Systems

Data from the Irish Companies Registration Office on more than 280,000 active and inactive companies. Complemented by the directory of businesses and their owner's name and addresses: *Business Names Database on CD-ROM* – ENKI Information Systems.

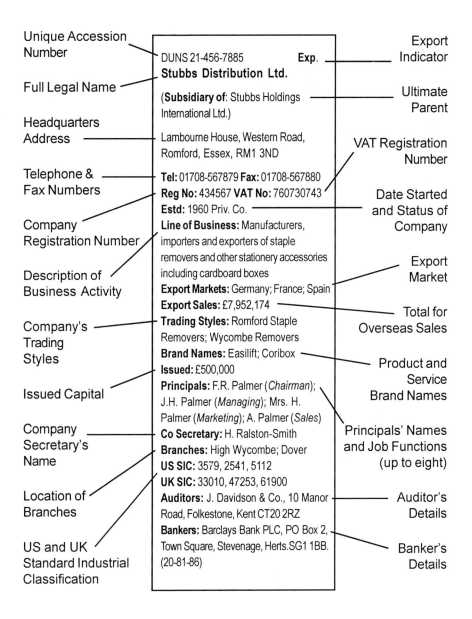

Unique Accession Number

Full Legal Name

Headquarters Address

Telephone & Fax Numbers

Company Registration Number

Description of Business Activity

Company's Trading Styles

Issued Capital

Company Secretary's Name

Location of Branches

US and UK Standard Industrial Classification

DUNS 21-456-7885   **Exp**.
Stubbs Distribution Ltd.
(**Subsidiary of**: Stubbs Holdings International Ltd.)
Lambourne House, Western Road, Romford, Essex, RM1 3ND
Tel: 01708-567879 **Fax:** 01708-567880
Reg No: 434567 **VAT No:** 760730743
Estd: 1960 Priv. Co.
Line of Business: Manufacturers, importers and exporters of staple removers and other stationery accessories including cardboard boxes
Export Markets: Germany; France; Spain
Export Sales: £7,952,174
Trading Styles: Romford Staple Removers; Wycombe Removers
Brand Names: Easilift; Coribox
Issued: £500,000
Principals: F.R. Palmer (*Chairman*); J.H. Palmer (*Managing*); Mrs. H. Palmer (*Marketing*); A. Palmer (*Sales*)
Co Secretary: H. Ralston-Smith
Branches: High Wycombe; Dover
US SIC: 3579, 2541, 5112
UK SIC: 33010, 47253, 61900
Auditors: J. Davidson & Co., 10 Manor Road, Folkestone, Kent CT20 2RZ
Bankers: Barclays Bank PLC, PO Box 2, Town Square, Stevenage, Herts.SG1 1BB. (20-81-86)

Export Indicator

Ultimate Parent

VAT Registration Number

Date Started and Status of Company

Export Market

Total for Overseas Sales

Product and Service Brand Names

Principals' Names and Job Functions (up to eight)

Auditor's Details

Banker's Details

Figure 9. Partial sample record from a printed edition of Key British Enterprises

Europe's Major Companies Directory. Euromonitor, 1996.

D&B Europa

4 volume directory of 60,000 European companies; country by country and ranked sequences.

Italy's...; Austria's...; Netherlands'...; Spain's...; France's... etc. Largest Companies. Dun & Bradstreet.

Specific Trades and Industries

Bankers' Almanac BANKbase. Reed Business Information; CD-ROM.

The 150 year old authority on ca. 28,000 banks around the world, now with all the features of electronic database format, including quarterly updates and an annual subscription price of £1,125.

Specific Business functions

CD-Export. Chambre de Commerce et d'Industrie de Paris; CD-ROM

French, Italian, Portugese, Spanish & Austrian importers and exporters.

Specific Types of Business: Quoted Companies

Macmillan Stock Exchange Yearbook 1998. M. Tumbrell and D. Tweedie (eds.). Waterlow, 1998; also available on CD-ROM.

Authoritative source of financial and general information on the 4,339+ London and Dublin quoted companies and securities.

Hemscott Company Guide. Hemmington Scott Publishing.

Details of 2,300 UK quoted companies, including, financial details, mergers and acquisitions, shareholders, directors, corporate and professional advisers. Quarterly issues.

Specific Types of Business: Limited Companies

Macmillan's Unquoted Companies: Top 20,000 1997. Waterlow, 1997

Financial and other data on the UK's top 20,000 by turnover, various approaches and listings.

Specific Types of Business: Multinational Companies

Directory of Multinationals. Waterlow, 1997.

Profiles of the world's top 500 multinational companies.

Local Areas

D&B Business Registers series – e.g. Birmingham; Kent; Wales. Dun & Bradstreet.

30 separate directories covering 600,000 businesses around the UK.

The Official Barnett Business Directory. Published in association with Barnett Council; annual.

Sheffield Industrial Estate Directory. ABC Info. Published serially.

Thames Valley Chamber of Commerce and Industry's own database

Chambers typically maintain such local directories: Thames Valley's contains information on approximately 4,500 member companies in the Thames Valley region. Records are said to be regularly updated and are therefore ideal for local sourcing of companies, for mailshots or identifying suppliers of products and services.

Intertrader Directory of Mid Wales Manufacturing Group Companies. MWMG; annual

Sources of Company Financial Information

For tactical and strategic decision making purposes, business at times need all of the following specific financial indications. As shown, they fall into three levels of sophistication or added value (investment rating services for companies and their equities and bonds, are covered in the 'Financial Information' chapter, in the section 'Financial Instruments Performance Guides; Ratings Services . . .'):

- Raw data
        - disclosed financial results
        - additional figures
- Numerical analysis
        - financial ratios
        - credit scores
        - performance on equities markets
        - industry comparisons and rankings
        - historical comparison
- Expert analysis
        - projected figures
        - expert analysis and prediction

The large selection of information products in this field, address one, two, or all three levels, in various degrees of detail. The 'comprehensive' type of database aims to satisfy most if not all these common needs for financial information, so aspects of them are also considered in this section. However, there are also sources which concentrate on company financial information, some of which provide great detail for a specific range of companies. The range of the above areas addressed varies between publishers and between their individual products, as does the level of detail, number and type of companies covered, time range of figures, update frequency, search and output functionality, accuracy and cost. Here are some examples of sources of detailed company financial data, gathered from product literature, grouped according to significant geographical or other scope:

Examples of Sources of Company Financial Information

UK Companies

FAME (*Financial Analysis Made Easy*). Jordans via Bureau van Dijk; CD-ROM and Internet versions. 280,000 British and Irish companies' records – equivalent of *Jordanwatch* database.

Corporate Financial Performance. Dun & Bradstreet. Three years' financial trend data for each of the UK's 50,000 largest companies.

Juniper (Windows); *Plum* (web) etc. ICC; other versions on various online hosts. Accounts data, ratios, industry comparisons and ICC scores on over 150,000 firms.

ROM:BUS: The Business Ratio Plus CD-ROM. Allows comparison of the financial performance of companies within their industry sectors.

Infocheck Equifax reports on UK Ltd companies – via their web site etc. Financial data includes ratios, credit profile, industry comparison, analyst's report.

Jordanwatch. Jordans; others versions on various online hosts. Three years accounts, ratios, trends; 200,000 UK companies with over £500,000 turnover.

Kompass CD Plus, volume 3: Financial Data. Extracted from the UK *Kompass*, financial snapshots of just under 30,000 companies.

D&B Marketplace UK. Dun & Bradstreet (CD-ROM, plus other versions via third parties). 1.6 million actively trading UK businesses, from multi-nationals to sole traders.

Creditmaster. Experian; online, CD-ROM, or via phone enquiry service. All limited companies' documents, plus payment, credit and risk information.

aRMadillo. RM Online; via web or offline. All limited and some non-limited companies, emphasis on credit analyses.

Major UK Companies Handbook 1997. Extel, 1997; also available in electronic formats.

Other Countries

Amadeus ('Analyse Major Databases from European Sources'). Jordans via Bureau van Dijk. CD-ROM and Internet versions. Data on top 150,000 European companies; from providers in each of 25 countries.

D&B US Companies Financial Statements/Dun's Financial records Plus. Dun & Bradstreet.The former is a database on e.g. the Biz@dvantage host, covering major US companies, the latter a CD-ROM version.

Moody's Company Data. CD-ROM available from Dun & Bradstreet. Covers over 10,000 US public companies listed on the NYSE, AMEX, Nasdaq, OTC and regional exchanges. Includes up to seven years' financial data.

EDGAR Database; FreeEDGAR (http://www.sec.gov/edgarhp.htm). U.S. Securities and Exchange Commission free official web source of the filings submitted by PLCs. Various non-official sites also repackage the EDGAR data in various advantageous ways.

Hoover's Online – web site *http://www.hoovers.com/*. Aimed at end-user subscribers, but includes free report formats. US company coverage includes 3,200 in-depth Hoover Company Profiles, 7,500 in-depth financials, real-time SEC documents from EDGAR, and subsidiary information. Profiles and Capsules (free) are linked to related industry snapshots and lists of companies.

SCRL Bilans Plus. SCRL; on Questel-Orbit host. Balance sheets and analysis for 350,000 French companies.

Teikoku Databank/Teikoku Japanese Companies – Summary Financials. Nikkei. Former title contains financial and other data on 200,000 listed and unlisted Japanese companies.

CFI Direct. CFI Online, Dublin (*http://www.formations.ie/direct.htm*). Online database of 'all' 290,000 Irish companies, including 42,000 analysed accounts.

ISI Emerging markets. Internet Securities (*http://www.securities.com*). Web-based source on companies (and related matters) in Central and Eastern Europe, Latin America, Asia.

Financial Publishing Highlights. ADC Diskont International/Eorocredit (Italy). Data for companies representing 80% of the Italian economy; CD-ROM.

International Coverage

D & B European Financial Records. Dun & Bradstreet , on FT Profile with other versions and titles on other hosts. Includes detailed financial data, including ratios, on 2.4 million companies in 13 countries.

Extel Financial Cards/Extel International Financials. Financial Times Electronic Publishing; the former is an FT Profile database, the latter and other versions exist on other hosts. British and selected non-UK companies, includes share data, ratios, balance sheets, profit and loss statements, and market capitalization.

Worldscope. Disclosure. Over 15,000 global companies representing more than 50 established and emerging markets. Includes financials, product and geographic segment data, growth rates and more.

Nikkei Asian Corporate Profile. Enterprises in China, South Korea, Singapore, Malaysia, Thailand, Taiwan and others.

Asia Pacific Handbook. Extel. Also available in electronic formats.

Global Scan (also branded as *International Reports Service*). Infocheck Equifax. Online financial and credit data on nine million companies worldwide.

PLCs or Quoted Companies

Major UK Companies Handbook; Smaller UK Companies Handbook; International Handbook; European Handbook; Asia Pacific Handbook. Financial Times Information. Quick reference to financial data on the leading PLCs inthe country or region concerned, published once or twice yearly.

FT Analysis Reports. Financial Times. Analysed financial and other data on approximately 4,000 quoted European companies.

FT CITIFAX. Financial Times Electronic Information; faxed service. Detailed overview of UK listed companies' activities: financial data; financial results; share price performance; the company's directors; and the latest three months press coverage.

Global Vantage. Standard & Poor's Compustat. 12,000 quoted companies, in 70 countries.

Moody's Company Data/Moody's Company Data Direct – Financial Information Services. The latter is the Internet version of the database of the financials and other EDGAR filings of more than 10,000 NYSE, AMEX and Nasdaq stock exchange companies, including archive.

Nikkei Corporate profile and Financial Data. All Japanese listed companies; over 25 years of financial data.

UK Quoted Company Intelligence; on the OneSource host, incorporating financial and other forms of company information from a variety of providers.

Companies in Specific Industries

Hadleigh Marketing Services quarterly surveys, e.g. *British Drinks Index*. Profiles of 250 leading beverage companies; similar for retail, food, & drinks.

FT World Insurance Yearbook/World Insurance Companies. Longman (annual)/FT Profile database. ('. . . standard reference book for the insurance industry'); financial & other information, country by country arrangement.

Specialist Sources of Business Ratios

Key Business Ratios. Dun & Bradstreet; print format. 'Over 800,000 sets of accounts are compiled to identify the average business ratios for 370 different industries in the UK over the last 3 years, giving you a comprehensive guide to British business performance . . . over 34 balance sheet and profit & loss percentages, as well as 20 key business ratios for each of the 370 business classifications. Upper, median and lower quartile percentages are provided to ensure appropriate comparisons.'

Ready-made Rankings

UK's 10,000/Sweden's 10,000/Denmark's 80,000/Europe's 15000/Asia's 7,500 Largest Companies. ELC International; CD-ROM and/or other formats.

Britain's Top Foreign Owned Companies 1994. Jordans, 1995; one of several, others cover particular regions, industries and other criteria. Financial data, including ratios, for 10,000 companies, some ranked. 5 printed vols, or CD-ROM; separate shareholders and regional disks available.

Times 1,000. Times Books; annual. Very popular ranking and profiles of UK companies.

Forbes. The top 500 US Companies and 500 largest foreign ones; appears in Forbes periodical.

D&B Business Rankings. Dun & Bradstreet. Over 25,000 US businesses from highest to lowest by sales volume, includes other data.

Fortune 500. USA. Issued twice yearly as special issue of *Fortune* business periodical; or from their web site.

The Web 100 (http://www.w100.com/). The top 100 companies by annual profit; separate US, global and industry rankings; entries link to free company data from a variety of information providers.

World's Most Respected Companies

Financial Times annual survey and ranking of corporate reptation, widened from European to worldwide companies from 1998 (supplement to *Financial Times* November 30th 1998).

Quoted Companies; Financial Services Companies

Because of the number of people and businesses having different kinds of relationship with PLCs, in particular with *quoted* PLCs, more sources concentrate on them in more detail than on ordinary limited companies. As well as the extremely detailed data disclosed to registration and regulatory authorities, and data on the issue and performance of stocks and shares, FT and Extel records even include selected press cuttings. The information providers featured in the 'PLCs or quoted companies' list above, specialise in providing the type and level of detail necessary for serious, systematic analysis for corporate investment and fund management. As is necessary for in-depth analysis, they devote special record structures and data items to the different categories of financial services companies – such as banks and insurers. An illustration of these additional types and levels of detail, is provided by Standard and Poor's Compustat *Global Vantage*:

- Up to 12 years of historical financial data
- Monthly currency files with cross-translation tables for more than 110 currencies
- Monthly pricing for more than 90 indexes
- Monthly price and dividend histories for over 13,500 company issues

Software for Ad Hoc Company Screening and Analysis

The data provides only part of the solution; portfolio managers and others need to match their own changing criteria against the details of perhaps thousands of potentially interesting companies. They often have their own software, or can insert their criteria into the software provided with sophisticated databases such as those under 'PLCs or quoted companies' above. Dow Jones, for instance, offers *Private Investor* and *Technical Analyst* editions of its *News/Retrieval* software, allowing the 6,000 companies in Dow Jones' database and current stock market price service to be screened by at least 20 criteria. Thus an investor could obtain a list of the companies whose share price was for some reason artificially depressed in relation to its performance.

Interpretation of Company Financial Data

Fortunately most of these secondary sources cut through the 'window dressing' and varying complexities of the figures released by companies. Some sources extract standard, comparable key figures, but especially where the full and original accounts are given, value is added in the form of standard and widely recognised ratios, comparisons with the industry as a whole; and various proprietary scoring systems. It can be seen from the full company record reproduced earlier in the chapter, how fairly typically Infocheck extract key accounts figures as a 'Financial analysis', make standard calculations on accounts figures as an 'Extended company ratio analysis', and present a table of key accounts figures for the industry sector as a whole, which the user can compare with the company's figures. Like the raw figures themselves, calculations and comparisons are normally given for three or more years, to reveal all-important trends.

Whatever the language and layout of the original accounts, the important figures to identify are :

- *Assets*   (property, stock, cash etc.)
- *Liabilities*   (owings)
- *Capital*   (mainly the initial shareholders' inputs)
- *Income*   (amount received over the period)
- *Expenses*   (costs incurred during the period)

The *profit and loss account* is normally present, and is very revealing. It is the difference between income and expenses; a positive or negative figure.

The *balance sheet* gives a fuller picture of financial standing, by adding the difference between assets and liabilities to capital.

Business and Financial Ratios

Some ratios may be volunteered by the company in its accounts, or a set calculated by the secondary source provider (as in the Infocheck sample record), indicating performance in general, financial performance, credit position, added value, efficiency, employee performance, investment performance. Since ratios are single figures resulting from meaningful combinations of other figures, they are ideal for making comparisons between individual companies, or with a company and the particular industry as a whole, as in *industry quartiles*, below. The *quick ratio,* for example, is the figure for current assets excluding stock, divided by current liabilities. In the hands of someone who knows what figure to expect, it indicates liquidity, and therefore the potential for cash flow problems.

Industry Quartiles

For each ratio value for a company, sources often give comparative *industry figures* in the form of three different industry quartile values. That is, figures delineating the four groups or 'quartiles' into which the industry as a whole has been divided for that ratio; a lower quartile, an upper quartile, and two more in between. Thus the company can be ranked for that criteria against those sharing the same SIC or other industry classification. This is how the data appears in, for example, a record from *ICC British Company Financial Datasheets*, on DataStar:

RATIOS (for a specific company or an industry)

Profitability Ratios	19970930	19960930	19950930
Pretax Profit/Capital Employed(%)	8.04	9.04	7.14
Pretax Profit/Total Assets(%)	7.13	8.13	6.18

[and other ratios]

INDUSTRY COMPARISONS

UK SIC code: 15960 Manufacture of beer
Year to : 19971231

Quartile:	Lower	Median	Upper
Pretax Prof/Cap Employed %	3.70	8.50	13.80
Pretax Profit/Total Assets %	3.20	6.60	10.60
Pretax Profit/Sales %	2.50	9.40	13.50
Sales/Total Assets %	67.60	92.00	129.00
Credit period (days)	42.30	36.10	25.60
Current ratio	80	.90	1.30
Value Added per employee	NA	NA	NA
Av.g empl. remuneration (GBP)	8,492.40	11,089.30	14,098.40
Sales per employee (GBP)	44,987.80	76,380.40	112,702.10
Employee remuneration/Sales %	18.90	16.90	13.80

[and others, usually for each of 3 years]

This following diagram shows the first industry ratio given above for the company, superimposed on the industry quartiles data for the same ratio, for the year to 31st December 1997. It can be seen how the three industry quartile figures precisely define the median ratio for the industry, the bottom of the upper quartile and the top of the lower quartile, but not the top and bottom of the whole range:

Figure 10. Company n's pre-tax profit/capital employed ratio, compared with 'industry quartiles' for the ratio

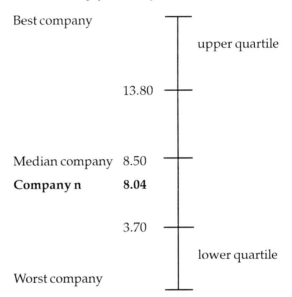

Scores

(*Credit* scores are dealt with in the section on 'Credit and Risk Asessment', below)

Certain information providers have their own way of arriving at scores which are intended as a simple instant indication of company's financial performance, enabling comparison with any other in the database; notably ICC where the up to 75 ratios given in a company record 'form an integral part of the ICC risk score model'. Here is an excerpt from a company's record in *ICC British Company Financial Datasheets*, on DataStar:

> *Corporate score*
>
> ICC Scores:
>
> > ICC credit scores are based on the company's financial performance and a comparison with the industry sector
>
> SIC code:
>
> > 15960 Manufacture of beer;

the score is out of 100 for the following years:

1997	60
1996	70
1995	71
1994	66

CD-ROM Products

The relatively stable nature of company financial data, and the frequent need to spend a long time manipulating it, makes CD-ROM distribution an attractive proposition. Most of the major providers offer a CD-ROM incorporating complete or nearly complete records from the central database for at least larger companies. A feature of CD-ROM products is software allowing elaborate in-house analysis and output formatting, unconstrained by telecommunications charges. Included above in 'Examples of Sources of Company Financial Information' are *FAME* (Jordan's data), and *Amadeus* (data from various providers), which have recently also been launched as web products.

Applications and Functions (taken from *FAME* product literature)

- Aggregate the accounts of groups of companies
- Analyse the evolution of a company
- Rank companies according to one variable for several years
- Modify the data of a company
- Add the accounts of a company to the group
- Calculate the statistical distribution of any financial variable
- Perform concentration analyses on groups of companies by any variable over five years
- Calculate the correlation coefficient between any two variables in a group of companies
- Graphics facility incorporating bar charts, pie charts, line graphs and Lorenz curves
- Navigable company tree facility displays holding companies and subsidiaries
- Software includes online statutory document ordering service (fax, post etc. delivery)
- Available as one disk (top 120,000 companies), or two (next 140,000 companies)
- Subscription includes monthly replacements

Credit and Risk Assessment

Managing cash-flow and minimising bad debt requires 'credit management'. Millions of tactical credit decisions are made daily: for instance, whether, or on what conditions, to extend credit to customers; when and whether to expect payment from a customer. A single default or a group of late settlements could seriously damage a creditor's financial health. Some businesses use credit insurance companies to protect themselves, some have credit control departments to carry out initial and regular credit worthiness checks on corporate and personal customers and suppliers. The credit status of a firm can have strategic as well as operational implications; for instance, as an indicator of value and performance to potential investors, collaborators, and takeover bidders. This section is concerned with services which rate companies for credit management purposes; those which primarily rate companies or financial instruments for investment purposes appear in the 'Financial Information' chapter under 'Financial Instruments Performance Guides; Ratings Services, ...'

Credit and risk management embraces the need to establish any or all of the following, in relation to other firms:

Overall credit status

- to assess value, performance and stability of the firm
- to assess whether the firm should be allowed credit, whether it can pay bills

Credit limit

- to assess how much the firm can be allowed to owe

Payment pattern

- to assess the time taken to pay, and likelihood of defaulting

Failure risk

- to assess likelihood of firm being suddenly and permanently unable to pay and honour commitments

Establishing these variables with any degree of confidence requires a combination of past financial performance data, and a variety of other indicators. The following table shows which primary source equates to which function of secondary credit and risk information sources.

Sources of Credit and Risk Assessment

Primary source	Role in credit & risk assessment		
	Credit assessment	Payment pattern	Failure risk
Statutory disclosed information:			
Figures, calculations from accounts	X		X
Directors' histories / records	X		X
Liquidation, administration bank-ruptcy orders; creditors' petitions	X	X	X
Voluntarily disclosed information:			
Press statements	X		X
Supplementary financial data	X		X
Information disclosed by third parties:			
County and other court judgements	X	X	X
Other firms' experiences	X	X	X
Consumer credit licensing data	X		X
Trade and bank references	X	X	X

Credit Assessment

Credit information providers add value by gathering the relevant diverse primary information and applying a combination of mathematical methods and experience to arrive at succinct, authoritative assessments. Built into proprietary credit and risk models are the company's financial figures and ratios, comparisons with industry figures and ratios, and the past outcomes of other companies with similar indicators. A company's exposure to others' financial insecurity and late-payment, can be assessed by cumulating the risk assessments of its customers. Dun & Bradstreet's *Risk Analysis* software compares a client's customer base with D&B records, using company and industry risk indicator and payment score fields to analyse the customer base by these criteria. Results could show that a client is exposed to cash flow difficulties because it has significantly more slow-paying customers than the industry norm.

Credit reference agencies, such as Qui, Graydons, Infocheck Equifax, Dimensione (in Italy) and Experian (a merger of the former CCN Group and TRW Information Systems and Services), developed specialist products in response to growing demand in the 1980s and 1990s. The last three mentioned, exemplify credit specialists expanding into broader company information provision. Since its association with Equifax, Infocheck has become a major supplier of general company information. Infocheck Equifax has claimed to be the UK's largest credit information provider, covering 3.5 million businesses, including many sole traders, and 45 million private citizens. They also employ collaboration and networking in order to offer financial and credit information on 9 million companies worldwide in their 'real-time' online *International Reports Service*. Conversely, generalist company information providers have adopted various strategies to meet this specialist need. Most have increased the credit information given in company records, in some cases achieved through collaboration with specialists – as between Jordans and Qui Credit Assessment Ltd, resulting in a credit rating and score in all *Jordanwatch* records. Dun and Bradstreet's secret formula for the 'D&B rating' can still be seen as the pinnacle of their business. In common with other company information generalists (examples below), ICC offers selective companies and data elements from its corporate database as the *Credit Index* CD-ROM. The *Company Search Reports* of the RM Group have a very strong credit information element, combining standard financial data with a credit limit figure and reports from all the public sources of adverse indications.

Providers tend to produce credit analyses automatically for a basic range of businesses – for example, Infocheck gives a wide range of credit-related data for live UK limited companies, and adds non-limited companies if and when researched on their own initiative, or for users of their ad hoc information service. As in the sample Infocheck report reproduced earlier in the chapter, credit-related ratios and other vital signs data may form part of the standard record – e.g. 'Credit limit £40,000 (assessed for monthly terms)'. However, for the searcher particularly concerned with credit or risk 'management', some sources collate, calculate and report much more information. The relevant sections of Infocheck reports include:

Analyst's Comments
*   Textual summary of relevant data, and credit recommendation
Gazette or Detrimental Information
*   Creditors meetings, winding up petitions etc., reported in official *Gazettes*
Credit Profile
*   County Court judgement details
*   Notifiable 'events' from official *Gazettes*
*   Profile of firm's compared with sector's payment period
*   Liquidity ratio of firm compared with sector
*   *Vital signs* – i.e. trends in firm's key financial indicators
*   Monthly trade credit limit (£)

In full versions of 'comprehensive' company databases such as ICC's, one of the pre-defined report formats often comprises data selected for credit and/ or risk management purposes. Alternatively, the relevant data is packaged with appropriate software and available separately:

CD-ROMs marketed for credit and/or risk management purposes
(All aiming to provide credit and selected financial and other information, at least for all UK limited companies; most updated monthly, and linkable to the 'parent' database; most available on annual subscription, payment for some by metered usage)

- *CD Credit Register* – Dun & Bradstreet
- *Credit Index* – ICC
- *Credit Decisions* – Infocheck Equifax
- *Creditmaster* – Experian

Specialist credit reference agencies usually go beyond supplying the relevant figures, ratios and other facts, and provide a succinct credit rating which the searcher can act on without further deliberation. Such ratings are the result of the provider's own algorithm applied to all the relevant numerical and non-numerical, hard and soft information they have on the company. The agencies charge from about £10 for a company rating, up to £50 if a more detailed format is requested, and from £1 for a private individual. The credit score sometimes takes the form of a monetary limit or range which the company could safely be allowed to owe. Experian's 'Snapshot credit categories', shown below, are an example of a verbal system, which requires and allows more interpretation by the user. The category given for a company is complemented by text and figures under the headings 'Detailed legal findings', 'Detailed payment behavior', 'Payment trend behavior', 'Company history' and 'Financial services history.'

Experian's 'Snapshot credit categories' (From product descriptions on their web site – *http://www.experian.com/*)

'Experian provides a credit category by analyzing the business's current trade experiences and the presence or absence of collection data and derogatory public record filings. We then classify the business into one of the following categories:

Acceptable: This company actively uses credit and pays its bills no later than nine days late, on average. There are no derogatory legal records on file for this company.

Caution: A company may fall into this category in one of two ways: If the company actively uses credit, the risk category is based on the current payment performance and/or legal records on file. If the company does not actively use credit, it may pose increased risk. In either case, the caution risk category suggests you investigate further before making credit or business decisions related to the company.

Warning: Derogatory payment performance information and/or derogatory legal records exist on file for this company. Fifteen percent of businesses fall into this higher-risk category. Experian recommends further investigation prior to making any credit or business decisions.

Serious risk: Based on seriously derogatory payment performance and/or seriously derogatory legal records on file, Experian strongly recommends further investigation prior to making any credit or business decisions. Fifteen percent of businesses fall into this higher-risk category.

Bankruptcy: This company has previously filed for bankruptcy.'

Payment Performance

Payment profile information may be given as an average number of *creditor days*, as Infocheck below:

Sector average	*31.57 days*
Company n	*40.81 days*

Or the data may be broken down into creditor days for different sized payments (as in Dun & Bradstreet's *DunsPAR* reports); or as in the Payment Trend Behavior data in Experian's *Business Snapshot Rating Reports*, the time taken by the company to pay its bills over a period may be shown, and compared with an industry average. A similar graph to the following one is included in Experian reports; it illustrates the payment performance of the firm concerned, compared with industry averages. The bars on the left side

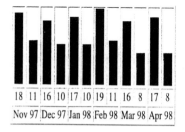

Figure 11. Graph from an Experian report

for each month show the average number of days beyond the invoice due date that a real estate development company paid its bills during the past six months. The bars on the right side for each month show the same information for the industry as a whole.

Alternatively, Experian, for example, offers a concise Days Beyond Terms (DBT) score – the average number of days a firm takes to pay its bills past the due date; or all the following elements in a *Payment Performance Report*:

- Latest days beyond terms figure, for both company and industry
- 6 month trend for the company and industry
- Number and value of accounts placed for collection by third parties
- Number of accounts on cash or pro forma terms
- Highlighting of any accounts remaining unpaid
- A summary of key points relating to payment behaviour
- A warning of any other adverse information relating to the company

Monitoring and Alerting

Because creditors and others obviously call for the earliest possible warning, particularly of detrimental changes in the liquidity of firms, the information providers usually offer monitoring and alerting additions to their services. Sometimes this is achieved through a user-defined, user-instigated online device which keeps a watching brief for the industries, companies and events specified – as in online host Profound's *Custom Alert*. Alternatively, the provider sets up a similar profile for a customer, for regular searching against relevant databases. Infocheck's *Priority Watch Out* monitors changes affecting specified firms or directors, and reports to the client by email. Instead non-selective alerting services can be subscribed to or consulted when needed, such as Jordans *Daily Reporting Service*, which lists firms with new liquidation, administration or wind-up orders.

Credit Decision Support Systems

In order to make many quick but reliable decisions on extending credit to businesses or individual consumers, traders need systems which automatically combine credit information on the client with the organisation's own policy. National Information Bureau's NIB-BACAS is such a 'decision support system'. The software integrates all the components of the proposed transaction, for the ease of the sales assistant; including checking Equifax, Experian and others for credit status. For international credit checking, NIB and others use the BIGNet company and credit information providers network, which delivers reports with standardised format and credit assessment. The firm Fair, Isaac provides 'comprehensive solutions to companies' business challenges by offering data management and data mining, analytic services, software and consulting.' Its products include both credit data, and scoring models for corporate and consumer credit, and 'behaviour' assessment. Fair, Isaac also sell software to analyse actual and potential client accounts, for the identification of payment behaviour and risk. The following are excerpts from credit decision support product descriptions on Experian's web site – *http://www.experian.com/index.html*:

Delphi

Uses advanced statistical techniques to combine the full range of credit reference information into single, highly predictive measures of risk.

Detect

The service draws on a unique database of credit applicant information provided by lenders to identify potentially fraudulent applications.

Motorfile

Protects consumers, motor trade, insurers and finance companies against fraud. The United Kingdom's most advanced vehicle identification system, Motorfile instantly identifies if a vehicle has been reported stolen or been subject to a total loss claim.

Autoscore

Experian's automated application processing system, has long been central to the lending operations of companies around the world. Autoscore processes more than 35 million credit applications each year.

Intelliscore

Quick and cost-effective way to process and monitor business accounts and to predict the likelihood of derogatory payment performance. Can help identify potential credit or payment risk among prospects. By screening high-risk accounts prior to marketing campaigns, users can better target potential customers and manage marketing programs to reduce cost and increase profitability.

Scope scorecard; Probe software

The Scope scorecard is a customer monitoring and information system; the Probe software is used by lenders around the world to implement behavioral scoring systems.

Company News

The section above, on primary sources of company information, established that extremely topical, potentially crucial, information may emerge through the general and business news media. Media coverage of a company, its directors, its products, its finances or its behaviour may update other sources, and pre-date statutory disclosure – private companies' reports and accounts do not have to be filed until 10 months after the end of the accounting period. What some of it lacks as *hard*, tested information, press reporting gains as *soft* information: leaks, rumours, speculation, indication of public image. All of which has a value in minimising uncertainty and risk in investment, credit and other decisions involving the company implicated.

Products have long existed to exploit systematically this particular source of company intelligence; both on a current awareness basis, and retrospectively. A press search is a standard complement to a search for financial and market information and so on when compiling a profile of a company. Few business information services maintain large cuttings files today, or even file printed McCarthy cards by company name. Press reports on companies are more often traced and obtained in one of three major ways: either included in the records in certain 'comprehensive' company databases; from general purpose business news indexing, abstracting or full-text databases; or from the few sources of the latter type which are dedicated to company news. Examples of each type are given here, and there is more on general business news sources in the 'Business News Sources; Industry Sources' chapter:

'Comprehensive' databases which include company news

> *Extel Financial Cards* – database of 11,000+ world companies; on FT Profile.

> *FT Analysis Reports* – database of 4,000 quoted European companies; on FT Profile.

> *Infocheck* – database report incorporates a trawl of national and regional UK newspapers for 'full and interim results, large contracts won, acquisitions etc.'.

General purpose business news sources

> *Financial Times Index* – Primary Source Media, monthly; includes a companies sequence.

> *Research Index* – Research Index Ltd; printed and web-based index to business periodicals; includes a companies sequence.

> Reuters *Textline* database (via various hosts; further details in 'Business News Sources; Industry Sources' chapter).

> *World Reporter* database (jointly produced by Dialog Corporation, Financial Times and Dow Jones; further details in 'Business News sources; Industry sources' chapter).

Company news services

> *FT McCarthy on CD-ROM* – Company and industry-specific articles selected from over 50 international newspapers and periodicals, indexed by company name etc.

Clover Newspaper Index Company Data Supplement – Clover Publications; print, CD-ROM, web site (*http://clover.niss.ac.uk/*). An index by company name to 12 broadsheet newspapers.

Moody's Corporate News database – international coverage of major companies; on Dialog.

UK Business Park (*http://www.ukbusinesspark.co.uk/*) – a UK oriented, database of brief news items. The chargeable *UK Activity Reports* on industry sectors are intended for corporate competitive monitoring, but there is currently free searching by company name:

> 'Comprehensive coverage of UK business activity, including information on acquisitions, new projects, expansion plans, strategy, major new products, and other important developments. A vital source of intelligence for your business. Used by sales & marketing managers, directors, researchers, investors, and other people who needed to keep up-to-date with the UK business news. Delivered to your email address every week.'

Standard & Poor's Daily News – full-text; mainly US public companies; on Dialog.

Where press items are included in records (the first group above), whether in the form of headlines or text, they can only serve as a briefing compared with the coverage and searching flexibility offered by dedicated news databases. The most sophisticated online hosts' interfaces are able to disguise the fact that a number of different sources may be necessary to assemble the full range of information on a company. By a click of the mouse a searcher can opt to add press reports to the data on a company, and full-text digitised image copy will automatically be assembled for viewing, from whatever appropriate databases the system has access to. The Dialog Corporation's web-based *Profound* is such an example; press items are not included in records in its *Companyline* virtual database, but the same navigational software can be used in *Newsline*, to automatically retrieve them from a number of different providers' sources. Infocheck's web interface similarly offers use of the Infocheck News Service, and the web version of Onesource's database of UK companies can be complemented with trade and press articles provided by RDS (Responsive Data Services). In the case of Reuters' *Business Briefing* suite of company databases, the balance is the other way round; their massive *News Wires* and *News Search* databases are complemented by a comparatively smaller file of 22,000 worldwide company profiles. Alerting and selective dissemination services naturally include the types of company news source discussed above. In for instance Dialog's *Alert*, most of the host's news sources are included among the databases which the user-defined parameters are frequently and automatically searched.

Stockbroker Research

(See also the section 'Rating Services' in the 'Financial Information' chapter, for sources of bond and other ratings.)

Variously called brokers' or analysts' reports, or investment research, this is a rather specialised source, applying to public, especially quoted companies. It is probably the ultimate in added value, in that it is a detailed, authoritative and timely judgement of a company's future prospects. It is the result of research done specifically to support investment decisions, by analysts in stock brokers firms, investment banks and the like. Morgan Stanley Dean Witter, Natwest Markets, Merrill Lynch and UBS figure prominently among the generators of such investment research; some others are given below. Data from all the available primary and secondary source material is combined with the analyst's expertise gained from close ongoing contact with the company and industry, which can include interviews with management on strategies, and other privileged access. Reports are more often on a specific company, but sometimes cover a number of companies in a particular industry. The reports are produced for clients who are mainly institutional investors, and sometimes for release to the press, to advise on the future prospects of companies' stocks or shares. Most only become widely available after an embargo of something like a month, when many securities firms release them to the information industry, by which time the critical 'buy', 'sell', or 'hold' advice, together with the rest of the evaluative data and text, has assumed more of an historical research value. These sections are typically present, a combination of textual and numerical data, some of them inevitably overlapping with the financial information in more typical company databases:

- Recommendation to investors
- Financial evaluation
- Sales analysis and divisional evaluation
- Financial outlook
- History
- Trading performance and outlook

There follows the heading and the all-important first section of a brokers report; the latest on MUFC in the ICC Stockbroker Research database on DataStar, in mid-October 1998:

Title

MANCHESTER UNITED – The biggest club in the world.

Source

UBS Limited

100 Liverpool Street

London

...

PUBLICATION DATE: 971010;

ANALYST: Easthope, J; Heath, P; Hastie, L;

TOTAL PAGES OF DOCUMENT: 8.

Text

1 OF 8

MANCHESTER UNITED – THE BIGGEST CLUB IN THE WORLD

BUY

Final figures for Manchester United prove that the club is the most profitable in the world. Excellent earnings growth of 62% and £39m net cash in the balance sheet add up to another strong year for the group. A new sponsorship agreement at three times last year's figure, the new BSkyB deal, pay-per-view, the announcement of a dedicated television channel and the European Superleague promise further excitement ahead.

PRELIMINARY PROFITS AT TOP OF EXPECTATIONS

Pre-tax profits in 1997 came in at £27.3m – an increase of 63%. After a 3 percentage point increase in the tax charge to 31%, net earnings increased by 62%. The dividend was raised by 19%, producing a cover just under 5x.

EXCELLENT UNDERLYING GROWTH TO CONTINUE

Renegotiation of the club sponsor should treble revenue from this area in 1999. This, together with a further 50% hike from BSkyB, will help the group achieve strong underlying profit growth. Headline earnings were boosted by £7.6m last year following the club's successful run in the European Champions League. We estimate that this will fall to £2.1m, on more conservative assumptions, in 1999.

MUTV – HERE WITHIN A YEAR

A new magazine-style television channel dedicated to Manchester United will start broadcasting on BSkyB's digital service in Autumn 1998. We estimate that this will contribute around £3m profits within five years.

COST RISES UNDER CONTROL

Cost control has been a concern for investors, with players' wages growing quickly. Total wages and salaries increased by £9.3m (£5.4m

due to players' wages). Wages as a percentage of revenue are reasonably steady at 25.5%. Other operating expenses increased by 67% last
year due to the big capacity increase. These will grow above inflation
in the medium term mainly due to a rising depreciation charge following the North Stand fit-out.

EARNINGS FORECASTS

[. . . continued]

Incités *Company and Industry Research Reports* was an early and major American example of brokers' research cumulation. *The Nelson Directory of Investment Research* (e.g. *Volume 2: International Companies*), as a printed cumulation
of analysts' reports on quoted companies worldwide, was also a forerunner
of the following full-text database examples:

Investext – Dialog, FT Profile.

Around 10,000 reports from 400 contributors; USA and worldwide
coverage.

The Research Bank – Ark Information Services; monthly CD-ROM; Western Europe.

Even smaller utterances from analysts are gathered up and flashed to waiting investors:

First Call Notes – First Call Corporation; available via web site (*http://
www.firstcall.com/*)

'Over 250 sell-side institutions worldwide, including 113 of North
America's top brokerage and investment research firms, distribute their
morning meeting comments, intra-day research broadcasts and special equity notes over this service.'

Research Direct – First Call Corporation

'Electronic, real-time access to more than 770,000 commingled original full-text equity research reports – including all text, charts, graphs,
color and formatting – directly from more than 250 leading brokerage
firms worldwide.' Also Japanese version, *Research Direct – Japanese*

Estimates Direct – First Call Corporation

15,000 share price and company performance estimates daily from
brokers worldwide, combined with estimates extracted from reports
in *Research Direct*. Includes consensus data.

The Estimate Directory ('*TED*') – Barra

Cumulates the opinions, recommendations and forecasts of brokers
and analysts, on UK quoted shares, includes a 'consensus line' for
each. A variety of delivery formats, including online from Barra (*http:/
/www.barra.com/home/default.asp*), who state: '*The Estimate Directory*
(TED) provides highest quality broker forecasts for more than 17,000

companies in over 60 countries. *TED* includes more than 1,000 contributing brokers globally. Its acceptance by leading global financial institutions has made *TED* the world's fastest growing source of company forecast data. Access is available by the following regions: United Kingdom, Continental Europe, Pacific Basin, North America, Emerging Markets, and Japan.'

As the first of the two lists above illustrates, most hosts provide at least one collection of analysts' reports, to complement other forms of company information. According to a *Profound* brochure, their *Brokerline* gives seamless access to 60,000 of them, from a number of different providers. Dial-up access to Investext Group's own Windows format *I/PLUS Direct*, or visiting Investext's *Research Bank Web* gives access to over a million 'business reports' from more than 700 of the world's investment banks, brokerage houses, market research firms and trade associations. Their *Investext* brokers' reports file, including image copies of the more recent reports, is complemented by the unusual *Industry Insider* collection of industry-specific reports and data from trade associations. The following are typical Investext company or industry investment research sources:

Disclosure and Ford Investor Services Inc.

Value Line Publishing

The Red Chip Review

Research Data Group

GEARS

Investor Responsibility Research Center

Renaissance Capital

IPO Maven

Boston Equity Research Group

Renaissance Capital

The Wall Street Transcript

Energy Security Analysis Inc.

Information on Other Specific Aspects of Companies

Some other aspects of companies are covered by 'comprehensive' sources, and are the subject of specialised ones. It is worth briefly considering here the often researched areas of company personnel, company ownership, including merger and acquisition activity, and share ownership.

In fact the viability of separate sources for such aspects is reduced by the increasing ability of software to retrieve and present satisfactory specialist information which exists in generalist company database records. This applies to formerly only printed ownership directories like *Who Owns Whom*

UK and Ireland (London: Dun & Bradstreet; annual, various editions and formats for various countries and regions, including UK and Ireland), and directories like *Crawford's Directory of City Connections* (Economist Newspaper Ltd.), which 'identifies the lawyers, accountants, insurance brokers, financial public relations consultants and stockbrokers used by many leading UK companies. It also lists the major clients of these professional advisers.'

Separate sources will no doubt continue for data which is too specialised or rarely needed to justify inclusion in general company databases, especially if the information has to be collected separately. For instance, Directory of Social Change's *A Guide to Company Giving* provides company by company data on the last annual donation, and donations policy.

Company Personnel – Including Directors and Principals

(Directors' share dealings are dealt with in the 'Share Ownership' section below.)

There is a substantial niche in the business information market for biographical information – not only obvious data on obvious people like directors or senior managers, but detail on a wider, unpredictable range of persons. Large businesses, charities, journalists and public relations firms and the media share a need for systematic full-text, full-colour access to the huge volume of articles and features relating to 'personalities'. This may be for headhunting of different kinds: selecting directors, trustees, or people to be involved in promotions.

Because standard biographical reference sources offer scant treatment of personalities who are or may be significant to business, business libraries have often maintained press cuttings files in anticipation of demand. These are to a large extent being replaced by searchable commercial databases of full-text, image copies of news items (treated in the 'Business News Sources; Industry Sources' chapter).

At the more mundane level, one of the few types of data extracted and sold as a separate product by Companies House is information on directors' and company secretaries' names, home addresses, and company affiliations. Their database includes past and present companies and directors (including disqualified directors), and is available online via the Mercury host, or incorporated into commercial company information providers' products. The information is valuable operationally for mail shots, tactically for marketing, headhunting, or 'credit management', and strategically for assessing the reliability or prospects of a company. Generalist company database records typically include abbreviated directors information – the listing of names of company secretary and directors' names under 'Background Information' in the basic 'Infocheck Report' is typical (reproduced in the 'Comprehensive Company Information' section above). However, fuller directors data may be offered, derived partially or entirely from the Companies House database. Certain specialist commercial databases incorporate the full disclosed data, such as Dun & Bradstreet's *DASH* (*Directors and Shareholdings*) on digital video disk. Otherwise directors data can be selected from 'comprehensive databases' via reports such as ICC Juniper's *Company Directors Report* – partially reproduced below. Companies House's own Directors databases is hosted by providers such as Infocheck, who also hold a consumer credit database where directors' and any other individuals' personal status can be further examined.

Company Registered No.:	**01800000**
Company Secretary	
COLIN RAYMOND GREEN	
Appointment Date:	01/08/1994
Date of Birth:	16/04/1949
Occupation:	–
Address:	81 NEWGATE STREET LONDON EC1A 7AJ
Present Directorships:	5
Resignations Since June 96:	0

Directors

JAMES IAIN WALKER ANDERSON

Appointment Date:	01/11/1995
Date of Birth:	30/06/1938
Occupation:	MANAGER
Address:	WEENA 241 3013 ROTTERHAM NETHERLANDS
Present Directorships:	2
Resignations Since June 96:	0

MALCOLM ARGENT

Appointment Date:	09/08/1992
Date of Birth:	14/08/1935
Occupation:	NON EXECUTIVE DIRECTOR
Address:	CHESTNUTS FRYERNING LANE FRYERNING INGATESTON ESSEX CM4 0DF
Present Directorships:	5
Resignations Since June 96:	0

SIR PETER LEAHY BONFIELD BSC HON F ENG CBE

[etc. etc. for all directors]

Information on company 'principals': managing director, financial director, sales manager and others, is rarer, since it has to be obtained voluntarily rather than disclosed by law. Detailed versions of company records from some providers, especially if intended for marketing purposes, do often include the heads of firms' major operational departments. ICC's records do, and also entries in Dun & Bradstreet's *Key British Enterprises* directory. The American *Standard & Poor's Register of Corporations* includes a considerable amount of personal, professional, and company affiliations detail for 70,000 people. The biographical information is available on Dialog as the separate file *Standard & Poor's Register – Biographical*. At £3,200 for a year's subscription, Chadwyck Healey offer *Leadership Directories* on CD-ROM; that is 12 'Yellow Books' which include contact details of business people and government decision makers, intended for many marketing and lobbying purposes.

A considerable number of business-oriented *Who's Who* style, usually printed, works exist, which, though infrequently published, can be a source of substantial biographical data. British titles have included:

Directory of Directors – Reed Business Information

In its 119th edition, 1998; vol. 1 details 50,000+ directors, vol. 2 companies over £10m turnover.

Who's Who in the City – Waterlow. 1999 edition, published 1998.

Business and personal details of 16,000 'decision makers' in 1,600 UK financial services firms.

Who's Who in Industry – Stock Exchange, and London and International Publishers.

Who's Who in European Business – Who's Who Edition GmbH, Germany; on DataStar etc.

Consists of around '8,500 biographies of managers in Europe's 7,000 largest companies'.

People – Hemmington Scott; database available direct or as an FT Profile 'Data collection'.

Biographies of UK quoted companies' directors, extracted from the quarterly periodical *PriceWaterhouse Corporate Register*

US Reference Book of Corporate Management – Dun & Bradstreet.

3 volume directory detailing the careers of over 12,000 key business leaders and decision makers.

Who's Who in World Petrochemicals and Plastics – Reed Business Information.

Contact details of decision making executives, arranged by company.

The British company The Reward Group issues regular surveys specifically of directors' remuneration. Directors, economists and politicians alike are interested in findings such as an average increase in pay over the year of 5%, with 79% owning company cars; and a lower forecast increase in pay for the following year.

Corporate Affiliations; Including Share Ownership and Merger and Acquisition Activity

Ownership of private and public companies is a strictly regulated and publicly notifiable matter. Perhaps because changes in ownership occur unpredictably, perhaps because knowledge of them has rather specialised uses; a specialised group of sources exists. For purposes like investment research and competitor monitoring, decision makers are interested even in micro level ownership changes, in particular movements and trends in the ownership of shares in quoted companies. Related to this are actual and potential merger and acquisition events.

Corporate Ownership and Structure

Ownership in terms of a single company's immediate parent or subsidiary (defined in the 'Primary Information' of the 'Company Information' chapter) is comparatively static, and easy to discover from primary sources, and to collate as *Who Owns Whom*-type secondary sources. However, especially for quoted companies, it is necessary to detect subtle changes in share holdings' as an indicator of takeover intentions, leading to change in share value or company strategy. Also complicated, and necessary for both tactical and strategic purposes, is the 'family tree' and operating structure of corporate groups.

As already mentioned, an alternative to printed or electronic ownership directories, is those company databases which include details of any parent (sometimes just the 'ultimate parent') or subsidiaries (often 'major' ones only), such as for instance ICC's records. The following is extracted from their *British Company Financial Datasheets* on DataStar.

> Parents and subsidiaries
>
> Up to 10 companies from the ICC Database that show MORLAND PLC as a holding company in their latest analysed accounts.
>
> Principal Subsidiary Companies:

Number	Name	Turnover GBP '000
02191112	MORLAND BREWERY ESTATES LTD	6,925
01374471	BELL AMUSEMENTS LTD	4,436

An advantage of company databases on CD-ROM compared with dial-up hosts is the sophisticated analytical and display software. Detailed sources such as

Jordan's *FAME* and various providers' *Amadeus* are able to costruct a graphic family tree in response to a corporate structure search. Versions of Dun & Bradstreet's *Who Owns Whom* on the major hosts normally yield a structured list of the whole group, in the record for the ultimate parent. The following is an indication of the data in the *Who Owns Whom: UK and Ireland* record for The News Corp. Ltd, Sydney, Australia (*before* they embraced Manchester United PLC):

Company type

    Ultimate parent

Number of subsidiaries

    679 in 22 groups

Subsidiaries

    1 OF 22.

    – Access Securities Pty. Ltd., Australia.

    2 OF 22.

    – Ansett Airlines Ltd. (A), Australia.

    3 OF 22.

    [etc.]

    6 OF 22.

    – British Sky Broadcasting Group PLC (A), United Kingdom.

    7 OF 22.

    – Harper and Collins U.S. Inc., USA

    – HarperCollins Publishers Inc., USA

    – Editora Harper & Row de Brasil Ltda., Brazil

    – Editora Vida Ltda., Brazil

    [etc]

    8 OF 22.

    – HarperCollins (UK), United Kingdom

    – Collins Desktop Publishing Ltd., New Zealand

    – Harper & Collins Investment (UK) Ltd., United Kingdom

    – HarperCollins B.V., Netherlands

    – HarperCollins Finance B.V., Netherlands

    – HarperCollins Holdings B.V., Netherlands

    – HarperCollins Publishers Ltd., United Kingdom

    – William Collins Holdings Ltd., United Kingdom

[etc]

16 OF 22.

– Newscorp Investments Ltd., United Kingdom

– 'News of the World' Ltd., United Kingdom

[etc]

– The Sun Ltd., United Kingdom

– The Sunday Times Ltd., United Kingdom

– The Times Educational Supplement Ltd., United Kingdom

– The Times Higher Education Supplement Ltd., United Kingdom

– The Times Literary Supplement Ltd. (d), United Kingdom

– The Times Ltd. (d), USA

– The Times Network Systems Ltd., United Kingdom

– The Times Pension Trust Ltd., United Kingdom

– The Times Supplements Ltd., United Kingdom

– Times Newspapers Holdings Ltd., United Kingdom

– Times Newspapers Ltd., United Kingdom

In common with many other monolithic printed business reference works, the five volume *Directory of Corporate Affiliations* has become a CD-ROM and an online database. Combined with financial data from *America's Corporate Finance Directory*, Bowker-Saur now distribute it as *Corporate Affiliations Plus* in the UK, and as *Corporate Affiliations* on Dialog and certain other hosts. Infocheck's products include a 'Holding company database', providing parent-subsidiary and group structures. Kompass' spin-off products include *Kompass CD Plus, volume 4: Parents and Subsidiaries*, profiles and shows the relationships between 29,000 ultimate or immediate parents and 11,000 subsidiaries.

Share Ownership

Major movements by major players in PLC share ownership reveal not only potential takeover or merger activity, but are also an early indication to investors and others of performance, structural or strategic change. Certain information providers analyse share movements by monitoring shareholders registers at Companies House, share transactions data emanating daily from stock exchanges, and changes notified to exchanges. The London Stock Exchange requires notification of directors' share dealings, and dealings of 5% or more of the company's share capital. Usually only principal shareholders and holdings are included in the records of general company databases, as in the Company Capitalisation section of the sample Infocheck record in the 'Comprehensive Company Information' section above. This is an example of a Company Shareholders Report for a specific company, from ICC's *Juniper* online service:

Share Capital Structure

Class of Shares	Par Value (pence)	Issued Capital (£)	Nominal Capital (£)	SEDOL
Ordinary shares	25	1,589,000,000	2,625,000,000	0140843
Total Issued Capital		1,589,000,000		

Shareholders

Shareholder Name	Class of Shares	Number of Shares	Shares (%)	Holder Type	Beneficial Owner*
Prudential Corp. Group of Cos	Ordinary Shares	205,000,000	3.20	Company	Beneficial Name

*Instead of an actual 'beneficial owner', the 'shareholder' may be a 'nominee', i.e. the person or organisation holding the shares in trust for someone else.

ICC provides similarly abbreviated data (as above) in standard company records, down to a certain percentage of holdings. ICC provide much more detail in the separate *Sharewatch* database on the joint London Stock Exchange/ICV *TOPIC 3* and *TOPIC PLUS* screen-based price information services. Amongst other detail, this shows latest reportable transactions for London quoted companies, and a descending list of shareholders and their holdings, down to a holding of 0.25%. An American equivalent is *Insider Trading Monitor*, on Dialog. The specialist information provider Technimetrics maintains a database of worldwide institutional and mutual fund, unit trust, investment trust, and similar ownership data; collected from the relevant exchanges, funds and investment companies and from surveys of shareholders themselves. In launching the *Technimetrics Share/World* database on DataStar, the Dialog Corporation's *Chronolog* periodical stated that typical searches allow you to:

- Identify all institutions holding a specific share
- Identify by location the holders of a specific share
- Identify the shareholdings of a specific institution
- Identify by market the shareholdings of a specific institution

A much more specialised service is the *Financial Times'* weekly 'Directors' dealings' column, with a listing divided into 'Sales' and 'Purchases' of the companies concerned during the week, and the size and value of transactions. Because directors' dealings in their own companies' shares are potentially so significant, a number of products specialise in monitoring them, such as Barra's *Directus*:

> '*Directus* monitors and reports the transactions made by more than 20,000 directors of every U.K. quoted company.

For every deal announced, *Directus* provides you with the context you need to evaluate it. Detailed briefings include the company's core activities, total director shareholdings, ordinary shares in issue, and consensus earnings, profit and dividend forecasts provided by *The Estimate Directory*. And with *Directus*, you receive more than just current buy and sell information. We also include a history of transactions and holdings for each director so you can see each one for what it is – a genuine signal of a director's sentiment or simply incidental to their position.' (From the Barra web site – *http://directus.barra.com/*.)

Disclosure's Internet updated CD-ROM *InsideTrade Asia* has a similar role: to detail the trading activity of Hong Kong insiders, company share buybacks, purchases and sales made by shareholders with sizeable positions, and Disclosure's analysts' reports of insider trading patterns and significant events for firms trading on the Hong Kong Stock Exchange.

Merger and Acquisition

Otherwise known as 'M & A', this activity can be indicated by share capital ownership changes, and strategic changes, and detected through statements or leaks to the press and rumours. Stock market regulations ensure that friendly or hostile intentions to buy control in a PLC are declared when the bidder gains a certain proportion of the equity. In the UK this may be confirmed or otherwise by Mergers and Monopolies Commission reports and the City Takeovers Panel, or publication of 'offer documents'. While *Who Owns Whom* type services are useful reference sources on established corporate structure, a number of sources specialise in reporting subtle changes. The *Financial Times* newspaper gives bidder, target, and bid price in the listing Current Takeover Bids and Mergers, and produces the separate *FT Acquisitions Weekly* charting M & A activity in major non-US markets. *M & A Filings* (Dialog) collates notifications to the US Securities and Exchange Commission. IFR Securities Data's *SDC Worldwide Mergers and Acquisitions* (Dialog and DataStar, excerpt from file description below) reports M & A transactions worldwide, which involve changes of ownership down to 5% of share capital. Onesource's web-based service uses data from the UK oriented *Acquisitions Monthly*.

SDCA – SDC Worldwide Mergers & Acquisitions (exerpt from the DataStar Datasheet)

Content

SDC Worldwide Mergers and Acquisitions includes information on all announced, completed, or pending transactions that involve a change in ownership of 5% or more. Information is given on target and acquiror companies and includes company names, business activities, US SIC codes and description, country and region, public/private status, and financial information.

For the deal itself announcement and effective dates are given together with the amount paid, and information on the form, attitude and status of the transaction. A brief text synopsis detailing the specifics of the deal is also available together with other information including advisors, techniques, fees, and information sources.

Use SDCA to answer questions like:

- how many deals have taken place where the amount paid for the target has been in excess of US$ 1 billion?
- which deals involve transactions between French and Spanish companies?
- are there details of any transactions involving companies involved in the soft-drinks industry?
- on which deals has S.G. Warburg acted as advisor?

Sources:

Sources include all worldwide major financial newspapers, press releases, offer documents, newswires, stock exchange circulars, annual reports, and surveys from advisors on the deals.

Company Sources Exhibiting Specialisms Other than Subject Scope

Geographical Specialism

A combination of detailed records, and flexible search and output software, allows 'comprehensive' company information sources to be used for unlimited purposes. Though as the above sections have shown, for certain subjects and approaches, the user is still best served by turning to specialist sources, though above sections have noted many sources of worldwide scope, sources providing in depth coverage of the maximum range of companies almost inevitably have a particular geographical scope; for example hosts approximately 50 company databases to cover Europe, including:

Germany	Company news	*FINF-TEXT*
	Trade directory	*German Buyers' Guide*
Austria	Company directory	*Hoppenstedt: Austria*

Fortunately geographical and database boundaries can be made insignificant, by means of visible or invisible cross-file searching software.

Company Information for Marketing and Sourcing

Company information is very often needed for the purpose of identifying firms as marketing targets; there is more on this subject in the 'Market Information' chapter. With this use in mind, many providers make their data searchable by for instance: line of business, sales volume, or geographic location. They include relevant details, such as names and addresses of buyers and plants; and provide output formats for direct incorporation into mail shots.

An almost universal need is information for 'sourcing'; that is, identifying suppliers of particular goods or services (the main coverage of which is the 'Sources of Basic Company Details: Company Directories' section of this chapter, and in the 'Product Information' chapter). Jordans *Acquisition Service* serves to identify companies which might *themselves* be acquired, or merged with. This is a 'service' rather than a separate database because it is achieved by searching the master company records by a specially constructed set of parameters, and outputting equally targeted data.

There follow a few more examples from the many specialised approaches taken by company information sources, and not specifically discussed in this chapter (specialising in terms of the companies, industry or subject, purpose or arrangement):

By Role of Company

Retailers/wholesalers
(Further coverage of retailers in the 'Retail Intelligence' section of the 'Market Information' chapter.)

> *European Directory of Retailers and Wholesalers*
> Euromonitor; considerable detail on 5,000 operators in 18 countries.
>
> *World Retail Directory*
> Euromonitor; 2,600 retailers in nearly 100 developed and less-developed countries.

Further Sources

European Business Information Sourcebook. Bowker-Saur, 1995. Useful information on the availability of the primary company information in different countries, as well as the secondary sources.

G. Holmes and A. Sugden. *Interpreting Company Reports and Accounts*, 6th edn. Woodhead-Faulkner, 1997.

P. Norkett. *Guide to Company Information in Great Britain*. Longman with ICC, 1986.

3

Market Information

The model of the business in its environments reproduced above and discussed in chapter 1, shows that the interaction of businesses, products, and the population, creates what we know as *the market*. This means that competitors, their products and services, and consumers comprise what is indisputably for a business the *immediate*, or *micro* external environment.

Figure 12. The interaction of individuals and businesses to create the market

Although companies and products concern business information for other reasons than as components of the market (hence separate chapters on company and product information), about the only reason *people* concern business information is as consumers! For a business person 'company information' is various aspects of potentially thousands of entities (other companies), 'market information' is essentially various aspects of one entity – a particular market. A 'market' being generally defined as the intersection of the potential sellers and buyers of any given range of products or services (not used here as the *Financial Times* uses 'markets', to mean just the markets for financial commodities). Thus 'market information' is information gathered for various purposes, on aspects of a given set of sellers, buyers and products, and their interaction.

At one level, a player in a market, potential player, or anyone else commercially affected by it, needs to know the present and future dimension and characteristics of the market. At a more direct level of involvement, players need specific details relating to specific products, including on the products' suppliers and consumers. Information at the 'whole-market' level is the stuff of longer-term, strategic decision making. It provides a composite picture on which to base non-marketing decisions, such as on investment in the company, structure of the company, or product development. On the other hand, information at the 'product level' is vital for strategic, tactical or operational marketing decisions, such as by marketing and sales people, to target products at potential customers. This requires much raw primary data, and will be dealt with first in the chapter. Information at the whole-market level requires further analysis of the primary information used for marketing decisions, together with information on the environments which affect the market.

Sources of Product-Level Information

Managers of marketing must have knowledge of the competitors, products and consumers in the market. Relevant sources of information rarely relate to a single one of these elements, but rather to the interaction of two or more; for example, dealing with retailing, or advertising. Some sources can be grouped according to the component of the market they report on (such as consumers), others the process (such as advertising); however, what characterises others is the specific type of information provided, and so are more obviously grouped by internal format (such as market research, and statistics).

The left hand side of the table below represents marketers' fundamental information needs. Along the top are the sources appropriate for those needs, categorised by subject or form, as explained above, including 'company' and 'product' information sources which are covered in other chapters. The columns show how needs and source types relate, revealing that a source type rarely addresses a single need. In the following sections each of those source types is examined, in each case relating its nature and contents to marketing intelligence needs.

Market Research

In this book the term 'market research' is used to distinguish what in marketing is also called 'primary market research', meaning original, field-based research: the work which results in what will be called here 'market research reports'. As the table below suggests, primary market research is the only means of answering very specific questions relating to actual and potential customers and/or products. It is very different from 'secondary market research' resulting in what will be called in a later section 'market surveys', which uses mainly data already available to answer whole-market level questions. Unfortunately, the terms 'market research' and 'market research reports' are often used to embrace both categories.

| | Primary Sources | | | | | | |
Needs / questions	Company Information	Product Information	Market Research	Business Statistics	Non-Bus Statistics	Advert. Monitor.	Opportunities Services
Competitors' Products							
– who is selling what	X	X		X			
– where bought & sold		X			X		
– branding policy	X	X					
– advertising policy/spend	X					X	
– pricing policy		X	X				
– product developments	X	X					
Own Products							
– effectiveness for customers			X				
– effectiveness of promotion			X			X	
– potential of new products			X				
Potential Customers							
– who are they			X		X		X
– where are they	X		X		X		X
– what spending power			X		X		

Table 2. The relationship of product-level market information needs to sources of information

Market or opinion research firms, such as MORI, Marplan, IRN, SGA, NOP Market Research Ltd., Euromonitor, Datamonitor or RGB (Research Surveys of Great Britain), charge large sums for the labour-intensive design, sampling, surveying, and statistical analysis necessary for reliable results. Most British firms guarantee standards by membership of the British Market Research Association, whose Quality Charter lays down minimum service standards of the Market Research Quality Standards Association. Most market research is ad hoc; that is, commissioned by a specific client for a specific purpose, the results never likely to be available to anyone else. Market researchers refer to this as the 'consultancy' side of their operations, as opposed to 'syndicated' or 'multi-client' studies which they have themselves initiated. Euromonitor described this side of their operations as follows:

> 'Euromonitor Consultancy, the company's ad hoc research division, also undertakes a wide range of projects tailored to the individual needs of our clients. The strategic unit specialises in international market entry studies, competitor intelligence and global industry studies, while the research unit focuses on the development of customised relational databases consisting of comparative economic, demographic and market statistics'.

Syndicated research reports are put on general sale, and although as in the example of *Marketstat* are still very expensive, they are acquired by certain firms and public sector libraries, especially the British Library. IRN (Information Research Network) combines ad hoc and syndicated primary research with market information consultancy and brokerage, they state:

> Our aim is to create a competitive edge for clients through market-research based solutions:
>
> MARKET RESEARCH – Business analysis and research.
>
> *INTERSTAT* – International and national business statistics enquiry service.
>
> *TRAVELSTAT* – Travel and tourism enquiry and reporting service.
>
> *WEBSTAT* – The gateway to electronic statistical information.
>
> SOURCES OF TRADE ASSOCIATION STATISTICS – Database of UK trade associations and their publications.
>
> TRAINING – In-house and public training seminars for business information and market research.
>
> *MARKETSTAT* – Syndicated survey of the online business information market (details below).
>
> PRESS RELEASES – *Marketstat* survey summaries, Learned Information survey summaries and our online *Newsletters*.

Data collection methods employed by the bespoke market research service include:

Desk research

Telephone interviews

Fax surveys

Postal questionnaires

Face to face interviews

Executive interviews

Group discussions

Data analysis

Business analysis

Report writing

These details of *Marketstat* syndicated research indicate not only the high cost, but also the level of detail provided by primary market research (from IRN promotional material

> '*Marketstat* is a confidential, regular survey of the UK online business information market. It offers the benefits of shared research costs and up-to-date high quality research data not available from any other service. The survey comprises 1,600 telephone interviews per year with online users and potential users in the UK, supported by group discussions. Quarterly survey results are produced every March, June, September and December. Press release summaries of results are posted on our Events page . . . Subscribers can include their own confidential questions in the survey. The cost is £300 per question per quarter, with the results only available to the sponsor.'

Marketstat Standard Service – £5,800 per year

> Quarterly summary of the survey
> Copy of full detailed interview results for further analysis

Marketstat Gold Service – £9,400 per year

> Quarterly summary of the survey
> Detailed review of group discussions
> Detailed quarterly report analysing the results
> Copy of the full detailed interview results for further analysis
> Individual presentations to selected staff, if required

Omnibus Research; Trade Association Research

Additionally, many market research firms collect and sell general purpose market intelligence as serial publications. Such omnibus research includes widely-sold series like British Market Research Bureau's (BMRB International Ltd) Target Group Index, based on an annual survey of the buying patterns of thousands of adults. Peter Hodgson & Associates' travel and tourism research products include the bimonthly Travel Agents Omnibus Survey. The web sites of market research companies, MR professional associations, such as ESOMAR (the world association of research professionals founded as the European Society for Opinion and Marketing Research – *http://www.esomar.nl/*), are useful for discovering very specialised publications, and sometimes free excerpts.

Trade associations are not an obvious source of reports of market intelligence value; however, Investext now collects reports from 150 around the world, and hosts them as its *Industry Insider* database to complement their more conventional market research and investment research databases. In promoting their use, Investext state:

> 'Trade association research reports contain industry growth trends, consumer spending habits, industry statistics and a variety of economic indicators including sales figures, production rates, export/import facts, factory shipments, manufacturing capacity, product developments, market share rankings, demographics, consumption spending habits, surveys, industry news and analysis.'

These samples illustrate both the associations which exist, and the topics covered by their reports (from the Investext site – *http://www.investext.com/*):

> February Mall Merchandise Vol. 8, No. 4
> Apr-01-97
> International Council of Shopping Centers
>
> New Medicine In Development for Heart Disease/
> Stroke
> Mar-07-97
> Pharmaceutical Research and Manufacturers of
> America
>
> Trends in Consumer Borrowing: Installment Credit
> 1996
> Dec-31-96
> American Bankers Association

The field research techniques employed in market research are either specified by the client, or applied by the market research firm as appropriate to the objectives. The alternatives offered by BMRB International include the typical range of consumer research techniques, two of which are further explained below the list:

Research Technique

Advertising Evaluation

Media Analysis Software

Brand and Product Research

Business-to-Business Research

Consultancy

Customer Satisfaction Measurement

Database Modelling

Employee Research

Innovative Techniques

Media Research

Minority Samples

Multi-Country Research

Omnibus Surveys

Public and Social Research

Qualitative

Statistical Services

Third Party Field and Tab

Usage and Attitude Research

Minority Samples – *Target Samples*

Target Group Index has a database of over 1 million individuals, all interviewed in the recent past on one of our ACCESS omnibus surveys. Because they have already been interviewed, their demographic classification is known to us. What really gives Target Samples the edge, however, is the ability to re-contact respondents to TGI and Premier TGI. Target Samples has access to 250,000 such individuals, whose product usage, media consumption and lifestyle attitudes are already logged. This greatly enhances the potential for detailed post-survey analysis, as well as providing vastly increased parameters for selecting samples. Target Samples can be used to construct accurate samples for product testing, studies of advertising effectiveness, readership surveys, audience surveys, tracking studies and much more.

Innovative Techniques – Multimedia CAPI

Face-to-face interviewing enters a new dimension with Multimedia CAPI. It brings high quality moving images, stills and audio clips to in-home interviewing, via highly-specified lap-top computers. It is already revolutionising the research we do for a number of clients, and has particular relevance to: advertising tracking and pre-testing, packaging and design research, social research, especially on sensitive issues, pricing research, media and sponsorship research.

Not detailed in the above are commonly used *focus groups*, and the rigorous but bizarre sounding technique of going through a consumer's dustbin to record weekly consumption! An alternative to targeting consumers to obtain data on branch shares of sales, product pricing and promotion, and geographical analysis of various factors is the *retail audit* or *store check*. Here a panel of stores is visited, and conclusions drawn from invoices, shelves, till data, and customers. A.C. Nielsen's *Market Statistics* (available on Dialog) is sales data direct from the check-outs of North American retail outlets. Amongst its complementary range of market research and product monitoring services, the UK-based Mintel firm IIS offers 'shelf surveys':

'At your given instruction, and within hours of your request, we can have one of our world-wide contacts out in a shop or supermarket, surveying the state of your and your competitor's products.

For each product or brand, any or all of the following information can be collected for you, depending on your own, individual requirements:

Shelf space devoted to each brand

Pack sizes available

In-store promotions

Sell-by dates

Brand name and manufacturer

General condition & presentation of goods

Price bands

On-pack promotions

In-store geographic positioning

Type of packaging

Main ingredients'.

Business Statistics

The term business *statistics* usually refers to the many series statistics on business activity used more than anything else as a raw material of market intelligence. Like any statistic, they are welcomed as concise, precise qualitative descriptions of industrial production, sales, import, export, trade and similar. Like any statistic, they are a simple, attractive and also often a wrong answer to an information need – at least not having quite the expected currency, accuracy and relevance expected.

Unlike the data resulting from market research, this is a raw form of information, not collected or presented for marketing purposes, and requiring much synthesis with other data, and interpretation to be of use. When re-launching the former *Production Monitor* series as *UK Markets*, partners CSO (now Office of National Statistics) and Taylor Nelson/AGB, suggested the statistics could answer 12 different information needs, many clearly more appropriate to strategic management than to marketing:

1. What is the total value and volume of its UK production?
2. What is your Company's share of UK production?
3. What is the average price/value of a unit of UK production? How does your price compare?
4. How much of UK production is exported?
5. What is your Company's share of exports?
6. What is the average export price/value of UK production? How does your price compare?
7. How much of your market is imported i.e. what is import penetration?
8. What is the average import price/value? How does your price compare?
9. What is the Net Supply to your UK market, i.e. the real value and volume, after deducting exports and adding imports?
10. What is your Company share of Net Supply?
11. What is the average price/value of the Net Supply to your UK market?
12. How does your price compare ?
    For all the questions above, what is the trend over previous periods: is it Up? Down? or Static?

The prime publicly-accessible library of *foreign* business and non-business, official and other statistics for market intelligence, is the DTI's Export Market Information Centre, in Westminster (*http://www.dti.gov.uk/ots/emic/*). Users can either help themselves, or pay for intelligence to be gathered by the Export Market Information Research Service. As well as statistics, EMIC's in-house resources have been categorised as directories, market research reports, country profiles, multilateral development agencies' documents on project funded – revealing business opportunities, DTI export publications, CD-ROMs, mail order catalogues, business travel guides, trade fair catalogues, development plans, documents and a database revealing export opportunities and sales leads, agreement and guides relating to outward investment from the UK. The market research firm Information Research Network or IRN, is an example of a specialist information broker's business statistics enquiry service; they also provide WebSTAT (*http://www.irnxxx.co.uk/webstat.html*), a source of and web gateway to statistical information of market intelligence value:

> 'Basic economic information and value added statistics calculated by IRN from reliable sources are available on WebSTAT. Forecasts are also provided for many countries. In addition top line data from reputable industry surveys including company rankings are available . . .'

Official Business Statistics

Official, that is government produced statistics have the advantage of wide subject coverage and comprehensive or large sample sizes. Though the identity of companies is always concealed – the UK Office for National Statistics (ONS) *UK Markets* covers 90% of industry, broken down into 5,000 product classifications. There is usually also comparability over a long time scale, and now compatability with most other European official statistics. Harmonisation of industry classification systems, and of statistics collection, is raising the value of international statistics. Official statistics are not only harmonised within the expanding EU, but countries throughout the world are now adopting the trade statistics classification, the Harmonised Commodity Description and Coding System.

Data collection on the UK services sector is only gradually reaching the level of the industrial sector. The Office of National Statistics is increasing the number and detail of annual and more frequent 'enquiries' on service sector indicators, such as volume, prices and labour costs; and increasing the coverage and frequency of price indices. The expanding service sector data appears in the quarterly *SDQ11 – The UK Service Sector.*

UK and EU examples of official business statistics

General
British Business – DTI.
> Weekly periodical which includes statistical extracts and summaries.

Annual Abstract of Statistics; Regional Trends; Monthly Digest of Statistics – ONS.
> Annual compilations of business and other statistics selected from more specialised and frequent series.

Basic Statistics of the European Union: Comparison with the Principal Partners... – Eurostat.
> Frequent.

Euro Indicators – Eurostat.
> A range of statistics available on the web site – *http://europa.eu.int/en/comm/eurostat/index.htm*

Industrial sector output, sales etc.
Product Sales and Trade series (version for all products, in whole EU, is EUROPROMS CD) – ONS.
> Annual for 89 UK products, quarterly for 35 – production, sales and trade data combined.

Sector Reviews (e.g. PRA4 Oils, Fats and Margarines) – ONS.
> Annual – 90 reviews which combine 30 data series on production, employment, R&D etc.

PACSTAT: Production and Construction Statistics (CD-ROM) – ONS.
> Annual – combines former Business Monitors, includes other industry-specific data series.

Directory of Manufacturing Inquiries (CD-ROM) – ONS.
> Details of over 7,000 businesses; price indices, output, turnover data.

Fisheries: Yearly Statistics – Eurostat.

Service sector output, sales etc.
UK Service Sector – ONS.
> Quarterly – a single report giving output, income & other data for different activities.

Retail Sales – ONS.
> Monthly.

Catering and Allied Trades – ONS.
> Annual – one of several titles giving turnover and other data for specific service industries.

Distributive Trade and Services – Eurostat.
> Monthly.

Labour market

Labour market Statistics – ONS.
> Series includes an annual employment survey, and quarterly labour force survey.

Unemployment – Eurostat.
> Monthly – current rate for each member state, with annual averages.

European Labour Force Survey – Eurostat.
> Annual.

Prices

Consumer Price Index – Eurostat.
> Monthly – figures for members states, and other countries.

Gas prices 1990-1996 – Eurostat, 1997.

Agricultural Markets: Prices – *EC Directorate General for Agriculture.*
> 4 issues per year.

Trade

Overseas Trade Statistics of the UK – ONS.
> Monthly breakdown of imports and exports by volume and value.

Tradstat – *available as gateway via DataStar etc.*
> Official trade figures of 24 important trading nations.

External Trade of the European Union with the ACP countries and the OCTs 1991-1995 – Eurostat.

The UK Government Statistical Service as a whole holds vast amounts of data of obvious and less obvious value to business. Most is available comparatively cheaply, some of it free – such as *UK in Figures* on the National Statistics web site; it is disseminated in printed form, on CD-ROM, online, and in other ways. Much is not published, but available on demand from the various government departments and agencies which collect it; the freephone *Data Analyses Service* advises on what can be done, and estimates for the work involved. To help exploit the published data there are tools such as, for the UK, the subject-indexed *Guide to Official Statistics* (including CD-ROM and Internet versions), and separate guides to specific groups of statistics. Visits or remote enquiries can be made to ONS libraries in London and Newport. ONS and other national statistics services disseminate much free data via their web sites. The ONS site provides links to other countries' equivalents; as does the *Statistical Data Locators* web site (*http://www.ntu.edu.sg/library/statdata.htm*). This is a free service of the Nanyang Technical University Library, Singapore; through its own resources and links to others, it offers an impressive range of country-related statistics, especially useful for the Far East. *Nomis* is an online labour market information service, with data on employment, unemployment, Jobcentre vacancies, and VAT registrations. Official statistics of the European Union can be consulted in Euro Info Centres in Britain and elsewhere, and via the *Eurostat* web site (*http://europa.eu.int/en/comm/eurostat/serven/home.htm*).

Annual periodical prices for 1998

The 1998 edition of this annual survey of periodical prices is based on a broad selection of journals made by Blackwell's Periodicals Division. It reflects as nearly as possible the annual pattern of periodical purchases in specialised and learned libraries, irrespective of language, price or country of origin. The sample is based on the more important journals in each subject field. The subjects have been chosen to approximate the subject divisions in special and academic libraries, regardless of individual classification scheme. Previous statistics have appeared annually in issues of the *Record* since 1966.

It must be emphasised that this survey is intended only as a guide to trends. It is primarily for the use of libraries within the United Kingdom. Figures produced by individual libraries will vary, depending upon the origin of the journals and the emphasis given to a particular subject area. It should be noted that the 1998 index is based on exchange rates applied in September 1997.

Humanities & Social Sciences

	No of titles	% increase over 1997	Index (1970=100)	Av price 1998 (£ sterling)
Accountancy	19	3.50	2,484.69	106.44
Architecture & Town planning	34	4.46	3,669.76	233.17
Art	28	-2.03	995.69	69.73
Classics & Archaeology	30	-5.29	1,386.09	70.89
Commonwealth, Oriental & African Studies	19	7.65	2,301.14	104.30
Economics & Trade	62	1.95	3,051.63	215.99
Education & Child Psychology	70	16.75	4,346.50	200.47
English Language & Literature	38	2.49	1,400.46	54.24
Entertainment, Theatre, Film, Ballet	23	4.75	1,463.96	58.06
European Language & Literature	57	-2.19	1,817.65	77.54
General & Popular	29	-1.68	1,252.10	65.70
Geography	34	6.95	1,825.30	100.05
History	50	6.65	1,988.46	80.16
Law & Criminology	35	4.79	1,916.80	140.23
Librarianship & Documentation	37	14.23	2,299.49	228.28
Management	40	40.78	6,753.54	377.02
Music & Recording	19	4.31	1,310.63	52.13
Philosophy	27	4.55	2,267.09	77.58
Photography	5	1.76	1,406.63	64.87
Political Economy & Politics	38	7.54	2,522.16	98.26
Psychology	32	3.22	2,261.32	220.65
Religion & Theology	47	2.01	1,696.09	59.38
Sociology	49	6.12	2,237.99	120.70
Sports & Pastimes	19	-0.72	1,680.94	46.31
Total	**841**	**9.48**	**2,508.95**	**134.12**

Analysis by country of origin

	No of titles	% incr. over 1997	Index (1970 =100)	Av price 98 (£ ster)
Great Britain	879	8.42	3,807.96	334.89
USA & Canada	698	6.40	2,532.70	366.80
Other countries	430	-6.69	3,425.09	391.71
Total	**2,007**	**3.78**	**3,158.74**	**358.16**

Analysis by subject category

	No of titles	% incr. over 1997	Index (1970 =100)	Av price 98 (£ ster)
Humanities & Social Sciences	841	9.48	2,508.95	134.12
Medicine	203	6.02	3,053.99	325.00
Science & Technology	963	2.40	3,354.22	560.81
Total	**2,007**	**3.78**	**3,158.74**	**358.16**

Medicine

	No of titles	% incr. over 1997	Index (1970 =100)	Av price 98 (£ ster)
Dentistry, Opthalmology, Audiology	17	1.55	2,757.77	295.11
General Medicine	27	3.61	2,160.76	204.32
Neurology, Psychiatry	25	4.53	3,256.09	326.66
Pathology & Clinical Medicine	52	6.28	3,052.96	358.91
Public Health, Nursing, General Practice	26	9.33	2,822.92	160.42
Surgery, Anatomy, Physicology	20	8.22	4,800.92	610.48
Pharmacology	21	5.51	2,886.59	417.31
Veterinary Medicine	15	8.75	2,233.17	231.16
Total	**203**	**6.02**	**3,053.99**	**325.00**

Science & Technology

	No of titles	% increase over 1997	Index (1970=100)	Av price 1998 (£ sterling)
Agriculture	46	12.16	3,162.93	219.73
Anthropology	16	3.56	2,503.21	189.87
Astronomy, Astrophysics	13	5.97	4,203.19	591.49
Biology	32	-0.30	2,623.28	768.01
Biophysics, Biochemistry, Microbiology	26	-0.32	3,571.87	1,317.10
Botany	25	2.75	4,538.36	419.34
Chemistry	66	0.74	3,161.39	1,276.93
Civil Engineering	26	5.04	3,225.70	257.20
Computers, Automation & Control	37	5.83	3,676.13	491.76
Electronics, Elect. Engineering, Aero'tics	73	6.66	3,142.56	537.69
Food, Soap, Cosmetic Industries	37	11.06	3,017.51	284.90
General Science	25	4.52	2,360.05	347.86
General Technology	33	3.45	2,939.05	577.48
Geology, Mineralogy, G'Physics, Meteorology	44	0.92	3,021.42	436.51
Glass, Ceramics	20	2.99	2,366.80	205.40
Heating, Lighting, Ventilating	13	-1.83	1,585.50	73.85
Industrial & Engineering Chemistry	22	-0.36	2,488.87	375.74
Mathematics & Statistics	51	4.65	3,187.83	441.20
Mechanical Engineering	30	3.68	3,075.54	359.74
Metallurgy	36	5.74	2,312.63	280.71
Nuclear Science & Technology	30	-4.96	3,655.54	1,236.42
Petroleum & Fuel Technology	22	0.66	4,347.81	389.68
Physics	58	0.86	4,891.74	1,276.03
Polymers, Paint, Rubber, Plastics	48	6.01	3,930.49	712.88
Printer, Paper, Packaging	20	-3.61	2,255.64	190.67
Production Engineering & Oper'l Research	28	8.49	3,092.65	276.75
Textiles, Leather, Dyeing	22	1.21	1,564.64	112.04
Transport	24	9.50	4,703.60	252.13
Zoology	40	4.67	3,592.67	332.69
Total	**963**	**2.40**	**3,354.22**	**560.81**

Figure 13. Annual periodical prices from **Library Association Record**

Non-official Business Statistics

Statistics produced by bodies other than government are likely to be more specific and detailed in their coverage, and more directly relatable to market intelligence purposes. They tend also to be less predictable in their coverage of periods and subjects, and because they emanate from innumerable different organisations, harder to trace. Time series – that is, regularly produced series, whether issues as separate publications or within other serials – can usually be traced via subject guides to statistics. A specialist finding tool here is *Sources of Unofficial UK Statistics*, compiled by David Mort; there follows an example of an entry from it, and from the statistical series it refers to:

Tracing a non-official statistic appearing in a non-statistical source

> In Subject index of *Sources of Unofficial UK Statistics*:
>> Periodicals – Prices 602
> In Sources sequence, entry no. 602:
>> Originator: *Library Association Record*
>> Title: Periodical prices, annual in monthly journal
>> Coverage [etc]: Average prices analysed by subject and origin... Survey usually appears in the May issue . . .

An alternative starting point for tracing such data is Euromonitor's *European Directory of Non-Official Statistical Sources*. Extremely timely and unique once-off statistics often appear in journals or other unexpected sources, but tracing them systematically is difficult. They are not likely to be covered in the statistical guides, and even if the item is traceable by subject in indexing and abstracting services, they may not distinguish statistical treatments from normal text. The attraction of Responsive Database Services' *TableBase* (direct on CD-ROM or web site, or via DataStar and Dialog) is its collection and indexing of hard *tabular* data, much of it production, sales, and market share figures, extracted from a wide range of mainly non-official sources:

> '*TableBase* contains tabular data about companies, products, industries, brands, markets, demographics, and countries. The data is derived from privately published statistical annuals and from trade associations, nonprofit research groups, government agencies, and international organizations. Industry reports prepared by investment research analysts from the source.' (From the description in Dialog Corporation's *Chronolog* periodical.)

Types of non-government bodies producing valuable business statistics include trade associations – such as the Pet Food Manufacturers Association in the list below, chambers of commerce, other national and local trade promotion organisations, consumer protection and lobby groups – and, of course, business information publishers. These include the publishers of statistically rich periodicals, including those often called industry newsletters. An example is Agra Europe, whose weekly periodical of that title is packed with statistical series from official and non-official sources, updated by a web site (*http://www.agra-food-news.com*).

Industry organisations are worth contacting directly because they can often provide statistical and other market data which is hard to find or not even published (they can be traced by subject in *Directory of British Associations & Associations in Ireland* (S.P.A. Henderson & A.J.W. Henderson editors; CBD Research Ltd) or similar, or some of the subject guides to business information sources given under 'Bibliographical Apparatus' in the final chapter). A rare compilation of some of this data is, as described under 'Market Research' in the 'Market Information' chapter, the *Industry Insider* database of trade associations' industry-specific reports and other data, hosted by Investext. The market research firm and information broker IRN also offers a database of UK trade associations' statistics. An idea of the variety and information value of trades organisations, is given by the following list, cited by Keynote as sources of information for their survey of the pet foods market:

> Nutrition Society
> Pet Food Manufacturers Association
> Pet Fostering Service Scotland
> Pet Health Council
> Pet Trade and Industry Association
> RSPCA
> Society for Companion Animal Studies

Non-business Statistics; Data on Consumers

Official data collection is the source of most of the omnibus data on the population – the consumers for many products or services. The vast amount of data collected, collated and harmonised by the EU for Europe as a whole is a boon in today's global markets. National and Eurostat services provide demographic data: numbers, age, sex and geographic distribution, and data on 'lifestyles', including on people's income, expenditure, possessions, work and leisure activities, health, transport and mobility patterns, all of potentially great market intelligence value. By comparing with earlier statistics in the series, or with those for other countries or regions collected to the same standards, patterns and trends can be identified, and translated into market opportunities or threats. The word 'trends' appears in some of the non-business statistical examples listed below, emphasising the value of such data for strategic purposes.

Examples

Demographic

> *1991 Census Topic Reports: Household and Family Composition* – ONS. One of many special analyses of the 10-yearly UK national census data.
>
> *Population Trends* – ONS. Quarterly – statistics and articles on a variety of population matters.
>
> *Population Projections for the UK and Constituent Countries Over the Next 40 years* – Government Actuaries Department.
>
> *Demographic Statistics* – Eurostat. Annual.

Lifestyle (see below for non-statistical data)

> *Social Trends* – ONS. Annual – 'combines text, table and charts to present a narrative of life and lifestyles in modern Britain . . . misses nothing, from employment to environment, from spending to sport.'

		5: Income and Wealth
		5.27

Adults holding selected forms of wealth[1]: by age, 1995-96
Great Britain — Percentages

	26-34[2]	35-54	55-74	75 and over	All adults[2]
Current account	78	83	74	60	77
Building society account[3]	42	51	51	46	48
Premium bonds	12	22	25	21	20
Stocks and shares	8	18	21	15	16
Other bank account[3]	13	14	16	16	14
TESSA[4]	3	10	16	6	9
Post Office account	6	6	7	13	7
PEPs[5]	2	7	10	3	6
Unit trusts	2	5	7	4	5
National Savings bonds	1	2	9	12	4
Other account[6]	1	2	2	1	2
Save as you earn	2	2	2	0	1
Gifts	-	1	2	2	1
Any	87	91	88	86	89

1 Percentage in each group holding each form of wealth.
2 Excluding 16 to 19 year olds in non-advanced full-time education.
3 Excluding current account and TESSAs.
4 Tax exempt special savings account.
5 Personal equity plans.
6 Any acount yielding interest not included in another category.
Source: Family Resources Survey, Department of Social Security

Figure 14. Example of statistics of business relevance from **Social Trends**

National Food Consumption and Expenditure (National Food Survey) – MAFF. Annual – consumption and expenditure by household.

Women and Men in the European Union: a Statistical Portrait – Eurostat, 1995.

Digest of Statistics on Social Protection in Europe: Volume 1 Old Age – Eurostat, 1992 (and 1996 update).

The Economic Activity of Women in the European Union – Eurostat, 1997.

Income and expenditure

Family Spending (Family Expenditure Survey) – ONS. Annual – household expenditure by broad subject categories, age and sex.

Consumer Trends – ONS. Quarterly – consumer spending data for specific markets.

Income Statistics for the Agricultural Household Sector: . . . – Eurostat, 1996.

Non-statistical 'Lifestyle' Data

To stay one step ahead in planning, designing and marketing products, businesses must try to understand current and future tastes and aspirations, and try to translate it into buying behaviour. Market research firms, government and others publish omnibus studies on different aspects of consumers and their behaviour, such as:

Consumer Niche Markets – Headland. Quarterly issues focussing on e.g. The Over 50s, Baby Boomers.

Third Agers – Mintel (i.e. 45+ and 50+ age groups; numbers, income, expenditure, activities, opinions).

Smoking Related Behaviour and Attitudes – ONS.

Socio-economic and Geodemographic Classification

Lists of names and addresses are of obvious value in direct marketing to private consumers if the raw data can be converted into valuable marketing intelligence by classifying individuals – or at least localities, according to likely purchasing patterns. The standard, now regarded as a poor minimum, is the groupings originally devised by JICNARS – the Joint Industry Committee for National Readership Surveys:

A	Higher managerial and professional
B	Intermediate managerial or professional
C1	Supervisory or clerical
C2	Skilled manual workers
D	Semi and unskilled manual workers
E	Widows, state pensioners (with no other earnings)

In November 1998 the British Government issued the new *National Statistics Socio-economic Classification* (*NS SEC*), to be used in official statistics. It replaced the *Registrar General's Social Class*, which was also based on occupation. It remains to be seen whether the classification will be widely adopted in market research.

National Statistics Socio-economic Classification (NS SEC), issued 1998

1. Higher managerial and professional ocupations
   1.1 Employers and managers in larger organistions
   1.2 Higher professionals
2. Lower managerial and professional occupations
3. Intermediate occupations
4. Small employers and own account workers
5. Lower supervisory, craft and related occupations
6. Semi-routine occupations
7. Routine occupations

A category covering those who have never had paid work, and the long-term unemployed, is to be added at a later date.

The most comprehensive and up-to-date publicly-available UK name and address listing is the electoral roll. Cumulated telephone directory databases are now also available, as are many more selective listings, such as a 'Windfall shareholders database' and a 'Gone-away suppression file'. Information providers market the electoral roll data along with geodemographic classifications and overlays for identifying areas with characteristics like high income, high unemployment, aged population or receiving a particular TV channel. Experian's *Mosaic* geodemographic classification system relates every British household to one of 52 lifestyle categories. Their pay-as-you-go *Prospect Locator* CD-ROM aims to help small businesses compile targeted lists of names and addresses. EuroDirect's products also allow complex screening of Britain's 46 million adults and 24 million households, and automatic addressing of mail-shots to the lucky people matching the user's criteria. The entire electoral roll is compressed into one CD-ROM, with one or more of their *RollCall* personal computer software products:

Data

Combines EuroDirect's geodemographic targeting systems with a name and address file; can produce targeted mailing lists at 6 million records per hour.

Batch

Allows in-house consumer databases to be 'cleaned' by comparison with the CD-ROM.

Profile

Allows targeting of postcode areas by EuroDirect's household classifications.

Look Up; Trace

Roll is searchable by name, address etc. to discover adults names, verify addresses.

Capture

Client incorporates EuroDirect consumer details and classification in own data entry.

Complementary software products are available to profile a district in marketing terms, compile marketing databases of consumers, identify branch and store catchment areas, exchange additional data items (such as dates of birth) between users. In fact, EuroDirect have software to predict an individual elector's age, called *IAN* – Indicating Age by Name.

While databases of business phone numbers have been marketed for some time, British Telecom has only recently had to release the monopoly on its 'white pages' of private subscribers. With its *UK Infodisk*, and since then a web site, the American firm i-CD Publishing was possibly the first to offer customers 42 million British names, addresses and phone numbers – a combination of electoral roll and phone subscribers data. Although people who don't like telesales can visit their *192.COM* (*http://www.192.com/*) site and remove their own telephone number, this is probably the signal for even more private subscribers to go ex-directory! The American web site called *555-1212* (*http://www.555-1212.com/*) is currently a favoured starting point for telephone numbers searches. Searches are not only carried out in their own databases, but through links to most significant others also. You can not only look up phone numbers and email addresses, but also addresses and post codes, and easily repeat a search in several databases. There is also reverse look-up, to find the owner of a number, look up by address, and the ability to list all the names and numbers in a particular street. Via links the service includes access to the white pages of at least 12 other countries, and many other yellow pages and specialised phone directories. *Infospace* is a free 'people-finding' search engine, taking in an impressive range of public domain personal records, including British ones (*http://www.infospace.com/*). *Whowhere?* (*http://www.whowhere.lycos.com/*) is another popular gateway to an international range of directories of personal and business telephone and email numbers and addresses.

Digests and Compilations of Market Data

The sections on business and non-business statistics, showed the potential value in market intelligence of data on an unlimited range of topics, from a huge and diverse range of sources. A range of secondary sources exists to do the leg-work for the business person in this large and unfamiliar field.

They trace, sift and re-present the primary data, producing manageable digests and compilations for the more predictable market intelligence purposes. Quantitative data on all the matters directly affecting *any* market – demographics, incomes, prices, sales– may be included in a single one of these 'digests', 'databooks' or 'handbooks', sometimes with international scope. A minority, like *Factfinder* and *Countryfile* CD-ROM (typical contents illustrated below), concentrate on matters which *affect* markets, such as consumers and the economy; while those like *Market Profiles* (also illustrated below) are mostly data *about* markets. Compilations can 'spin-off' the market information publishers' core work of examining primary sources to create surveys on markets, consumers, retailing and so on. Although some such compilations are now in electronic form, these sources rarely exist in online hosts' portfolios. *Market Size Digest* and *IAC Forecasts* have a specialised bibliographic role, in that the relevant market data is abstracted from other sources.

Typical statistical data per country in Countryfile *CD-ROM (from flyer of ca. 1997)*

Overview – All 175 countries

Review of recent and projected political and economic developments, supplementary to a front page of general information on population size, population density, ethnic groups, main languages, religions, GDP, GDP per capita, main trading partners and capital city, detailed map of each country outlining its main cities and key features.

Key Variables:

Population

Total Population: Trends	1990-1995	Million
Total Population: Forecast	2000-2025	Million
Male Population Age 0-14yrs	1990-1995	Million
Male Population Age 0-14yrs	2000-2025	Million
Male Population Age 15-64yrs	1990-1995	Million
Male Population Age 15-64yrs	2000-2025	Million
Male Population Age 65yrs +	1990-1995	Million
Male Population Age 65yrs +	2000-2025	Million
Female Population Age 0-14yrs	1990-1995	Million
Female Population Age 0-14yrs	2000-2025	Million
Female Population Age 15-64yrs	1990-1995	Million
Female Population Age 15-64yrs	2000-2025	Million
Female Population Age 65yrs +	1990-1995	Million
Female Population Age 65yrs +	2000-2025	Million

Macro-economic Indicators

GDP Trends	1990-1995	USD Billion
Real GDP Growth	1990-1995	% (+/-)
Consumer Price Inflation	1990-1995	Ave. Annual %
Exchange Rates	1990-1995	Loc Cur/LISD
Lending Rates	1990-1995	%
Unemployment Rate	1990-1995	% of Workforce
GDP Growth per Capita	1990-1995	USD

Trade and Industry Data

Total Imports Trends	1990-1995	USD Billion
Total Exports, Trends	1990-1995	USD Billion
Industrial Production Index	1990-1995	1990=100
Manufacturing Index	1990-1995	1990=100
Agricultural Output Index	1990-1995	1990=100
Level of Unemployment	1990-1995	Unemployed 000's
Level of Employment	1990-1995	Workforce 000's
Employment in Manufacturing	1990-1995	Workforce
Working Week Manufacturing	1990-1995	Av. Hrs/Week

Retailing — 25 major developed countries.

Total Retail Sales	1994	Local currency
Structure of Retail Market	1994	% of retail outlets
Leading Retailers	1994	By turnover

Advertising — 25 major developed countries

Total Advertising Expenditure	1995	Local currency
Main Advertising Categories	1995	Top 5 by spend
Leading Advertisers	1995	Top 5 by spend

Consumer Expenditure

Total Consumer Spend	Latest Years	USD Billion
Spend on Food	Latest Years	USD Billion
Spend on Alcoholic Bevs.	Latest Years	USD Billion
Spend on Tobacco	Latest Years	USD Billion
Spend on Household Prods.	Latest Years	USD Billion
Spend on Housing	Latest Years	USD Billion

Spend on Fuel	Latest Years	USD Billion
Spend on Clothing/Footwear	Latest Years	USD Billion
Spend on Health/Medical Care	Latest Years	USD Billion
Spend on Leisure/Education	Latest Years	USD Billion
Spend on Transport/Comms	Latest Years	USD Billion

Consumer Durables

Penetration of Motor Vehicles	Latest Years	% Households
Penetration of TVs	Latest Years	% Households
Penetration of Radios	Latest Years	% Households
Penetration of Telephones	Latest Years	% Households
Penetration of CD Players	Latest Years	% Households
Penetration of Video Recorders	Latest Years	% Households
Penetration of Personal Computers	Latest Years	% Households
Penetration of Satellite TV	Latest Years	% Households
Penetration of Washing Machines	Latest Years	% Households
Penetration of Freezers	Latest Years	% Households
Penetration of Cookers	Latest Years	% Households
Penetration of Microwave Ovens	Latest Years	% Households
Penetration of Refrigerators	Latest Years	% Households

Sociocultural Data

Number of Households	1990-1995	Million
Number of Persons/Household	1990-1995	Number
Marriage Rate	1990-1995	Rate
Divorce Rate	1990-1995	Rate
Population Density	1990-1995	Pop/Sq Km
Diet (Calorific/Protein Intake)	1985-1990	% Daily Req.
Health Spend by Govt.	Latest Years	USD Billion
Birth Rate	Latest Years	Rate/'000
Death Rate	1990-1995	Rate/'000
Infant Mortality rate	1990-1995	Rate/'000
Rural/Urban Population	1990 & 1995	% Breakdown

Examples of market data compilations

– Market data in general
United Kingdom

> *Factfinder*. Mintel; demographic, lifestyle, financial, economic & other figures and trends.
>
> *Market Pocketbook*. Advertising Association; demographic, market size, distribution, advertising data.
>
> *Market Profiles*. Headland; brief import, export, sales, and value data and trends for each market.
>
> *UK Market Facts*. Business Information Associates; wide range of data on a range of specific markets.
>
> *The British Shopper*. AC Nielsen, 1997; a compilation of data for marketing purposes.

Europe

> *European Marketing Data and Statistics*. Euromonitor; the 1998 edition is the 33rd. 'Far-reaching coverage of socio-economic indicators, detailed breakdowns of demographic trends, historical data spanning 20 years and 207 countries in two comprehensive volumes'. Also on CD-ROM.
>
> *Consumer Europe*. Euromonitor; data on 300 product categories for 20 European countries.

Worldwide

> *Consumer Asia* (plus editions for other continents and countries). Euromonitor.
>
> *Countryfile*. Market Tracking International; CD-ROM or printed; data for 175 countries.
>
> *International Marketing Data and Statistics/World Marketing Data and Statistics*. Euromonitor; annual; similar scope to European Marketing Data and Statistics above, for 200+ countries; latter CD-ROM, former both print and CD-ROM.
>
> *China Marketing Data and Statistics*, 1998. Euromonitor; 'the first comprehensive source of accurate, official Chinese market data to be published in English', compiled from official and non-official sources.

Market-specific

> *Foodline: International Food Market Data*. Dialog and DataStar. Leatherhead Food Research Association's database, combining market values, volumes, shares; production, sales and trade figures.
>
> *The Market for Food Retailing in Eastern Europe*. Euromonitor, 1996; socio-economic indicators, retail infrastructure, retailer profiles, market opportunities and forecasts.

– Specialised types of market data
Market forecasts

> *European Marketing Forecasts; International Marketing Forecasts; World Marketing Forecasts.* Euromonitor; collected macroeconomic, market size/value, socio-economic forecasts.

> *IAC Forecasts.* Database available direct, or via DataStar and other hosts. IAC; numeric forecast data on products, industries, markets, demographics etc.

Economic indicators

> *Industrial Economic Indicators.* DTI statistics. Business and trade statistics; 90 series, 300 industries; sales, prices, market size.

Retail Intelligence

There are two reasons for a need to know about retailing: because almost every business depends on those processes to sell their products, and because the retail sector is an enormous service industry in its own right. A plethora of information sources is aimed at either or both points of view. While most of the large market information providers include one-off or serial reports on or for the retail industry, some, like Corporate Intelligence on Retailing (CIR below) specialise in 'retail intelligence'. The sources, illustrated below, tend to be either guides to retailers and/or outlets (as below), aimed primarily at firms distributing through retail outlets or data on the retail market for those involved in it (as 'Retail market' below). Information on retailers themselves could of course also be obtained from the more general company information sources, covered in chapter 2.

Retailers and retail outlets

> *European Directory of Retailers and Wholesalers; World Retail Directory.* Euromonitor. 5,000 European operators, 2,600 world; overviews and national profiles.

> *British Drinks Index; British Foods Index; British Retail Index.* Hadleigh Marketing Services. Quarterly; detailed profiles of retail companies.

> *Retail Directory.* Newman Books. Retailers in UK and Ireland.

> *Retail Rankings.* CIR. Profiles of the top 775 UK retailers, ranked by various retail operations.

> *United Kingdom's Leading Retailers.* Management Horizons Europe. Approximately annual financial and trading profiles.

Retail market – general

> *Retail Pocketbook.* AC Nielsen, 1998. Facts and figures on UK retail markets and retailers, including sections on Irish and European retailing.

European Retail Handbook. CIR. Lists of retailers, outlets; reviews of 27 countries, product sectors; market statistics.

Retail Trade Review. EIU. Quarterly serial.

Retail Pocket Book. NTC. Small, inexpensive, wide-ranging compendium of UK retail market statistics.

Retail Trade in the UK. Euromonitor. Regularly reissued market survey of the retail sector.

Retail Trade International. Euromonitor. World overviews, plus separate market surveys of retailing in 50 countries.

Retailing in Eastern Europe. CIR. Survey data on retail markets in central and Eastern European countries.

Verdict Reports. Verdict Research. Approximately 15 per year, each on a specific aspect of the retail market; annual forecast. Titles include: Electronic Shopping; Neighbourhood Retailing; Department Stores; Retail Demand 2001.

Specific aspects of the retail market

International Private Label Retailing – Indicators and Trends. AC Nielsen, 1998. Data and analysis for up to 20 product categories in 40 countries worldwide.

Retail market – sectors

In-store Catering in the UK. CIR. Trends and developments in different sectors, profiles of retailers and caterers.

Grocery Retailing in the UK. CIR. Market structure and value, distribution channels, profiles of 30 major retailers.

A considerable number of periodicals make regular contributions on retailing, retailers, and the retail market, for example:

UK Retail Report. CIR. Monthly summary of each sector, and twice-yearly analysis, plus features and news.

Retail News Fax. CIR. Daily email or fax; UK, European and international retail news monitoring.

Retail Monitor International. Euromonitor. Monthly – major reviews of sectors, retailer profiles, retail markets news.

Advertising, Media and Image Monitoring

In the knowledge that the image of company and products is strongly linked to success, most firms spend heavily on advertising and promotion. It follows that their own and their competitors' promotional policy and results should be carefully evaluated. Firms achieve this partly through in-depth analysis of their own advertising expenditure, and researching the effect on sales, and partly by comparison with competitors. It is possible at least to observe competitors' methods and estimate their expenditure, then to make tentative connections with what can be discovered about their sales, brand share, financial performance. A number of information providers specialise in recording details about advertising, including product and company involved, advertising agency, cost, and media organ involved; they even copy the advertisement itself. Expenditure is periodically totalled by company, media type, media company, brand and advertising agency, and usually sold on subscription to some of the firms concerned. Alternatively users can connect to the supplier's database when a need arises, and use the software to manipulate and output required data. *ACNielsen•MEAL* (formerly *MEAL* – i.e. Media Expenditure Analysis Ltd, then *Register-MEAL*) is the best known source of UK advertising expenditure. Advertising expenditure data is rarely included in company database records; however, there is a *Register-MEAL* database on the FT Profile host, details and sample data below:

> *MEAL* monitors advertising for 15,000 different brands, classified into nearly 500 product groups within 34 broad product categories. For each brand *MEAL* lists:
>
> > Brand name
> >
> > Agency
> >
> > Media buyer
> >
> > Client company
> >
> > Expenditure (previous quarter; each of previous 3 months; previous 12 months; moving annual total – MAT). Plus totals for each product group.

Sample record from FT Profile File Guide (1997) for the Register-MEAL Quarterly Digest database

1 Jun 96   FOOD (FOO) / STOCK & STOCKCUBES
PRODUCT DESCRIPTION
AGENCY

(MEDIA BUYER)	TOT.	APR	MAY	JUN	<u>MAT</u>
ADVERTISER	000s	000s	000s	000s	000s

BISTO BEST GRANULES					
ABBOTT MEAD VICKERS BBDO	0.3	0.3	—	—	2872.6
(BBJMED)					
RHM FOODS LTD					
BOVRIL BEEF & CHICKEN PASTE					
BMP DDB NEEDHAM	—	—	—	—	407.4
(BMPDDB)					
CPC UNITED KINGDOM LID					

KNORR STIRR FRY CUBES
BMP DDB NEEDHAM   —   —   —   —   693.7
(BMPDDB)
CPC UNITED KINGDOM LTD

KNORR STOCK CUBES FOR RICE
BMP DDB NEEDHAM   —   —   —   —   740.6
(BMPDDB)
CPC UNITED KINGDOM LTD

	TOT.	APR	MAY	JUN	MAT
	000s	000s	000s	000s	000s

MARMITE SPREAD
BMP DDB NEEDHAM
(BMPDDB)
CPC UNITED KINGDOM ijtb

	TOT.	APR	MAY	JUN	MAT
MARMITE SPREAD	391.4	297.8	89.9	3.7	2941.6

MARMITE STOCK CUBES
BMP DDB NEEDHAM 3
(BMPDDB)
CPC UNITED KINGDOM LTD

	TOT.	APR	MAY	JUN	MAT
MARMITE STOCK CUBES	9.7	27.7	12.1	—	299.2

OXO CHICKEN STOCK CUBES
J WALTER THOMPSON
(IN MED)
UNILEVER BROOKE BOND FOODS

	TOT.	APR	MAY	JUN	MAT
OXO CHICKEN STOCK CUBES	12.5	—	12.5	—	1801.0

OXO RED STOCK CUBES
J WALTER THOMPSON CO LTD   —   —   —   —   1645.5
(IN MED)
UNILEVER BROOKE BOND FOODS

	TOT.	APR	MAY	JUN	MAT
Sub-threshold Brands 7	32.1	—	32.1	—	233.2
TOT(F0076) STOCK&STOCKCUBES	476	326	147	4	11635

Neilsen Media Research produces ratings of North American TV programmes and networks, while FT Electronic Information's Broadcast Monitoring Company (BMC) views and listens to a very wide of local, national and global printed and broadcast media, covering editorial material as well as advertisements. Perhaps to check who is saying what about them, in order to try to adjust their image, a client can ask for the name of any subject, person, company or organisation to be monitored, and receive copies and recordings of relevant text. From BMC's prospectus:

UK Press Monitoring

Team of 40 readers work through the night providing articles, summaries and abstracts from national the press by 0730 each morning.

International Press Monitoring

Early morning delivery of keypoint summaries of articles from main national and business titles across Europe and the rest of the world.

Broadcast Monitoring

Monitors UK national TV and radio; provides summaries, transcripts and tapes 24 hours a day, 7 days a week.

'Tear sheet' services are more modest, simply providing subscribers with paper cuttings of advertisements for specified companies or products. Mintel Group's International Information Services' *IIS Tearsheets* covers approximately 25 different product categories, such as 'Gardening products', in main consumer general interest periodicals in a given country or region, for £300 per category.

There is a chance of tracing forms of promotion other than advertisements, in sources which index or abstract the trade press. The *MARS* database, from IAC's own web-based InSite Pro host, provides full-text or abstracts of items from advertising, marketing and public relations periodicals. This includes items on these as professional activities, but also promotions of specific companies and products. The UK's Profile Group, established in 1987, calls itself '... the most comprehensive and extensive source for future events information in the UK', providing over 2000 top UK organisations ... with promotional and market opportunities, sponsorship openings, editorial ideas, PR links and sales & new business leads'. Even more than the MEAL data mentioned above, Profile's products are for and about the advertising, media and PR industry itself, forthcoming PR events, and corporate client account activities and opportunities. However, of wider interest is their weekly *Advance Media & Marketing Opportunities* (*AMMO*; print or web site), which has sections abstracting news from the general and trade press on marketing and PR 'People' in industry in general or the media industry. Another section gives general news on potential corporate clients, and another on industry activities which might result in business for PR firms, for example:

An entry from the Activity section of the December 12th 1997 issue of AMMO:

Divino (George Best)

London-based wine distributor Divino has launched a range of wines in the UK in conjunction with footballing legend George Best. The range, whose labels feature Best's face and signature, comprises four Italian wines: two white and two red.
oln [Off Licence News]
Divino 0171-486 9171 (London)

Sources of Market Opportunities

Levels of opportunities, types of source

Opportunity level	Example	Primary information source
Possible	High income or profit, so likely to buy new vehicle	Organisations: disclosed details. Individuals: data at level of group/district
Probable	Planning permission; new contract, grant; public sector project	Planning announcements; press releases; media coverage
Actual	Tenders for local or central government works/supply	Press, trade or official serial publications

At any given time marketing opportunities exist, of varying degrees of certainty. As in the diagram, three points in the spectrum of certainty can be identified. A range of primary sources useful for the identification of leads and opportunities corresponds with each. Some of these primary sources categories are covered in other chapters or sections; however, specialised primary and secondary sources are treated below.

Identifying 'Possible' Market Opportunities

First the normal, low level of opportunity, where different private or business customers' potential can only be surmised by analysing factors like their income, or size. In relation to private consumers, this is the normal role of the market research, geodemographic, socio-economic and other data covered in other sections. Targetting consumers via lists such as those of electors and telephone subscribers, appears under 'Non-statistical "Lifestyle" Data' above.

Normal opportunities for marketing to *businesses* can be also be identified from the various market information sources covered in this chapter. They can be further narrowed down to specific targets via the wide variety of company information sources discussed in chapter 2. The more detailed the records in company directories or databases, the better they are likely to be for selecting companies as marketing targets, especially if they are searchable at least by business classification, geographical area and size. Most electronic company sources offer this approach, together with the ability to sort and rank output by various criteria, and to transfer name and address data into in-house marketing and mail-shot software. However, a number of company sources are marketed or even primarily intended for market opportunity identification. Infocheck Equifax, for instance, produces *Marketing Decisions* CD-ROM, representing data on 220,000 companies selected from its core database, packaged with search and output 'functionality' tailored to marketing purposes. The role in marketing of Infocheck's normal features: directors' details and credit information is emphasised in the promotional literature. ICC's equivalent spin-off database of 130,000 'actively trading' UK companies is *Target Business*. *D&B MarketPlace UK* is the CD-ROM version of Dun & Bradstreet's marketing-oriented database of over 1.6 million businesses; the data is available via Dialog and DataStar as *Dun's Market Identifiers* (*European Marketing CD* has a similar function) The web-based *D&B Direct Marketing Database* represents an amalgamation between D&B's records for larger British companies, and the 1.8 million small firms covered by Thomson Directories. Data fields, such as the following in *D&B MarketPlace UK*, enable marketers to create their own target databases:

Town	Company size (sales)
County	Fax indicator
Postcode area	Legal status
Postcode district	Date of relocation
Economic region	Year started
Number of branches	Import/export
Line of business	Site status
Company size (employes)	Sales increase/decrease

Trade fairs at home or abroad are used to promote products to potential customers. The DTI facilitates British exports by maintaining the free overseas *Trade Fairs Database* (*http://dti2info1.dti.gov.uk/public/exp1.html*).

Identifying 'Probable' Market Opportunities

The buying potential of a minority of customers is, however, heightened by certain events; for example, in the case of private individuals, a forthcoming wedding; in the case of a business, previous orders, or a contract to manufacture a new product. Special marketing effort is justified by the raised level of certainty, and the reduced number of targets. Because such events occurring in businesses and other organisations are more easily detectable and generate more business than do private consumers' equivalent events, commercial sources exist to provide systematic access to them. Most of these sources are very different from company databases in content and format; each tends to collate opportunities arising from 'events' of a particular kind. They are either a version of the primary source of information (if any) on one of the following 'events', or a secondary source based on one or more of them:

> Local planning decisions
>
> Plans announced by business and other organisations
>
> Developing countries' forward plans
>
> Contracts awarded to business and other organisations
>
> Public sector contracts awarded
>
> Previous purchasers; importers of goods
>
> Manifests of cargos loaded or discharged at ports
>
> Development banks' projects
>
> International or bilateral aid projects
>
> Opportunities reported by overseas trade missions
>
> Licenses or permissions gained for new activities
>
> Items to be sold by auction (including online auctions)

Although planning consents are published, because most are at local authority level it requires a secondary source, such as in this case a press database, to sort and collate the data into useful form. *DMS/FI Contract Awards* is a database, on Dialog, representing the US government's 'non-classified prime contract actions of $25,000 or more'. Some trade journals collate relevant opportunities data for their readers, as does *Construction News*; its Business Leads column includes local planning applications and approvals, and major construction contracts tendered and awarded. The *Scan-a-Bid: Business Opportunities* database, on DataStar, is compiled by scanning the more diverse range of primary documents, which reports development projects in developing countries and similar. Amongst others, the *Internet Auction List* is a 'web portal to the action community', providing lists of auctions and a calendar (*http://www.internetauctionlist.com/*).

Leads from Customs Records

The public nature of most countries' customs records provides a rare opportunity to know exactly which company is trading what quantity and value of raw materials or goods with whom. The US-based Trade Inc. acquires and adapts such records to produce CD-ROM databases for countries including the USA and China. *UK Importers* (on DataStar) is a British equivalent, whereas Eurostat's *Comext-CD* covers imports and exports to and from the EU, as well as between individual member states. The table below shows the uses suggested by Trade Inc. for such data, and the information elements available in their China records:

Uses of customs data	Fields in TRADE Intelligence-China
Finding and evaluating new suppliers	Company code and/or name
Finding and evaluating sales prospects	Company contact information
Tracking competitors, customers and suppliers	Product code and description Shipment value – US$ or RMB
Analysing industry activity	Value per unit – US$ or RMB
Investigating new markets	Quantity of units shipped

Uses of customs data	Fields in TRADE Intelligence-China
	Method of transportation
Questions	Country of origin/destination
Are my customers or distributors	Routing country
buying from my competition?	Shipment type
How much are my competitors exporting	Month of shipment
to the country, who are their customers?	Customs locations
Can I obtain information to improve my	Consumption/production region
negotiating position with my customer	Software allows searching
or distributor?	and analysis by most attributes above

Companies Seeking Foreign Partners

Athough it is left to the 'Product Information' chapter to deal with opportunities presented by the advertising or appearance in directories of products and services, it is worth mentioning here the opportunities presented to potential foreign partners of firms actively seeking introductions. *TradeUK* is a British example of the many government sponsored initiatives to promote small and medium sized companies abroad (*http://www.tradeuk.com/*). On *TradeUK* since 1997 the free *National Exporters* database has held details of 53,000 British exporters, and has received over 100,000 enquiries from 91 countries. *TradeUK* now includes the *Export Sales Leads* service, operated for the DTI's Overseas Trade Services by the Dialog Corporation, whereby leads notified by embassy staff and others are e-mailed to relevant firms on the database. *Export Affaires* is a database and service run by Chambre de Commerce et d'Industrie de Paris, enabling participating companies to be brought to the attention of potential business partners in France. *IBCC-Net* is the database of the 'Global Business Exchange' operated by the worldwide network of chambers of commerce. Businesses post their offers for a small fee, including, if they wish, a hypertext link, while consultation of the database on the web is free. There are many similar databases in which Central and Eastern European companies offer their services to, or seek partnerships with Western counterparts – for obvious reasons, many of them include the word 'Partner' in the title.

Examples of source and host coverage of 'probable' opportunities

Type of 'probable' opportunity	Database example	FT Profile	DataStar	Dialog
Opportunities reported by overseas trade missions				
UK	*Export Sales Leads Service – Dialog for DTI 'Export Intelligence Online'*	X		
USA	*FMIRs – Foreign Market Intelligence Reports* (distributed by Microinfo)			
Contracts awarded:				
US Government	*DMS/FI Contract Awards*			X
European Union	*Tenders Electronic Daily*	X	X	
Aid projects	1. *Scan-a-Bid: Business Opportunities*		X	
	2. *Programme d'Aide des pays de la CEE*		X	
Development banks' projects	*Summary of Proposed Projects*		X	
Importers/exporters of goods				
USA customs records	*Trade Intelligence* (CD-ROM)			
UK customs records	*UK Importers*		X	
UK exporters	*TradeUK.com* (*http://www.tradeuk.com/*)			

Identifying 'Actual' Market Opportunities

The highest point in a spectrum of marketing opportunities is where the consumer actually declares the intention to buy a product or service, and all that has to be decided is the supplier and the price. The visible evidence is often published tenders for goods or services, invitations to architects to submit competitive designs for building projects, or business to business invitations to collaborate in more general ways. The possibility of business is even greater, the product clearly identified, and the number of potential buyers even further reduced, so potential suppliers may devote even more time and effort to finding and pursuing such opportunities. Such opportunities are normally given by corporate purchasers, and because they are by definition advertised, are even easier for information providers to discover and collate.

FT Profile has added *Tenders Electronic Daily* (*TED*) to the DTI export sales leads database referred to above, and relevant items from the *Predicasts Newsletters* database, to create the simultaneously searchable *Business Opportunities* data collection. *TED* (also listed above as a source of probable business opportunities because it also records details of the *winner* of contracts, and the price) is the electronic version of the EU states' transparent system of offering and awarding public procurement contracts, public expenditure representing 12% of gross national product. Up to 500 contract offers are added to *TED* each day, as they are made public. DataStar similarly has a *Business Opportunities* 'cross file' searchable group of 9 databases, including *TED* among several listing actual invitations to tender. These, and the further examples given above, again show a the combination of very specific, primary sources, and commercial secondary sources adding the value of collecting from diverse origins.

Examples of source and host coverage of 'actual' opportunities:

Type of 'actual' opportunity	Database example	FT Profile	DataStar	Dialog
EU public supply and works tenders	*Tenders Electronic Daily*	X	X	
US Government announcements of products or services wanted	*Commerce Business Daily*			X
European companies' adverts for suppliers partnerships etc.	*Advertise: Business Opportunities*			X
General offers and demands for goods, services and corporate relationships	*International Business Opportunities Service*	X		

Sample record from the Advertise *database, on DataStar*

Accession number & update
990381 199810.
Title
Young Turkish company with large production potential of frozen food is looking for commercial and technical agreements.
Source
AN13275 040/96003
Deutscher Sparkassenverlag / DSGV.
Entry date
15 November 1996 (19961115).
Language
EN.
Company name
Mayadag Gida San. Ihracat Ltd. STI.
CONTACT:
Mehmet Genc – Bekir Savas
[address etc.]
Country
Tuerkei (C8TUR).
Branches
OBST – UND GEMUESEVERARBEITUNG (28600)
Product names and codes
Tiefkuehlkost (Grosshandel) (S5142),
Tiefkuehlobst, Tiefkuehlgemuese (S2037).
Abstract
Activities: Frozen food (vegetable and fruit) production and marketing type of cooperation. New young dynamic firm with large production potential is looking for product design agreement, manufacturing agreement, technical agreement, marketing agreement – Turkish producer of frozen fruits and vegetables with target capacitiy of 2000 tons for the first year is eager to penetrate foreign markets and is searching cooperation on various levels like technical assistance, marketing and distribution agreements in EU member countries, USA and Canada as well as to produce upon request.
Target countries: Germany, France, Italy, Luxembourg, The Netherlands, Belgium, Denmark, Spain, Portugal, Sweden, Finland, Austria, Norway, Switzerland, USA, Canada, United Kingdom
Date established: 1995
Banking reference: Yapi Kredi – Kuveyt Turk.
Notes
Language spoken: English.
Descriptors
[etc.]

Sources of 'Whole-Market' Level Information

The introduction to the chapter referred to the need for information at a 'whole-market' level, not for those directly involved in marketing, but to inform those making longer term, strategic decisions about the company. A business' most obvious strategic objective is to at least maintain its position in relation to the market or markets it is in. Porter's model of competitive industry identifies the five essential competitive forces: competitors, buyers, suppliers, substitute products (i.e. other than the industry's own), and new entrants to the industry (M.E. Porter, *Competitive Strategy*, Free Press, 1980, p. 4). Thus, there are these five elements for a business to fear or to beat; or at least to research and monitor, and orient itself towards.

Absolute figures for a firm's own turnover, sales or profits, are woefully insufficient in revealing changes in relation to the external market environment. Selective information must be gathered on the 'five forces', and appropriately manipulated and integrated to achieve the level of understanding necessary to orient the company to the market. Only hard data on the past and present is available, so definite answers to the key questions about the future are not forthcoming; nevertheless, competitive success equates to the extent that uncertainty and risk is reduced. The following list is a generalised representation of information needs at the whole-market level:

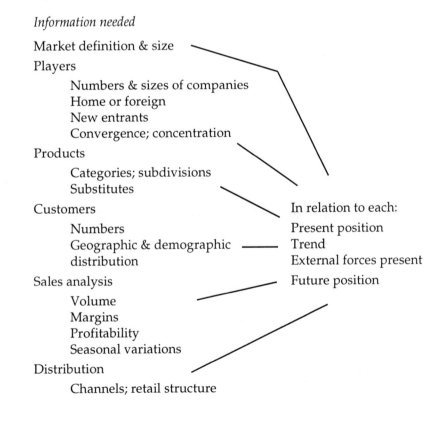

Information needed

Market definition & size

Players

    Numbers & sizes of companies
    Home or foreign
    New entrants
    Convergence; concentration

Products

    Categories; subdivisions
    Substitutes

Customers

    Numbers
    Geographic & demographic
    distribution

Sales analysis

    Volume
    Margins
    Profitability
    Seasonal variations

Distribution

    Channels; retail structure

In relation to each:

Present position
Trend
External forces present
Future position

Market Surveys

The rounded picture required can only be achieved through sophisticated collation and analysis of data on the many separate elements portrayed above. Fortunately for players, the fact that they can all use the same overview of their market makes it a viable proposition for publishers. Indeed such 'secondary market research' is available and frequently updated for most market sectors from a large number of publishers. Since compilation largely involves 'desk research', that is, using primary sources rather than *creating* them, the resulting reports will be referred to here as 'market surveys', despite the fact that publishers, hosts and others often include them with market research reports and refer to them as market research.

Market surveys typically range between 20 and 100 pages of mixed textual and numeric material. The best known are published in series of 100 or 200 market sectors. Publishers often have a broad subject and/or geographical focus, such as consumer markets, or British industrial products – as is apparent in the list below. By contrast, some surveys may be the only one produced by a specialised publisher. Their price, expensive but much cheaper than ad hoc and wholly primary market research, depends partly on the size, but also on how much original data collection is involved, and expected sales. Illustrated below are the four different price bands of surveys from MSI (Marketing Strategies for Industry), a major British publisher of surveys covering UK and European consumer, industrial and business-to-business market sectors:

£285 – example: *Fasteners, Industrial: UK*

£385 – example: *Express Delivery Services: France*

£510 – example: *Electronic Security Equipment: UK*

£635 – example: *Pharmaceutical Packaging: UK*

The two less expensive categories predominate, though 'multi-client studies' such as *Water and Effluent Treatment Plant: Europe* are more expensive than all of the above. MSI's titles amount to approximately 200 separate reports on market sectors. In this particular publisher's list, 'industrial' and 'business-to-business' markets predominate, as the examples show. Printed versions of the well-known *Key Note* reports also fall into detail and price categories, namely Market Reports – £245, Market Reports Plus – £335 and Market Reviews – £435.

Market surveys are normally dated with the year and month of publication, and more than three years rarely passes without an updated edition. Printed reports are normally available individually, or the series by subscription. Many series are available in full text via online hosts, where the software allows economical selection and viewing of specific sections. Heavy users prefer the storage and data manipulation advantages of CD-ROM versions, which are either bought outright, or bought cheaply and paid for by metered usage. The recent Euromonitor product provides search software and a quarterly updated CD-ROM holding all of their reports, for a mere £75. However, further payments purchase credit, in the form of access codes, which can be used to view a section of a report for as little as £10. By 1997 half of Mintel's turnover was said to be electronically based (*Information World Review,* January 1997, p. 23).

The promotional literature of another publisher, Market Assessment Ltd, showed typical source material and analysis:

'In order to compile a report, our researchers first look to published data sources:

Government statistics

Trade statistics

MEAL data (i.e. advertising expenditure)

Trade and general press

Company reports and accounts

In order to qualify these statistics, and render them more meaningful to marketing and sales personnel, we go on to conduct an intesive interviewing programme carried out among major manufacturers . . . Lastly consumer research is done on our behalf . . . based on questionnaires compiled in-house.'

The stated typical contents of their reports closely match the standard information needs, identified in the list above; as do MSI's and Datamonitor's, given below for comparison.

Market Assessment Ltd	Datamonitor	MSI
Market definition	Definition of the area	Market segmentation
Market size	Key issues affecting the market	Industry structure
Production	Market size and growth rates	Market trends
Foreign trade	Market segmentation	Distribution
Distribution	Competitive analysis	Advertising
Market segmentation	Advertising; ratio to sales	Company profiles
Competitive structure	Retailing; distribution channels	Brand shares
Advertising expenditure	Consumer analysis, behaviour	Production analysis
Consumer profiles	Forecasts	Prospects & forecasts
Market forecasts		

Contents list of a typical Key Note report, showing the many detailed sections and tables. Each 'TX' number is a 'text paragraph' which can be separately displayed and paid for on the DataStar host:

ICC Key Note Market Analysis (ICKN)

AN 100355 9806.

KEY NOTE REPORT *BREWERIES & THE BEER MARKET*
PUBLICATION DATE: 980515

CHAPTER/SECTION HEADING:

1. MARKET DEFINITION TX 1
MARKET SECTORS TX 1
MARKET POSITION TX 1
TOTAL ALCOHOLIC DRINKS MARKET TX 1
BEER AND OTHER ALCOHOLIC DRINKS TX 1

INTERNATIONAL POSITION TX 2
MARKET TRENDS TX 2
BEER CONSUMPTION TX 2
MARKET SEGMENTATION TX 2

BEER PRICES AND TAXATION TX 3
CROSS-CHANNEL SHOPPING TX 3
VERTICAL INTEGRATION AND THE 1991 BEER ORDERS TX 3
CONCENTRATION OF MARKET SHARE TX 3
SMALLER BREWERS TX 3

GROWTH OF NATIONAL AND INTERNATIONAL BRANDS TX 4
BRAND STRETCHING TX 4
NEW PRODUCTS TX 4
DIVERSIFICATION BY BREWERS TX 4
PATTERNS OF DISTRIBUTION TX 4

2. MARKET SIZE TX 5
THE TOTAL MARKET TX 5
BY MARKET SECTOR TX 5
BASIC PRODUCT DIVISIONS TX 5
LAGER VERSUS DARK BEERS TX 5
SEGMENTATION IN THE ON-TRADE TX 5

SEGMENTATION IN THE OFF-TRADE (TAKE HOME) TX 6
GROWTH CATEGORIES TX 6

ALE AND STOUT ADVERTISING TX 22
PROMINENT CAMPAIGNS TX 22

5. STRENGTHS, WEAKNESSES, OPPORTUNITIES AND THREATS
(SWOT) TX 23
STRENGTHS TX 23
WEAKNESSES TX 23
OPPORTUNITIES TX 23
THREATS TX 23

6. BUYING BEHAVIOUR TX 24
CONSUMER PENETRATION TX 24
DRAUGHT BEER DRINKERS TX 24
PACKAGED BEER DRINKERS TX 24

LOW ALCOHOL BEERS TX 25
REGIONAL PATTERNS TX 25
REGIONAL PENETRATION TX 25
REGIONAL EXPENDITURE LEVELS TX 25
PER CAPITA CONSUMPTION TX 25

7. OUTSIDE SUPPLIERS TO THE INDUSTRY TX 26
PACKAGING TX 26
IMPORTERS AND WHOLESALERS TX 26

8. CURRENT ISSUES TX 27
CORPORATE DEVELOPMENTS TX 27
BASS TX 27
CARLSBERG-TETLEY TX 27
DIAGEO TX 27
SCOTTISH AND NEWCASTLE TX 27
WHITBREAD TX 27
OTHER BREWERS TX 27
WOLVERHAMPTON AND DUDLEY TX 27
MORLAND TX 27
ENTERPRISE INNS TX 27
USHERS OF TROWBRIDGE TX 27

8. CURRENT ISSUES CONTINUED TX 28
WH BRAKSPEAR TX 28
SA BRAIN TX 28

DIRECTORIES TX 38

GENERAL SOURCES TX 39

HBI UK INFORMATION SOURCES TX 40

GOVERNMENT PUBLICATIONS TX 41

OTHER SOURCES TX 42

TABLE HEADING:

TABLE 1: SEGMENTATION OF THE BEER MARKET BY VOLUME (%), 1989-1997 TX 1

TABLE 2: CONSUMER EXPENDITURE ON ALCOHOLIC DRINKS AT CURRENT AND CONSTANT 1990 PRICES (LM AT RSP), 1990-1997 TX1

TABLE 3: BEER IN THE ALCOHOLIC DRINKS MARKET (LM AND %), 1990, 1996 AND 1997 TX 1

TABLE 4: PER CAPITA CONSUMPTION OF VARIOUS DRINKS (LITRES AND VOLUME INDEX 1980=100), 1980-1996 TX 2

TABLE 5: THE TOTAL UK BEER MARKET BY VALUE AND VOLUME (LM AT RSP, MILLION LITRES AND L PER LITRE), 1993-1997 TX 5

TABLE 6: ON-TRADE SEGMENTATION BY TYPE OF BEER AND PACKAGING BY VOLUME (MILLION LITRES AND %), 1997 TX 5

TABLE 7: OFF-TRADE SEGMENTATION OF THE PACKAGED BEER MARKET BY TYPE OF BEER AND CHANNEL OF DISTRIBUTION BY VOLUME (MILLION LITRES) TX6

TABLE 8: PRODUCTION AND EXPORTS OF BEER BY UK BREWERS (MILLION LITRES), 1992-1997   TX 7

TABLE 7: OFF-TRADE SEGMENTATION OF THE PACKAGED BEER

TABLE 8: PRODUCTION AND EXPORTS OF BEER BY UK BREWERS (MILLION LITRES), 1992-1997   TX 8

TABLE 9: EXPORTS OF BEER BY MAIN DESTINATION COUNTRY BY VALUE (%), 1994 AND 1997 TX 8

TABLE 10: IMPORTS OF BEER BY MAIN COUNTRY OF ORIGIN BY VALUE (%), 1997 TX 9

TABLE 11: ESTIMATED TOTAL NUMBER OF BREWERIES IN THE UK, 1998 TX 11

TABLE 12: NUMBER OF BREWERIES ESTABLISHED, 1985-1998 TX 11

TABLE 13: ON-TRADE AND OFF-TRADE BREAKDOWN OF BEER DISTRIBUTION BY VALUE AND VOLUME (%), 1990-1997 TX 12

TABLE 14: TYPES OF RETAIL OUTLETS FOR BEER BY VOLUME (%), 1997 TX 12

TABLE 15: LEADING OWNERS OF FULLY LICENSED ON-TRADE OUTLETS (OUTLETS AND %), 1998 TX 13

TABLE 16: NATIONAL BREWERS MARKET SHARES IN UK BREWING (% VOLUME), 1991 AND 1997 TX 15

TABLE 17: LEADING FOREIGN BRANDS IN THE UK, 1998 TX 16

TABLE 18: THE WORLDS LARGEST BREWERS BY OUTPUT VOLUME (MILLION HECTOLITRES), 1996 TX 16

TABLE 19: THE LARGEST REGIONAL BREWERS AND THEIR BRANDS, 1998 TX 17

TABLE 20: MAJOR BEER COMPANIES AND THEIR BRANDS, 1998 TX 17

TABLE 21: MAIN MEDIA ADVERTISING EXPENDITURE ON BEER (LM), 1992-1997 TX 21

TABLE 22: MAIN MEDIA EXPENDITURE ON LAGER BRANDS (L000), 1995-1997 TX 22

TABLE 23: MAIN MEDIA EXPENDITURE ON DARK BEER BRANDS (L000), 1995-1997 TX 22

TABLE 24: CHANGES IN PENETRATION OF BEER BY TYPE (% ADULTS 18-PLUS), 1994 AND 1997 TX 24

TABLE 25: PENETRATION OF DRAUGHT BEER BY SEX, AGE AND SOCIAL GRADE (% OF ADULTS 18-PLUS), 1997 TX 24

TABLE 26: PENETRATION OF PACKAGED BEER BY SEX, AGE AND SOCIAL GRADE (% OF ADULTS 18-PLUS), 1997 TX 24

TABLE 27: REGIONAL PENETRATION OF DRAUGHT BEERS (% OF ADULTS 18-PLUS), 1997 TX 25

TABLE 28: SALES OF PACKAGED BEER BY PACK TYPE BY VOLUME (%), 1985-1997 TX 26

TABLE 29: FORECAST BEER SALES (LM), 1998-2002 TX 30

COMPANY PROFILES CONTINUED:

BASS PLC TX 32

CARLSBERG-TETLEY PLC TX 33

DIAGEO PLC TX 34

WHITBREAD PLC TX 35

Series of market surveys

The Annual Business Information Resources Survey, 1998 (*Business Information Review* 15(1), March 1998, pp. 5-21) found that UK librarians ranked usage of series as 1 to 5 below. Details of most of the other series known to British users have been added below them in alphabetical order. The major hosts each include a wide and different selection of providers' reports, Profound having 70 series, more than 20 of which are said to be exclusive to them.

Notes in the table indicate the scope, and availability of the series from prominent hosts (the first three hosts particularly are subject to change resulting from their convergence within the Dialog Corporation), i.e.:

P	Profound
DS	DataStar
D	Dialog
FTP	FT Profile
I	Investext

Provide/Series (and ranking 1-5)	Market focus	Geographical focus	Hosts coverage
1. *Key Note* (ICC Group)	Consumer, service, & industrial sectors	UK	P, DS, D, FTP, I
2. *Mintel*	Consumer goods & services; retailing	UK, Europe	D, FTP
3. EIU	Broad spectrum: consumer, raw materials, industrial	European & Asian markets	P, DS, D, FTP, I
4. *Euromonitor*	Consumer products; retailing	UK, Europe, US, Japan etc.	P, DS, D, FTP, I
5. *Corporate Intelligence on UK* (Janet Matthews IS)	Originally retail market now includes consumer markets	UK and Europe	DS, FTP
Corporate & Marketing Intelligence	Business to business food and packaging market	CAMI are South Africa specialists	P
BCC Market Research	Industrial markets	US	D
Beverage Marketing Research Reports	Beverage industry	Global	D, I
Business Communications Company	Industrial materials; high tech	North America, global	I
Business Trend Analysts	Consumer and industrial products	US	I
Butler Bloor			

Provide/Series (and ranking 1-5)	Market focus	Geographical focus	Hosts coverage
China Business Resources	Industrial materials and services	China, Hong Kong, Taiwan	
Countryline International	Countries' service industries	Global	I
Databank	Wide range of European markets	Europe	
Datamonitor	Consumer products & services	UK, Europe, Americas, Asia-Pacific	P, DS, D, FTP, I
Datapro Reports and Analysis	Information & Communications		D
Decision Resources *Industry Trends. . .	Pharmaceutical, health care, and other industries	North America, Europe, Asia	D*, I
Electronic Trend Publications	Computers; electronic components	Global	I
Find/SVP	Wide range of market sectors	North America, global	D, FTP, I
Information Research Network	Continuous survey of electronic business information	Global	
Forecast International	Aerospace and defence industries	Global	I
Frost & Sullivan	Wide range of markets specialist in high technology	US, Europe, global	P, DS, D, FTP, I
Freedonia	Industrial markets	US, global	D, FTP, I
Fuji-Keizai USA	Computers and communications technology	USA	D
Future Technology Surveys	Various engineering fields	US, global	I

Provide/Series (and ranking 1-5)	*Market focus*	*Geographical focus*	*Hosts coverage*
Global Trade Intelligence	Consumer products; service industries	Africa, Asia, Europe, Latin America	I
Headland	Approx 10, focussing on leisure markets	UK	
IMS World Drug Markets	Pharmaceutical & health care industries	Global	DS, D
IIS – European Food & Drink	Consumer food & products	France, Germany, Italy, Spain	FTP
Jupiter Communications	Information and communications technology	US, global	I
Lafferty	Financial services industries	Global	I
Leatherhead Food Research/*Foodline	Food products	UK, Europe, global	*DS,*D I
Market & Business Development	Engineering, construction, service industries	UK	DS, FTP, I
Market Assessment	Consumer, business & financial markets	UK	FTP
Market Direction	Consumer & retail markets	US	I
Market Structure & Trends in Italy	Industrial and service sectors	Italy	DS
Market Tracking International	Consumer & industrial markets	Global	
Market Vision	Information & communications technologies	US	I
Marketdata Enterprises	Health and social services	US	P, I

Provide/Series (and ranking 1-5)	Market focus	Geographical focus	Hosts coverage	
MarketLine	Industrial, service, consumer markets worldwide	Global	P,	FTP, I
Marketpower	Specialist markets in various countries	Global		
MDIS Country Healthcare	Medical equipment and services	Global	DS	
MSI	Industrial & business to business markets	UK, Europe	DS,	FTP, I
Market Tracking International MTI	ca. 20 reports on consumer and other markets	UK		
A.C. Neilsen	Consumer products; packaged goods	North America		I
Packaged Facts	wide range of consumer markets	North America, Europe, global		FTP, I
Projection 2000	Comparatively inexpensive, small niche markets			
Pyramid Research (owned by EIU)	Telecoms oriented reports on emerging markets	Asia, Latin America, E. Europe, CIS, Africa		FTP
Sector Reports UK DTI	Low-priced research on selected sectors	Global		
SIMBA Information	Business information & other info industry topics	Global		
Snapshots (Extracted from Datamonitor, etc)	Standard format 15-20 page introductory reports	Global		
Specialists in Business	Consumer goods & services business to business	North America		FTP, I

Provide/Series (and ranking 1-5)	Market focus	Geographical focus	Hosts coverage	
SRI Consulting/* Speciality Chemicals	Chemicals industry	Global	*D,	I
Strategic Directions International	Analytical instrumentation	Global		I
Verdict Research	Retail industries	UK, Europe, US		I
Veronis, Suhler & Associates	Media & communications industries	US, global		I

As the scope notes above show, series overlap in content and in their subject and geographical coverage, several alternative reports being available on bigger markets. Nevertheless there is also great variation, in the nature and amount of data presented, the conclusions reached, and in the currency of the report and data within it.

Less Conventional Market Surveys

It may require bibliographic research to discover one-off surveys, such as *Marketstat*, IRN's syndicated ongoing survey of the online business information market, and series less prominent than some of those above. *Market Research: A Guide to British Library Holdings* lists over 400 publishers in the world. Some series are published as serials, and many reports tantamount to market surveys appear on an ad hoc basis from unpredictable sources. Euromonitor publish three separate monthly serials: *Market Research GB, Market Research Europe,* and *Market Research International,* each issue of each title featuring the equivalent of six different market surveys. The Economist Intelligence Unit (EIU) publishes several serial titles containing market-specific primary or secondary research. Each of the three issues per quarter of *Marketing in Europe* covers specific consumer market sectors: the first food, drink and tobacco, the second clothing, furniture and leather goods, the third chemist's goods, household goods and domestic appliances. This occasionally includes complete surveys of specific markets, and regularly includes consumer spending forecasts for the product groups covered. *Marketing in Europe* concentrates on Germany, France, Italy, Belgium, Luxembourg and the Netherlands. The EIU's companion serial *Retail Business* follows a very similar pattern and coverage for British consumer markets. There are also EIU serials devoted to research on specific markets, namely the quarterly *Components Business International; Motor Business Asia-Pacific;*

Motor Business Japan; *Rubber Trends*; *Motor Business Europe*; *Motor Business International*. The last is described by EIU as:

> '. . . the definitive regular research report on the world's automotive industries and markets. It provides authoritative analysis of important developments and trends: sales analysis and forecasts for over 30 national and regional markets, new models, new mergers and investment plans, global vehicle analysis by product sector and detailed strategic forecasts examining the impact of industry trends.'

Certain periodicals, notably *Financial Times* and *The Economist,* include occasional supplements, which, though not structured like a typical market survey, cover some of the same ground for a particular industry. Even embassy officials can generate unconventional market surveys; *FMIRs* or *Foreign Market Intelligence Reports* (distributed by Microinfo in the UK) are more than 300 inexpensive reports on European markets, based on market research data gathered by U.S. embassy officials.

Market analysts or industry analysts in the financial services industry also occasionally publish substantial reviews or forecasts of specific markets. These might be incorporated in their broker's or analyst's reports (discussed in the 'Company Information' chapter) as articles in the business press, or in 'industry newsletters' (discussed in the 'Business News Sources; Industry Sources' chapter). Less expectedly, government sometimes initiates a survey of a market, such as for example the European Commission's *Overview of the CD-ROM Market* some years ago.

Tracing Primary and Secondary Market Research

Because there are so many reports and surveys, used by so many business people, a healthy bibliographical apparatus exists to lead users to what is available. Additionally, individual online hosts pool a number of series as actual or virtual collections – such as Investext's *Markintel* collection of 100,000 market surveys from 50 different providers, and FT Profile's *Market Research* 'data collection'. Some additionally allow cross-database searching. Joint access is available via the host International Market Research Mall or instead to the reports of Freedonia, Beverage Marketing, Business Communications, Euromonitor, Quest Economics and FIND/SVP at a much cheaper rate, it is claimed, than via third party hosts. There is also a considerable number of published lists, directories and indexes, each normally integrating series of secondary surveys with multi-client and syndicated studies. Brief details of major examples are given below, showing which are available via online hosts.

Directories, guides, indexes to published market research

		Hosts' coverage	
Series Profile FT	Scope	DataStar	Dialog
Findex (Cambridge Scientific Abstracts)	Index to all industry and market research reports from 900 publishers worldwide. Print, online CD-ROM. 50+ word summaries		X
International Market Research Information (Norton Sterling,UK)	As well as abstracts of articles about marketing, etc.; includes abstracts of reports and surveys	X	
Market Research: a guide to British Library Collections	Catalogue of the British Library's unmatched collections of reports, surveys etc.		
Marketing Surveys Index (MSI) – Marketing Answers on FT-P	Worldwide coverage of published market research reports and surveys. Synopses.		X
Marketsearch: International Directory of Published Market Research (Arlington, UK)	'More than 20,000 studies from 680 organisations worldwide'; abstracts in some entries. Printed version also; published in UK	X	

Sample record from the FINDEX database on Dialog

DIY SUPPLIES: UK

1996
Publ: Datamonitor Publications Ltd
[address etc.]
Availability: PUBLISHER
Document Type: MARKET/INDUSTRY STUDY

This report presents data on the UK market for DIY supplies, including market size, segment, and market share information; market forecasts by segment; views of top industry executives on competitive positioning, key success factors, and future trends; and profiles of the top companies in the industry, including product portfolios and financial analyses.

Descriptors: HOME CENTERS & HARDWARE STORES ; HOME IM-
PROVEMENT; UNITED KINGDOM

Formal surveys with the typical whole-market coverage are desirable, but
even an answer to some of the key questions can be useful, from broad
issues like lifestyle trends to market-specific factors such as brand shares or
a sales forecast. Studies of simultaneous relevance to a number of markets
often emerge from the publishers of surveys series; for example:

> *Consumer Lifestyles in Eastern Europe.* Euromonitor, 1997.
>
> *British Lifestyles.* Mintel, 1998.
>
> *Customer Loyalty in Retailing.* Mintel, 1998.

Snippets of such information, often on markets too abstruse to appear in a
formal survey, but often more up to date and detailed, can appear at any
time and anywhere, including titles like 'Friends of the Earth launches savings account' picked up from *The Guardian* by Mintel and indexed as relating to the 'green consumer'. Small or highly specific items appearing in
market research and trade periodicals and in 'industry newsletters' are difficult to trace systematically. The 'Business Statistics' and 'Non-business
Statistics' sections of this chapter include relevant sources and related bibliographical tools. As was pointed out there, much raw, often unpublished,
data is available from bodies like trade associations, so it is useful to be able
to trace and contact them via the *Industry Insider* collection of 140 trade
associations' reports, available through the Investext host. Specialist bibliographical tools are necessary for confidence in discovering diverse gems of
market information. Such tools appear in the section below: 'Tracing Other
Forms of Market Information'. The bibliographical sources which cover business information appearing in periodicals are also relevant as detailed under 'Tracing Other Forms of Market Information' below.

Publication Formats

Most of the long established series of surveys are still published in their
original printed form, but are also now in full text on CD-ROM, or online
direct from the provider or via a host. The approximately 12 publishers'
series on FT Profile alone must amount to around 1000 reports, and there is
even greater coverage on the CD-ROM, dial-up or web versions of
Investext's collection. Electronic versions are advantageous for reasons of
retrieval and output, and economy. Hosts usually include a commercially
published index to market research (see the list above), a cross-file searching function to select the most appropriate reports on the system, and full-
text which is structured in such a way that sections can be selectively
identified, viewed and paid for. CD-ROM versions such as Euromonitor's
emulate most hosts in charging for the amount of use rather than an enormous sum in advance. On receipt of a payment, the publisher issues the
user a code number representing a certain credit value; encrypted reports
can then be 'unlocked', up to the limit of the credit.

Tracing Other Forms of Market Information

Bibliographic tools for specific categories of market information, have been mentioned in the appropriate section above. Other tools cover a wider range of types of market intelligence, so are needed for the more comprehensive search. At this whole-market level, bibliographical tools tend to be either general guides to market information, including to documentary and or-ganisational sources, or services which index or abstract the market infor-mation appearing randomly in periodicals. Details of major examples follow:

General guides to market information

> *World Directory of Marketing Information Sources*. Euromonitor, 1996. Libraries, market research agencies, associations, databases, journals.
>
> *Market Research Sourcebook*. Headland, 1999 edn, published 1998; ed. David Mort. Evaluative guide to documentary and non-documen-tary sources od statistics, market research reports, surveys, etc.
>
> *The Source Book*. ICC Key Note, 2nd edn, 1990. Under each industry classification, details of organisational and documentary sources are given under the headings: Trade bodies, Trade directories, Statistical and Other Sources – including published market reports and sur-veys, periodicals, online databases.

Indexes and abstracts of market information appearing in trade and other journals

> *Business and Industry*. Responsive Database Services Inc. Its breadth of source coverage, subject matter, and search functionality make this database an important source of market as well as other areas of busi-ness information. Items can be searched by text keywords, geographi-cal codes, and SIC codes for specific industries and products, as well as over 90 concept terms – e.g. 'Market share', and 70 marketing terms – e.g. 'Distribution channels'. Abstracts or full text of original arti-cles. Available from the provider's web site, and major hosts.
>
> *Market Share Reporter/World Market Share Reporter*. Data compiled from large and wide range of publications; hosted by Investext's *I/PLUS Direct*.
>
> *Mintel Market Intelligence*. Current awareness service available on sub-scription from Mintel. A wide range of general and specialised cur-rent information sources is scanned, and information of market intelligence value abstracted.
>
> *PROMT – Predicasts Overview of Markets and Technology*. IAC, USA; full text or abstracts from 1000+ newspapers, trade journals and other sources worldwide. Searchable by codes for industries, countries, and article type – such as 'market information' – from IAC's InSite Pro, and other hosts.

Research Index. Research Index Ltd; long-established, now web-based, current index to market and other business information appearing in UK newspapers and periodicals; searchable by market sector:
'Research Index is a database that indexes the news, views and comments on industries and companies worldwide, as reported in the UK national press and a range of quality business magazines. Every significant daily and Sunday newspaper, business magazine and periodical is indexed.'

Reports Index. Langley Associates; 6 issues per year; subject index to reports of business value.

International Business Directory. The data in Dialog's recent addition is derived from non-USA company, industry and product databases. As such it covers any and every aspect of business, including much market intelligence.

Further Sources

D. Mort. 'UK Official Statistics: recent changes and initiatives', *Business Information Review* 14(2), June 1997, pp. 65-69.

L. Nichols. 'Retail Intelligence in the UK', *Business Information Review* 9(3), January 1993, pp. 2-17.

4

Financial Information

Introduction

The ultimate aim of this chapter is to show how sources of information on the financial markets meet the various needs. Before doing so, it may be helpful to explain 'financial information', and to outline the workings of 'the City'. What goes on in our financial institutions affects every business and every individual to varying degrees, so information on it is a core area of business information. Another reason to know something about City activities is that because they are so dependent on uncertain future outcomes, financial industry institutions are heavy consumers of business information of all kinds.

'Financial information' is generally accepted within business information as information on trading in financial commodities. It is sometimes also called 'City information' because the organisations involved in have always gathered together in an identifiable commercial centre, such as the 'Square Mile' within the City of London. These financial commodities and trading activities centre on the advancing by some, and acquisition by others of money in different forms and for different reasons. The diversity and volume of 'financial instruments', and even more so the volume of secondary transactions in them, leads to many financial services intermediaries, and a large, lucrative industry.

This 'financial information' is not to be confused with information on companies' finances, as covered in chapter 2. This is despite the fact that share ownership in companies, and other forms of raising capital by companies, are among the financial commodities to be discussed here. Similarly, 'markets' as discussed below, and as used in the *Financial Times*, refers to 'the financial markets' rather than as in chapter 3, to markets in general. This chapter explains the 'money' domain of the external commercial environment. It examines the sources which report on it in relation to the needs of players in the financial markets, as well as of every other business or private individual directly or indirectly affected by those markets. It should be remembered that the sources discussed here are those which generally report on financial trading, not those on the wide range of other environments which traders and investors also scan in order to make their decisions. Though equally important to City decision makers, those are of course the topics of other chapters. The column 'Reason for change' in the table reproduced below, illustrates how different environmental events affect share prices – just as in turn the reporting of these prices will have have a further effect.

Major Share Movements summary table, **Sunday Times** *business supplement 'Databank', 13th September 1998*

RISERS	*Friday close price*	*Change on week price*	*1998 high*	*1998 low*	*Reason for change*
Leeds Sporting	24 3/4	12	25 1/4	12	Football frenzy
Newcastle Utd	89	26 1/2	102 1/2	56 1/2	Football frenzy
PSD Group	365	105	780	255	Profits up
Manchester Utd	221 1/2	62 1/2	225 1/2	123 1/2	BSkyB deal
Simon Group	52	12	74	38	Profits up
BAT	454	116 1/2	485	310 1/2	Cuts financial arm

FALLERS	*Friday close price*	*Change on week price*	*1998 high*	*1998 low*	*Reason for change*
Telspec	75	100	365	73	Profits down
Royal Doulton	104	35	227 1/2	99	Poor results
Coats Viyella	33	18 1/2	100	32 1/2	Demerger postponed
Booker	144 1/2	43 1/2	360	141	Profits fall
Brammer	392 1/2	95	735	390	Sector downbeat
Dewhirst Group	108 1/2	21	267 1/2	104	Profits down

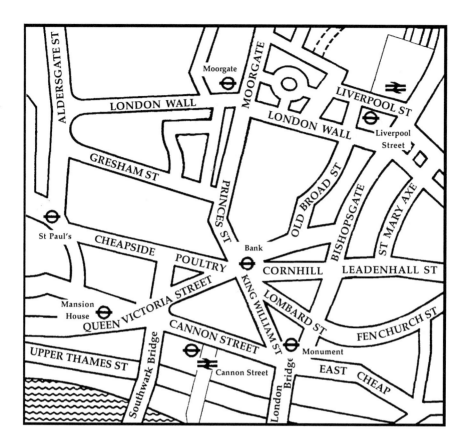

Figure 15. The City of London

The City

The business meaning of 'the City' relates to the activities at the very hub of commerce and power. In national terms, the City assumes a central role in both indicating and determining the economy; physically close to government, it is vital channel for monetary and economic policy. Even more importance accrues to the City of London as a centre of world importance for certain financial trading, well situated between the time zones of other major markets including New York and Tokyo. Institutions make their living by encouraging those with a surplus of money from their business activities to advance it to those who need money. Assisted by the non-tangible, quickly and easily traded nature of money, centralised dealing creates well-defined markets within a monetary area, and worldwide for some of the commodities. Governments and self-regulatory bodies ensure the transparency rarely now provided by 'open outcry' in trading floor or auction environment. Today real-time quotes and trading systems, and controlled simultaneous dissemination of price-sensitive announcements, have replaced most physical markets with virtual ones, networked far beyond a 'square mile'.

Financial markets could be represented as follows:

E.g.s of Those With Money	via	E.g.s of Those Needing Money
Individuals' & firms' working surpluses	Equity	Firms, for long-term growth
Individuals' and firms' savings	Capital Money	Individuals and firms, for immediate purchases
	Currency	Individuals and firms, for purchases in foreign currency
Private pensions; pension funds	Commodities	Governments, for short and long-term purposes

The Financial Markets

The following sections provide more information on each of the significant financial commodities, on the actual or virtual markets represented by the City of London. Even in its financial sense, 'market' or 'markets' is used confusingly in the literature. Sometimes it describes an actual exchange where a number of financial commodities are traded, as in 'the Stock Exchange'. Sometimes it describes a specific financial commodity or instrument, as in 'the gilt market', while at other times the definition is related to the reason for going to the market, as in 'the capital market'. In the sections following 'Derivatives' markets are categorised on the basis of the underlying financial commodity involved – though that may not be obvious from their familiar names.

Derivatives

Although 'derivatives', such as futures, options and interest rate swaps, are often traded in dedicated exchanges, they are treated in this chapter with the commodity they are derived from. An indirect way of investing in or otherwise using a particular financial market is for instance to buy the *right* to purchase a commodity rather than take possession of the commodity itself. The financial instruments which confer different kinds of rights in relation to different kinds of commodity are called derivatives. The best known are 'futures' and 'options', and secondary trading in them is a high volume business carried out in some of the normal markets and in some dedicated markets. Both equities and the options which are derived from them are traded in at the London Stock Exchange, whereas the comparatively new high volume London International Financial Futures Exchange (LIFFE) specialises in derivatives of equity, capital and currency. LIFFE is a physical market place where trading involves the traditional open outcry and people whose role is distinguished by the colour of their jackets.

Derivatives also attract investment by spreading risk. They usually involve 'forward' purchases of the various financial commodities, the ownership of which, or 'options' on the ownership of which, are tradeable many times before delivery – hence 'tradeable options'. While reducing risk for investors, and for those with a real need for money, currency, or raw materials at a future date, much business is created for the dealers and speculators who are willing to accept the calculated risks. Derivatives and their markets are often difficult to comprehend, and have a specialised vocabulary. Their prices and other data do appear in financial information sources, when it is necessary at least to know the difference between a 'put' and 'call' option. A 'put' option is the tradeable instrument purchased to acquire the right to *sell* a given amount of a financial commodity at a given price at a given time; for instance, it may cost £5 today for the right to sell to a dealer 100 ICI shares at today's price in one month's time. In one month the ultimate holder of the option will look at the market price of the shares to decide whether to take up or relinquish the right to sell. A 'call' option is the converse: the right to *buy* from the seller of the option.

The table below gives the financial commodities in the first column; other columns provide a the vocabulary for related concepts.

Market (alt. terms)	*Financial commodity*	*Other terms*	*Description*	*Exchange/s* (example)
Equity (Stock; Stock market)	Shares	Securities	Part ownership in PLCs, sold to raise capital	London Stock Exchange
	Investment Trusts		Shares in companies investing in securities	As above
	Unit trusts		Units in managed portfolios of securities	As above
Capital (Fixed income market)	Bonds; gilts	Securities; fixed interest stocks	Transferrable bills representing loan on specified terms	As above
Money (Eurodollar market, discount market, parallel markets	Bills, certificates of deposit, treasury bills, bank bills		Short-term secured or unsecured loans for fixed period and sum	Discount houses, banks, Bank of England
Currency			Money in a particular currency	Designated banks&brokers
Commodities			Raw materials – oil, coffee, sugar, tin etc.	London Futures& Options Exchange, Intl. Petroleum Exchange, London Metal Exchange

Each can be seen as a market sector within the City, and although they overlap, each has a range of institutions and sometimes physical locations associated with it. Most important for present purposes, each is separately reported on by information sources. The aim of these sections is to provide the understanding of the commodities, mechanisms and institutions, including of the related terminology, necessary to make effective use of the information sources. No attempt is made to cover important but less directly financial markets, such as London's insurance, shipping, and gold markets. More information on the City itself is best obtained from the recommended further reading.

The Equities Market

Shares are the best known and most widely owned and traded financial commodity. They are a form of *equity* since they represent *ownership* in a particular company. The value of a share rises and falls according to the value of the whole Public Limited Company, and the payment of dividends to shareholders represents their share of any profit taking. The availability to companies of strictly regulated markets for shares encourages them to register as PLCs, and to gain a 'listing' or 'quotation' on a stock exchange to raise capital by an initial 'flotation' or subsequent issues of shares. Even in the UK the regulatory authorities sanction other markets than the London Stock Exchange (formally the International Stock Exchange, or ISE) also operates a 'junior market': AIM or the Alternative Investment Market. AIM opened in 1995 for trading in the shares of 'young and growing companies', soon replacing the similar USM or Unlisted Securities Market. Stock markets compete for company listings, citing features such as efficient trading systems, and transparency of dealing. The *Financial Times* regularly lists indicative prices for the some 120 shares traded on the unregulated British 'OFEX'. The 'over the counter market' or OTC refers to dealings in shares (or other financial commodities) without recourse to a formal market. In the USA the Securities and Exchange Commission permits a number of competing markets, including also the high volume New York Stock Exchange, American Stock Exchange, and NASDAQ. The latter is a business venture of the National Association of Securities Dealers, who also own and regulate the US OTC market and Bulletin Board Quotation System.

The standards enforced by bodies such the London Stock Exchange (as a Recognised Investment Exchange under the UK Financial Services Authority) and NASDAQ on trading practices, company fitness, and practices including the dissemination of price-sensitive information likewise attract investors into the market. The 'primary market' for any financial commodity describes the initial purchase of a new share or other instrument, while the 'secondary market', much more important in terms of stock market volume and value, describes the subsequent transactions which holders of shares and other financial instruments are free to make. The London Stock Exchange is an example of an actual City market, though even it is defined more by regulation, membership, procedures and electronic systems, than by a physical location. NASDAQ is very much an electronic 'virtual' stock market. Transactions are carried out through members of stock exchanges, whose offers and/or bids are visible to all via in London for example the SEAQ electronic quotations system. This is gradually being replaced by SETS which automatically matches bids with offers. The CREST system takes the paperwork out of transferring ownership, registration, and payment. In the further interests of the free market, on NASDAQ for instance there must be at least two market makers, that is competing 'wholesalers', for each listed company's shares.

Collective Investment; Mutual and Managed Funds

There are other ways of investing in companies shares than owning them directly (the same applies to the other securities covered under 'The Capital Market', below). For the small investor in particular, buying into a professionally managed portfolio offers advantages of expertise and scale, and spreads risk. One way of collectively investing is purchasing shares in investment trust companies, the role of which is investing in the stock market. A more popular and slightly less indirect alternative is to buy 'units' in the portfolios of unit trust companies. Units are bought and sold back to the unit trust company at a cost which depends on the changing fortunes of the portfolio, with administrative charges added on.

The Capital Market

There are similarities between shares in the equities market, and bonds and related instruments in the capital market. Bonds and gilts are also issued in return for perhaps £100 each, and are sold and resold alongside shares in exchanges such as the London Stock Exchange. The main difference is that these securities do not confer part ownership of the issuing body, but an agreed income, usually a fixed rate of interest payable on a fixed redemption date. Thus companies, governments and other organisations issue bonds, usually via merchant banks, as a means of acquiring capital for medium to long periods. UK government securities are called gilts, referring to the original gilt-edged certificates denoting the fact that the government's bond was reliable. Gilts can be 'long', 'medium' or 'short', depending on whether redeemable in 15 or more, 7 to 15, or 7 or fewer years.

Bonds become 'eurobonds' when sold on foreign financial markets, in foreign currencies, constituting what are called the international capital markets, or 'euromarkets'. 'Junk bonds' are those whose value has become very low because of the apparent inability of the issuer to redeem them.

The Money Market

This is the wholesale market for money. Though not a single or physical location, it is the market in which 'bills' are bought and sold representing large short-term loans. It brings together lenders in possession of temporary surpluses of liquid cash, such as clearing banks and industrial companies, and those who are willing to pay interest to borrow it, such as companies, investors, banks and local authorities. In the traditional 'discount market' 'discount houses' buffer secured loans, known as 'short term securities', between banks. Also, so that government can both use the markets and influence them, the discount houses broker loans between the Bank of England and the money market. In the larger 'parallel market', largely unsecured short-term funds are either arranged directly between commercial firms, banks and other financial institutions, or via brokers. Secured loans or funds are those where the borrower holds resources of equivalent value, which could if necessary be realised to pay the debt. As in the capital market, the 'euro' in 'eurodollar market' relates to the fact that deposits are also attracted in foreign currencies.

The Currency Market

Money becomes 'currency' when you want to transfer it across monetary boundaries. 'Foreign exchange is purchased for many practical purposes, most of all for imports by industry from other countries. Currency is also a tradeable financial commodity, but although there is a vigorous market, there is only a need for financial instruments other than the currency itself for futures and options trading. Currencies whose exchange value is not fixed by issuing governments, constitute the currencies market; their value is established according to the comparative strengths of economies. Currencies of large and stable economies, especially the US dollar, are disproportionately traded in for their predictable value and ready exchangeability. By definition the market is international, trading taking place continuously between screens and telephones around the world, between brokers licensed in the countries for the purpose. There is a spot market, for currency for immediate delivery, and a large forward market. The latter allows the advance purchase of foreign currency needed at a future date, to avoid exposure to future fluctuations. The only way that relative values of currencies can be gauged, is as done by the *Financial Times* – periodically to sample the buy and sell prices of a number of major dealers. Prices of other currencies are then quoted in terms of one's own, as in a bureau de change, or against the dollar. London's is said to be the world's largest currency market, centering on around 50 banks and a dozen brokers.

The Commodities Market

Raw materials are a curious financial commodity, but the City is involved in their trading because of their huge financial and strategic value. Large funds are required for their purchase, and they provide much scope for speculative investment. London is of world importance for many commodities and has many separate, regulated, actual or virtual exchanges. Among 'hard' commodities there is the gold market, and the London Metals Exchange. 'Softs' include sugar and coffee. In some cases members of the exchange transact electronic deals at specific times of a day or week; in others the goods are sampled and traded in real auctions or sales rooms. Gold bullion dealers still meet twice daily at N.M. Rothschild's offices. The best known and highest volume markets are for tradable futures, rather than contracts for immediate or forward delivery of the commodity. Commodities purchasers often buy in advance, 'forward', in order to ensure future supply at a predictable price, then temporarily also buy 'hedges' on the futures market, which would cancel out any major difference in price by the time of delivery. Speculators help create a large secondary market in the consumers' surplus futures contracts.

Financial Information and its Users

The above glance at the workings of the City reveals many professionals who through their activities establish City prices at the same time as rarely taking their eyes off them. Those people seen in news reports in dealers' 'front offices' surrounded by screens and telephones are the most obvious users of raw data on the financial markets. They expect continuous real-time bids and offers and indices from all the dealers and exchanges involved in a market, wherever they are in the world. So instantaneous must the response be to certain developments that computers are programmed to buy or sell in automatic response to certain price or index thresholds. Dealers, and certainly the analysts in the 'back offices' who instruct the dealers, must monitor interdependent markets more widely. In order to act quickly and wisely they must be fed with news on the environments affecting their dealings, from company profits announcements to earthquakes, from to political scandals to the inflation rate.

Because so much rides on the prediction of future values, financial services firms are major users of financial and all other categories of business information. But almost everyone outside the City is also more or less directly affected by it, and so to varying degrees also needs City information. Some simply seeking the prices of specific financial commodities, perhaps to revalue a portfolio, or prior to a purchase or sale. Other private or corporate investors may have longer-term needs, perhaps seeking considered reports with expert advice and trend analysis. The cost of money affects public and private sector spending: when the pound is low UK exporters get more orders and importers have to pay more; when it is high consumers buy more imported goods at the expense of local industry, and funds tend to flow from the stock market to the money markets. Because the financial markets are both determinants and indicators of the economy, economists and politicians also monitor their underlying movements.

It is already apparent that much financial information consists of fast changing bid and offer price figures on electronic trading systems. For a market to be transparent, competitive and therefore attractive to all participants, these data have to be widely communicated and simultaneously visible. All other data follow from these: official records of the transactions on exchanges, numerical averages of the buy and sell prices of each financial instrument, indices of markets-level price changes, statistics on transaction volume. The financial media are full of these and many other numerical and textual reports and analyses. Prices are analysed, and then react to the analyses, and so on. One financial market instantly reacts to an environmental event, or to change in another market; it reacts again on more considered research and analysis.

Financial Information Sources

It is apparent that both numerical and textual data have a role, for both real-time and retrospective information. Real-time numerical data preponderates in terms of volume and also income to the information industry, and truly historical data has a comparatively small role in financial decision making. In the following sections sources are categorised according to their level of currency and comprehensiveness. Significant differences in delivery format are discussed within that structure, where most appropriate. Detailed explanations of the different types of numerical and textual financial data are given in the coverage of 'Sources of Intermediate Currency'.

Real-time Data Feeds

Though highly specialised and unfamiliar to most business people and information professionals, commercial distributors of real-time financial information generate more income for their owners than the whole of the rest of the business information industry. This is despite the fact that real-time price data feeds and much other data are often directly and economically available from individual exchanges: for example, as stated by the London Stock Exchange on one of its web pages (*http://www.stockex.co.uk/factbook/glossary.htm*):

> 'The Exchange distributes a wide range of market and securities data through its direct datafeeds to customers:
>
> *London Market Information Link (LMIL)*
> LMIL is the Exchange's datafeed for information services. The primary information is order, quote and trade data, regulatory company news and reference information. 'Value-added' information (such as indices) is also included.
>
> *Electronic Data Services*
> Electronic Data Services give turnover statistics for all securities traded on the London Stock Exchange. Trading volumes cover UK equities, fixed interest and overseas securities. The information is provided to customers either daily or weekly, on disk or as a hard copy report.

The Daily Official List (DOL)
DOL is published by FT Information on behalf of the London Stock Exchange. It is the Exchange's register of listed and AIM securities and contains prices of trades published each day.

The Weekly Official Intelligence (WOI)
WOI publishes data about companies on the main market – including details of new listings, official notices, dividend payments, company announcements and changes to the rules.

Securities Masterfile (SMF)
SMF provides up-to-date information on more than 180,000 securities traded on the UK and international markets. SMF data is available in hard copy or electronically to suit the individual needs of market participants.'

Among approximately 12 providers, the four biggest – Bloomberg, Bridge, Dow Jones and Reuters – have been dubbed the 'big money news gatherers'. The value is added and income generated through the firms' geographical coverage, financial markets coverage, range of information and software products, and depth of historical coverage. Other business information providers strive for viability and jealously credit these four with approximately $4.5 billion of sales per year. Their success is related to the size and wealth of the financial markets, and the dependence on information of those who trade in them. These firms maintain customer loyalty through providing a wide if not complete and integrated range of information and systems. In some cases this ranges from providing the exchange's dealing system itself, to transmission of the data generated there to dealers around the world, plus transmission of any other current and historical data which could inform deals (65% of Reuters revenue 1996), to the transaction systems in dealers offices (28% of Reuters revenue 1996). Their influence is further enhanced by distributing the data through closed networks to dedicated end-user terminals and software. In promotional material Reuter state:

> 'Reuters Holdings PLC supplies the global business community and the news media with real-time financial data, transaction systems, information management systems, access to numerical and textual databases, news, graphics, photos and news video. Information is obtained from around 270 exchanges and over-the-counter markets, from 4,800 subscribers who contribute data directly directly to Reuters, and from a network of 1,975 journalists, photographers and cameramen. Some 966,000 clients access reuters information.'

'Data for the money, commodities and securities markets is collected, processed and distributed via a series of computer centres linked by the world's biggest private global communications network. Reuters dealing systems serve the world's foreign exchange and securities markets, allowing dealers around the globe to buy and sell currencies and securities. Through our subsidiary companies we are also the leading supplier of dealing room technology, and are building historical databases to add value to all our services.'

Their last point is relevant to the accepted wisdom that Reuters' has the advantage over competitors in terms of the 'historical' data which brokers' 'back offices' need for research purposes. *Reuters 3000* series began 'rolling out' to clients in 1996, offering new levels of historical data, integration of data and systems, and usage of the World Wide Web:

'The *Reuters Markets 3000* service is Reuters flagship product. On one simple, integrated and open platform, it provides the full range of real-time data across the global financial markets, sophisticated analytics and extensive historical information for the equity, money and fixed income markets.'

Real-time Providers' News Services

Reuters feed direct to their subscribers the same raw news on market sensitive events that they supply to journalists in their capacity as news agencies. Textual data is made manageable alongside numerical data on traders' screens, using devices like expandable headlines windows, or scrolling 'ticker bars' along the bottoms of screens. Additionally or alternatively, software allows 'alerts' to be set up, so that news appears if it matches personally pre-determined subject and other criteria. *Reuters 3000* users are offered *Reuters News* 'real-time access to [Reuters and other agencies' coverage of] global and local events . . . relaying market moving news from 161 bureaux in 98 countries, 24 hours a day'. *Reuters Financial Television* provides multimedia information such as important live speeches and announcements.

Real-time Providers' Historical Services

Historical information, numerical in particular, is marketed by the providers to professionals as an essential complement to the real-time feeds. The suppliers are currently increasing and promoting their archives to match those of Bloomberg, whose strength in this area may well explain their lead in the real-time market.

> '*Reuters 3000* series marks a new chapter in the supply of information to the world's financial markets, marrying real-time prices and news to a huge new database of historical information' Reuters' annual report, 1996.'

Retrospective price and other data on most of the markets and individual financial instruments which Reuters cover, is included in *Markets 3000* complete integrated product, and in their specialised *Treasury 3000, Securities 3000* and *Money 3000* products (further details below).

Competitors seek a part of the lucrative action by breaking the link between data, networks and software. Some have plans to purchase the necessary real-time and historical data from various sources, and distribute it to finance professionals via an openly available web site. Dealers obviously need current and historical information which is authoritative, reliable, and available constantly. Front office staff expect a constantly updated display of selective raw price data and indices, and individualised analyses of incoming data. Back office staff need further retrieval and analysis facilities, including access to historical numerical and editorial data. Thus traders and fund managers pay large sums to one or more providers for unlimited access to their data feeds and databases, resulting in many permanently lit screens. Managing ever-increasingly available information, and integrating it into automated deal matching, records and other systems, is possible through the integration of systems, and so gives continuing advantage to the large 'comprehensive' information providers. It is apparent why neither information intermediaries nor more casual users of financial information are familiar with these real-time services; they come as complete packages, including information which is inappropriately presented and unnecessarily sophisticated and expensive for them. As will be seen, more appropriate products are available for these users, including some from the 'Big money news gatherers'.

One provider's information products range – Reuters

Branded as the *Reuters 3000 series*

*   Combined product:

    Reuters Markets 3000
    Includes Reuters full range of real-time numerical and textual data on global financial markets, analytical software and historical data on equity, money, and capital markets.

    Specialised versions:
    Reuters Treasury 3000
    The above data and software for the bonds, fixed income – i.e. capital markets.

Reuters Securities 3000
Real-time, historical data and analytics, selected for the equities markets.
Reuters Money 3000
As above, for money market traders.
Commodities 2000
An extant component of the Reuters 3000 predecessor, for commodities futures and options.

- Other relevant options available with the above packages:

Reuters Business Briefing
Suite of online news and other databases of value to financial professionals (further details in the 'Online Hosts' section of the final chapter).
Reuters Financial Television
Live coverage of relevant events, receivable via Reuters News, via the web.
Reuters News
'Unrivalled real-time access to global and local events through text and television.'

Examples of the software behind Reuters 3000 packages:

Bond Equation
User-defined 'tick by tick' analyses of incoming price movements of Japanese government bonds.
Chartist
User defined combination of windows on screens, including selecting alternative analyses of incoming real-time price data, and alternative real-time news feeds.
Reveal
Organises and updates professional equities portfolios and reporting systems, on own PC.

Example of the display and analytical facilities available from screens (From Reuters' description of Commodities 2000)

'Up to 32 items of clearly designated information for any futures contract month or option strike price can be viewed in a single display, and up to three such displays can be seen on screen at once. Both futures and options data can be chained at a single keystroke to track all price movements in all tradable months for any selected contract. Without disturbing the main display, instant data on any instrument can be simultaneously called to the screen by using a snap quote facility. Users can define for themselves up to 50 quote lists . . . A multi-window display system enables quotes to be displayed alongside supporting news and alert information.'

Brief details of some of the real-time financial information providers

- *Bloomberg*

    One of the top four; major player in information and transaction products.

- *Bridge*

    One of the top four; they acquired the heavily-used Telerate service from Dow Jones.

- *Dow Jones Markets*

    Dow Jones Markets, Inc. is one of the top four suppliers of real-time prices, news, market commentary, trading room systems and decision-support products to traders, dealers, brokers and other market professionals around the world. It is a wholly-owned subsidiary of Dow Jones & Company, Inc. Customers can gain access to the 60,000 pages of information on the Markets network through Dow Jones terminal products, such as the new Dow Jones Workstation, or via Digital Feed. The Dow Jones Trading Room System group has equipped and installed hundreds of multiple position trading rooms around the world. Dow Jones Markets is one of the financial community's principal sources for real-time prices of government and corporate bonds, money-market instruments, asset-backed securities, foreign exchange, stocks, futures, options, commodities, swaps and derivatives. The Markets global network delivers prices on exchange-traded instruments, with quotes from more than 100 exchanges worldwide and contributed prices on non-exchange-traded instruments, such as bonds and currencies from major dealers and brokers in virtually every trading center in the world. The regional head office for Europe is in London. (Based on information on the Dow Jones web site, 1998).

- *Extel*

    Part of the Financial Times Group, its market data is now integrated with another subsidiary, Interactive Data. In its own words:

    > 'Extel provides a comprehensive range of specialist financial information services to the global financial community. These include market data, company information and taxation services.

    > *Extel Market Data*
    > Serving the fund valuation and administration operations of the global asset management community, Extel is the leading supplier of global market data. Tailored to customer requirements, data is supplied in line with valuation points, from real-time through intra-day and close of market snapshots.

EXSHARE and *EXBOND* are computer-readable datafeeds covering global security prices, income and corporate actions, as well as bond terms and conditions, foreign exchange rates and indices. EXSHARE covers over 230,000 securities from over 160 markets worldwide.

The Snapshot Valuation Service – SVS – provides access to global pricing in real-time or via intra-day and close of market snapshots.

The FTS service is a flexible desktop tool, providing PC access to intra-day and end-of-day EXSHARE, EXBOND and SVS data which may be viewed, analysed or downloaded.

Extel Research Data
Delivered as PC, web and CD-ROM based services or digital feeds, on a daily, weekly or monthly basis, the research data services combine comprehensive data with powerful PC tools supporting international investment decisions.The Research Products range includes: *Referencer, Extelnet, Company Analysis, Company Research* and *Equity Research.*

- *First Call Corporation*

  The emphasis of this division of Thomson Financial Services is real-time global broker research and corporate news. However, that is complemented by their *World Equities* 'global fundamentals' pricing and news data for over 200 data items and ratios per company. It includes 10 years of historical pricing and two years of corporate news. Research Direct is First Call's dedicated terminal, dial-up or Internet interface to their products.

- *Interactive Data*

  US supplier of world capital and securities pricing data; its market data is now integrated with Extel's, another Financial Times subsidiary.

- *Micrognosis*

  Major player in financial information management systems.

- *Reuters*

  Reuters Holdings; British; one of the top four; major player in information and transaction products (details of products in section above).

- *Primark group*

  The established real-time financial information provider ICV was acquired by the U.S. Primark Corporation in 1996, and teamed with

Datastream for the combined delivery of price and price-sensitive company and other data. Datastream/ICV 'Provides real-time and historical financial information services to the investment community worldwide. Over 5,000 organisations in 50 countries benefit from Datastream/ICV's dynamic range of products'. The firm delivers real-time equity and news information and analytics through *Market Eye*, and ICV's collaborative venture with the London Stock Exchange *TOPIC3* and its variants. Historical and research data products cover equities, bonds, derivatives, economics, and investment trusts. Services delivered via the web and aimed at private investors include *Primark Investment Research Center* and *Market Eye*.

Other relevant Primark subsidiaries include:

Baseline – Fundamental financial information for portfolio managers, with decision software; Primark Investment Management Services (PIMS) – UK-based source of fund accounting and portfolio analysis software.

- *Vestek*

Investment software for portfolio construction, risk management, portfolio optimisation and performance measurement.

- *Data Downlink Corporation's XLS web site – http://www.xls.com/*

New York based, founded in 1996, an aggregator of data from different providers for investment decision purposes; according to its CEO:

'The service aggregates and indexes 24 databases licensed from 17 content providers, including: In-depth Data (SEC filing information in spreadsheet form); Data Analysis Group (computer industry forecasts from leading trade journals); Frost & Sullivan; IPO Data Systems; Mergerstat (M&A data); Leadership Directories (Corporate, Financial and Association Yellow Books); and Media General Financial Services (financial information on US public companies). .xls works with either Netscape Navigator or Microsoft Internet Explorer, and offers its data in six categories: Companies, Industries, Financial Markets, Demographics, Countries, and Economic Statistics. Each company and industry has a contents page with links to specific content, and all accessed data can be directly loaded or saved as a Lotus or Excel file for later copying, pasting, or manipulation.'

Real-time to Near Real-time Sources

A considerable range of products is available for the many users of financial information who are less directly involved in dealing on the markets. These may be the clients of the brokers and dealers: corporate treasurers, corporate and private investors, and even researchers and analysts in the financial services industry may seek different sources from their dealing colleagues. These users, and anyone else with an occasional and less predictable financial information need, are also much more likely to seek answers via an intermediary, partly because efficient use is required of sources which charge according to data retrieved.

These sources are also electronic, and provide 'Near-time and potentially real-time information from and on a wide range of financial markets'. However, each is limited and selective by comparison with the real-time data feed services, sometimes covering a particular financial market or geographical area, sometimes covering just the most actively traded instruments in a market, and often having modest analytical functions, currency, or historical archive. These are more conventional electronic information sources than the 'comprehensive' packages, where the user has to choose the appropriate source for a particular need, from many, requiring wide knowledge of sources' content and interfaces. In considering these sources, the following sections categorise them according to the distribution route – a fairly arbitrary division as far as their information content is concerned, i.e.:

- Web sites
- Online hosts
- Videotext
- Audiotext and fax

Web Sites and Gateways

Because of its ability to disseminate real-time data very widely and cheaply, the World Wide Web has spawned a great variety of sources of financial data. Both exchanges themselves, and established financial publishers and information providers, commonly offer free selections from their services: especially headline price, index, and news data. This diverse and ever changing range of sources can be accessed fairly systematically through web browser software, search engines and search directories. Several web gateways exist to direct users to the often free data disseminated by stock exchanges and other markets themselves; such as Asia Online (*http://www.asiadragons.com/business_and_finance/stock/exchanges.shtml*), which has links to some 100 exchanges worldwide:

> 'Stock Exchanges
>
> AFRICA – ASIA – EUROPE – MIDDLE EAST – NORTH AMERICA – SOUTH AMERICA
>
> African Stock Exchanges
>
> Ghana Stock Exchange, Ghana
> Johannesburg Stock Exchange, South Africa
> The South African Futures Exchange (SAFEX), South Africa

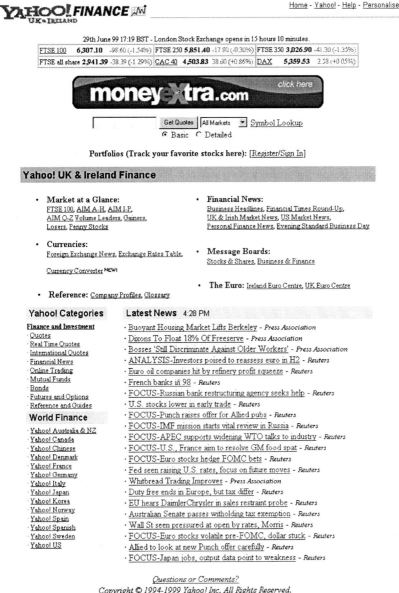

Figure 16. Yahoo! UK & Ireland Finance : opening page

Asian Stock Exchanges

Sydney Futures Exchange, Australia
Australia Stock Exchange, Australia
China Stock Exchanges, China
Shenzhen Stock Exchange, China
Stock Exchange of Hong Kong, Hong Kong
. . .'

The new information hosts with their 'preferred providers' can give the user a limited impression of what is actually available – such as the Microsoft *Investor* web site's relationship with Disclosure, and the Economist Intelligence Unit with America Online on their *International* and *Personal Finance* Channels. Although Yahoo! is essentially a web search tool, its Yahoo! Finance is an example of ready-made links to the web sites of a wide variety of sources on financial markets worldwide, as illustrated below:

The web site *Virtual Stock Exchange* (*http://www.virtualstockexchange.com/*) is another American and US orientated gateway to a great range of other provider's stock market prices, statistics and more. Although it is principally an interactive way for investors to learn about the stock market, it is a convenient and structured source of free data from a wide range of providers, and of complementary resources such as financial news, glossaries and software.

Among other free web gateways, the British information brokerage RBA Information Services maintains its *Stock Market and Company Financial Data* directory of and links to web sites (*http://www.rba.co.uk/sources/index.htm*). This includes other more specialised gateways, such as *Stock Exchange Markets in the World*, which in turn links to exchanges which provide an impressive range of data and other information services, of course centred around their own market; such as the American NASDAQ (*http://www.nasdaq.com/*). RBA's *Stock Market and Company Financial Data* gateway also leads to the web sites of commercial financial information providers. For instance, at the time of writing details and links are given for free and charged sites in 12 different countries. It shows that authoritative providers such as Datastream currently offer free end-of-day quotes for over 32,000 shares, and certain statistics. The following extract introduces Datastream's *Market-Eye* (*http://www.market-eye.co.uk/*), including the free *World Equity Quotes* service:

'Welcome to *Market-Eye* Internet

– the premier web site for UK stock market investors brought to you by Datastream/ICV, providers of real-time and historical financial information services worldwide. Click on Site Info for a detailed description of what's available. To access delayed prices, news and closing price historical data free of charge Register for our Investor Service. Alternatively you can subscribe for our Premium Service for real-time prices, news and historical data.

Investor and Premium service users can now test our new Discussion Forum 'Eye-to-Eye', visit the 'Investors Mall' for the largest online selection of investment books and periodicals in the world, or trade online through the 'Trading Floor'.

World Equity Quotes provides end-of-day quotes for over 32,000 World Equities. It is updated daily as closing prices become available. Choose your option for which to search on. This can be the ISIN code, Datastream Mnemonic, Datastream Code, or Datastream Company Name. Select Option.'

FT.com (*http://www.FT.com/* – more details in the 'News Information' chapter) is a gateway to Financial Times Electronic Publishing's own commercial products, and also a source of much free world financial markets news and prices. FT.com's *Financial Times World Share* service provides free headline numerical data for a plethora of markets, and links to them for further information. Qualisteam's *Worldwide Stock Exchanges* (*http://www.qualisteam.com/*) is another notable (free) gateway to worldwide stock exchanges and other financial web sites, presented by country.

The much respected gateway to business information web sites *Business Information on the Internet* maintained at Strathclyde University also has a section on stock market and related data. Equally authoritative, UK-oriented and impressively structured are the business sections on the NISS gateway to web information resources on the UK JANET academic network (*http://www.niss.ac.uk/news/index.html*).

Such gateways are an excellent way to discover, evaluate and connect to diverse web-based sources of financial information, most of which have a free level of service. Gateways themselves can be discovered via the *Alphasearch* 'gateway to gateways' (*http://www.calvin.edu/library/as/*), and some appear in the bibliography of sources in the final chapter.

RBA warns that for serious purposes there is no substitute for the established charged services. The free services can be frustratingly slow, highly selective, deliberately delayed in currency for 15 minutes, and in many cases you have to register your contact details in order to use them. Nevertheless, using a program such as *Quote Ticker Bar* from the *Filedudes* free software web site, it is possible to set up a free continuous Wall Street 'ticker' service at the bottom of your PC screen (*http://www.filedudes.com*). A recent bonus for users of Nokia 9000 Communicator mobile phones is free access to the Profound host's *Global Markets* web pages. Thus, price data and even graphics can be requested and displayed on the LCD screen. This was hailed as the first mobile phone to provide full live Internet access.

Online Hosts

Perhaps because the data and many users are contracted to the 'Big money news gatherers', perhaps because dial-up technology is inappropriate for the purpose, very little real-time price data is available through the generalist business information hosts. *Quotes* and *Foreign Exchange* are the modules on the more subject-specialised host *Reuters Business Briefing* (more details under 'Online Hosts' in the final chapter). Both include automatically updatable portfolio facilities. *RBB* offers 'share price, market index and foreign exchange data from the world's financial markets'. Available through the News Wires screen is 'the full range of Reuters' global news', including company announcements and regulatory news; the Quotes screen gives market index data and share prices for over 22,000 companies worldwide.

Dialog offers a gateway to the menu-based Dialog *Quotes and Trading*; this gives stock and option quotes provided by Trade*Plus from the various US exchanges, delayed by 20 minutes. Its *Stock Watch* and *Option Watch* software allows monitoring of up to 18 stocks at a time, portfolio management, and buying and selling via participating brokers. Price data is complemented by a range of analytical statistics. *Dialog/Moneycenter,* however, provides access to some of Dialog former owner Knight Ridder Financial Information's real-time US money, capital and currency markets quotes screens. It is '. . . a menu-driven price and rate quotations and news service covering major US and non-US cash, futures and options markets. Real-time cash prices, yields, and rates are updated continuously for US treasury, money markets, and mortgage backed securities, plus rates on corporate, municipal and foreign government bonds, foreign exchange, and commodities in both composite form and by individual contributor. Some quotes are delayed for 15 minutes'. The file includes related news and statistics.

An obvious strength of Financial Times Electronic Publishing, provider of FT Profile and FT Discovery, is its current and retrospective news data. It hosts the full text of *Reuter News, Dow Jones News Database,* and *AFX News,* as well as current and back files of *The Financial Times* and other financial and general newspapers, newswires, and the London Stock Exchange's full *Regulatory News Service* updated three times daily. 'Data Collections' such as 'UK News' allow all the relevant files to be searched at once if required. *The Financial Times' News Alert* (more in the 'News Information' chapter) delivers news as soon as it is published from a very wide range of wires, periodicals, databases and more, to subscribers' desktops according to their personal profile.

Matching Reuters for Japanese information, Nikkei Telecom offers the general user a dial-up PC-based financial information service. *Japan News and Retrieval* is the English language interface to the *Nikkei Economic Electronic Databank System – NEEDS.* The Windows version includes current quotes (for example, stock quotes updated 10 times daily) and historical data for all the financial commodities, market indices, and a whole range of complementary information, including bond rating service, company databases, economic indicators and a real-time news wire.

While they are major players in the real-time direct feed market, Dow Jones also offer pay-per-view access to selected financial data on their web-based host *Dow Jones Interactive Publishing*, including share price histories. The *Business Newsstand* option is an economical way of accessing '11 exclusive Dow Jones newswires, press release wires, international wires . . . all dating back 90 days'. There is also the full text of the most important financial and other newspapers (on the day of publication), an industry-categorised *Today's News Highlights* service, and *Custom Clips* which delivers news on selected topics to your mailbox as it appears'.

Historical data services are prominent in the financial information packages aimed at the pay-per-view user. Indeed, the web-based Dow Jones Interactive's *Historical Market Data Center* obtains from Tradeline up to 25 years pricing on more than 250,000 financial issues from around the world, including stocks, mutual funds, corporate bonds, government securities, market indexes, options and exchange rates – in charts, graphs, text and downloadable files – covering pricing history, dividends and capital changes.

Such pay-per-view services are suitable for the research needs of professional and other investors, and for information intermediaries. They offer economical access to the products of the major providers of historical price data. By contrast with Dow Jones, the dial-up Windows- or web-based *Reuters Business Briefing* emphasises currency in its complementary numerical and news data. Although 10 years of the news database is available, *Reuters Business Briefing* does not include the full range of the retrospective price data available to *Reuters 3000* customers.

Of the few financial information databases mentioned on the generalist business information hosts (Dialog, DataStar, Profound, FT Profile and others), only the Dialog gateway service *Tradeline*, and the FT Profile gateway to Nikkei, can be considered significant sources of retrospective financial information.

Summary of examples of online hosts' electronic financial prices and news sources

Service Current price and numerical data (some include historical data):	**Host/supplier**
Quotes (share prices, market indices)	Reuters – RBB
Foreign Exchange (exchange values)	Reuters – RBB
Markets (current&historical quotes& indices)	Nikkei – Japan News and Retrieval
Dialog/Moneycenter (US money, capital, and currency markets; information provided by Knight Ridder Financial)	Dialog Corp. – Dialog

Service	Host/supplier
Dialog Quotes and Trading (stock and option quotes provided by Trade*Plus from US exchanges	Dialog Corp. – Dialog
Stock Quotes (world price & other data; incl. historical)	Dialog Corp. – Profound
Historical price and numerical data (see also above):	
Historical Market Data Center (up to 25 years of quotes& indices, provided by Tradeline)	Dow Jones Interactive (web site)
Real-time financial news:	
Dowvision	Dow Jones – broadcast feed
Dowvision on Demand	Dow Jones – dial-up service
Business News Stand	Dow Jones Interactive (web site)
News Wires (financial and general global news)	Reuters – RBB
News (real-time updates of financial & business news incl. contents of Nikkei periodicals)	Nikkei – Japan News and Retrieval
Dialog/Moneycenter (data on US money, capital, and currency markets, includes news)	Dialog Corp. – Dialog
Wireline (news from 27 global newswires)	Dialog Corp. – Profound
Dow Jones News Database	FT Profile
AFX News database (European oriented world financial and related news, updated five times per day)	FT Profile
Retrospective financial news:	
News Search (10-year archive of Reuters' and others' business and general news)	Reuters – RBB
Text Search (Up to 10-year archive of translated financial & business articles from Japanese & Asian periodicals)	Nikkei – Japan News and Retrieval

Videotext

Although up-to-date information on UK financial markets has not been available from the conventional online hosts until the proliferation of web sites, sources using 'viewdata' and 'teletext' technology (generic name 'videotext') have in fact been available to the general user. Viewdata is a dial-up online system, where 'pages' of data are called up from remote providers', by users with special TV sets or PCs, connected to telephone lines. Teletext (below) is more limited in speed and volume, because pages of data are broadcast by the TV networks along with the signals for their programmes.

The 'public' viewdata host Prestel (which became New Prestel) was never taken up in as many British homes and offices as the technology justified, and now has web and cable to compete with. Nevertheless, an enduring service available on the latest incarnation, Prestel Online (*http:// www.prestel.co.uk/one.htm*) is *Citiservice*, from the mainstream financial information provider ICV. *Citiservice* constituted an economical alternative to the 'professional' services for the more occasional user, and was more akin to them than videotext services in terms of currency and market coverage. Today Prestel Online functions as an Internet service provider with a number of preferred content providers, and though *Citiservice* is only one of many easily accessible web-based financial information sevices, it still has the advantage of being UK oriented:

> 'CitiService gives you a unique blend of specialist financial news and data – just like your favourite financial newspaper – but up-to-the-minute, not a day late. Because profit opportunities can appear at any time and in many different places, you'll get authoritative news, analysis and commentary as well as live prices, trades and volumes. In short, everything you need to make winning investments.'

TOPIC was a videotext-based price service offered directly by the London Stock Exchange, and available to the public in general on BT's former Prestel. As *TOPIC3*, *TOPIC3 Trader* and other variations, it is now largely 'outsourced' to the Primark Corporation's Datastream/ICV division. *TOPIC* still uses LSE data feeds, but now delivers via more conventional communications technology, and is integrated with historical data and trading software to make it primarily a product for dealers.

Teletext

The City or financial information services on the major TV channels' teletext pages are popular in every sense of the word. Since *Ceefax* (BBC) and *Oracle* (ITV) can be received on appropriately adapted TV sets at no extra cost and manipulated using the remote control numeric keypad, they are probably in more homes than the financial pages of a newspaper. Popular usage of the City pages is confirmed by logjams on stockbrokers' switchboards caused by private investors issuing buy or sell instructions immediately after the three daily BBC1 *Ceefax* price updates. Brokers wish that more people were aware that BBC2 *Ceefax* prices are updated every 20 minutes, and the prices, statistics and news are more detailed than on other TV networks! The teletext services are all quite selective compared with 'popular' web financial information services and even audiotext.

Audiotext and Fax

Audiotext is the generic name for accessing remote databases using just a telephone as the output device. Thus it is a cheap, portable and widely available technology, appropriate for disseminating small units of information which can be synthesised into the human voice. For at least a decade there has been a choice of audiotext financial information services in the UK, including *FT Cityline*, *BT Citycall*, *The Telegraph* newspaper's *ShareCheck* and *The Guardian's Teleshare*, which includes services by fax. As the extract below suggests, prices of specific financial instruments, index figures and reports are all available for a call charge of approximately 50 pence per minute. Having connected, users 'dial' further digits to select the individual stock or other price, news or other data, from a printed directory of codes usually supplied free of charge. Services are linked directly to the London Stock Exchange's quotations and trading systems, so prices and other data are real-time. Where more complex data or textual reports are involved, some services allow users to request delivery by fax.

Example: services of Teleshare, *provided for* The Guardian.

- *Equities prices*

    Real-time price of approximately 3000 London Stock Exchange Shares, day's high and low, and the number of movements in the day.

- *Gilts prices*

    Similar details to above.

- *Personal Portfolio*

    Up to 50 entries can be input and changed by phone keypad, instant revaluation available on dialing and entering free membership number.

- *Portfolio Faxtrack*

    Details of the entries in the personal portfolio, by fax on demand.

- *Indices*

    Latest calculation of approximately 25 UK and foreign equities market indicies.

- *Forex Bulletins*

    Latest rates of major currencies against the pound, available individually or collectively.

- *Travelex Tourist Currency Call*

    Hourly-updated sterling prices for any of over 50 world currencies.

- *Sector Faxtrack*

    Faxed market news and price information, on any of over 30 industry sectors.

- *Personal Finance Faxtrack*

    Faxed messages can be dialed, on topics including fixed rate bonds, TESSAs, different aspects of mortgages and annuities.

Audiotext should be considered a cheap and convenient way of obtaining very current but highly selective numerical and editorial financial data, very appropriate for the business person on the move.

Sources of Intermediate Currency

There is a large group of sources identifiable by their analysis of the markets, rather than their mere reporting of them. They need, and take time to consider the significance of the prices and indices, in the light of the diverse environmental factors affecting the individual financial instruments and the markets as a whole. Such sources have an important role in the formation of considered, longer term buy, sell and investment decisions. These sources are still 'current' by most documents' standards, but though they do record prices and news, it is not these but the analysis that most influences dealing. The printed daily financial newspapers, *Financial Times*, *Wall Street Journal* and others, typify these sources of intermediate currency.

Several different roles can be identified for them, and will be used as the basis for the sections below:

Numerical data
    Concise but precise indication of values and trends of individual instruments
    Concise but precise indication of values and trends of markets
    Wide ranging, authoritative record

Editorial matter
    Reports on significant individual instrument and market activities
    Analyses of significant individual instrument and market activities
    Reports of less time-critical and price-sensitive news on the above
    News reports on the environments affecting the individual instruments and markets

Analysis of the environments affecting individual instruments and markets

Forecasts and advice on individual instruments and markets

Sources undertaking the above functions can have very wide appeal. For the person only indirectly or occasionally affected by the markets, financial newspapers or financial supplements in newspapers may provide the complete service. For the professional investment analyst, researcher or decision maker, even in their printed form financial newspapers are indispensable for the breadth and authority of reporting, and certainly for their analysis of non-stop market activity.

Price Data

It should not be overlooked that the most authoritative and comprehensive record of an exchange's transactions are its own equivalent of the London Stock Exchange's *Daily Official List*, which records each transaction and its price. Lengthy listings such as appear in the the *Financial Times* are inevitably selective: that is, they omit less traded stocks and other instruments, and only periodically publish listings for markets less important to the particular readership. It is very apparent in newspapers that analysed data in particular is often supplied by the real-time market leaders, or extracted by the journalists from their databases. 'Source: Datastream' commonly appears under ad hoc calculations and graphs of, for instance, the performance of a particular stock in relation to the market. A prominent credit on the *The Guardian*'s 'Prices' page states 'Price service supplied by Bloomberg', while 'Independent on Sunday Bloomberg Business' currently appears above that newspaper's Sunday business supplement.

The prices given in listings are necessarily averages of all the transactions in a particular instrument in a particular period, and normally half way between the buy and sell average. Nevertheless, the calculating, recording and daily dissemination of such figures is adequate for many current purposes; a sound snapshot for many users' comparisons and calculation. In common with business or financial sections in other news organs, the *Financial Times* uses an instrument's daily average price (for the London Stock Exchange this is the day's closing price) as the basis for further analysis, and further measures of the instrument's and the market's performance. The the *Financial Times*'s London Share Service lists shares and UK government bonds traded in London. It covers the more than 3,000 active PLCs which have a LSE listing, including the 'junior' Alternative Investment Market, or AIM. These data appear daily in the *Financial Times*' 'Companies and Markets' section (as well as on the the *Financial Times* web site, and the *FT Cityline* audiotext service, described in other sections).

The 'London Share Service' lists stocks (that is company name plus further details where there is more than one issue) alphabetically under 40 or so industry classifications. The data given in separate columns against each include:

Price	Normally in pence and midway between the day's closing buy and sell averages
+ or −	Change, to the nearest 1/4 penny, from the previous day's figure
52 week high & low	Highest and lowest price during the last 52 weeks
Volume	The number of shares traded during the day
Yield	(explained below)
P/E	Price/Earnings performance (explained below)

Some publishers' equities listings are arranged alphabetically by company name, which makes it easier to locate a company's share than in the London Share Service above, but harder to make the all-important comparison with others in the industry. For further ease of comparison, the *FT*'s industry categories above coincide with those of the FTSE Actuaries Share Indices (discussed later). The statistics given for financial instruments, and/or the way they are calculated, varies to some extent from publisher to publisher, making comparison difficult.

The performance ratios commonly calculated for equities can be further explained as follows:

> *Yield*
> A measure of dividend income, arrived at by comparing the dividend paid with the current purchase price of the share; expressed as a ratio as follows:
>
> $$\frac{\text{Dividend in pence (before tax)} \times 100}{\text{Current share price in pence}} = \text{Yield}$$

A healthy company, that is a share of high value because of its future dividend earning potential, is likely to have a low yield figure.

> *Price/earnings – p/e*
> The most used measure of share value; it measures a share's price against the company's last year's earnings:
>
> $$\frac{\text{Current share price in pence}}{\text{Company's annual earnings per share}} = \text{p/e}$$

This time a high p/e ratio, that is an apparently high share price in view of the company's current earnings, generally shows that higher earnings and higher dividends to shareholders are expected. If these market-related ratios do not reflect an analyst's impression of the company's future prospects, they can obviously be a trigger to buy or sell.

Similar listings and calculations to the London equities prices above are published by financial information providers for other countries and financial markets. They are also based on an average mid-price for a given instrument, taken at close of trading or at a specific cut-off point. If there is no single or physical exchange in a market, data is obtained and averaged from leading brokers in the commodity. The *Financial Times* is a major source for UK users on the world's financial markets, taken over a week its coverage is probably the widest of any newspaper, but is nevertheless selective. Foreign coverage concentrates on countries with the highest market capitalisation (such as Japan and USA for equities), and commodities in which foreigners can invest without restriction. Regularly appearing price listings for other financial commodities and other countries' markets are listed below (the financial commodities categories are used below as previously in this chapter). The *Guide to Financial Times Statistics* (details at end of chapter) provides further explanations of the *Financial Times'* prices, indices and other statistics, and a guide to the data given on specific days of the week.

Examples

Equity

The *FT's* listing of the main LSE market is decribed above. Similar data are given in a separate table for the Alternative Investment Market. Similar data are also given by country under 'World Stock Markets', with listings for example for NASDAQ-AMEX (USA); OFEX (an unregulated UK trading facility for unquoted PLCs); EASDAQ (a regulated independent market for internationally active European companies); and EURO.NM (a pan-European grouping of regulated specialist stock markets).

Capital

For the London market the *FT* gives prices for 'UK Gilts', 'International Bonds', and 'Benchmark Government Bonds' issued in the UK and certain other countries. Selected bonds futures, options and other derivatives prices are also given country by country, mainly from London's LIFFE. Data given for each bond typically include the bid price, highs and lows over time, and a range of yield data.

Money

On a page headed 'Currencies and Money' *FT* listings show interest rates in London and other countries for various periods, as well as for 'Eurocurrencies' traded in London. Typical tables include 'London Money Rates', with percentage lending rates for overnight, 7 day's notice, one month, etc.; for Interbank Sterling, Sterling CDs, Treasury Bills, etc. UK rates are given for sterling futures, and 'calls' and 'puts' prices from LIFFE given for options. A number of specific UK and other banks' base lending rates are listed. 'World Interest Rates' are given in terms of for example: overnight, one month, etc. lending rates for the Euro-zone, Switzerland, the USA and Japan.

Currency

The *FT*'s 'Currencies and Money' pages show current relative values of world currencies, and some currency futures prices. Exchange rates between countries are given in the form of a two-way table, the rate for the currency named along the top of the table is given in the currency named in the left column. Other listings include the futures and options prices of specific major currencies, mainly from LIFFE trading.

Commodities

Tradeable commodities futures prices predominate in tables in the *FT*. Average prices of lead, zinc, crude oil, natural gas, coffee, sugar, pork bellies and so on are reported from trading at the London Metals Exchange, London Bullion Market, LIFFE, the Chicago Mercantile Exchange and others. Spot market prices (commodities for immediate delivery), and prices of options for the purchase or sale of certain commodities futures are also given.

By virtue of their 'longer view', the financial media are able to identify significant performers among the financial commodities. The *Financial Times* regularly or occasionally includes special lists of:

New 52 Week Highs and Lows (i.e. share prices)
New International Bond Issues

Indices of Financial Market Performance

While the tables seen above provide a snapshot in time of an individual instrument's performance, for other purposes a sum of performances is necessary as an assessment of the market as a whole. An indication of the state of a market at any given time is vital for those dealing on it, but necessary also for almost everyone else, because we are all directly or indirectly affected. The state and trend of a financial market has obvious implications for current and future values of individual 'goods' in it, as well as being the best yardstick to judge them by. But it also has implications for other financial markets, imports and exports, consumer spending, corporate profitability, employment, and to complete the circle, political policy.

The common measure of the state of a whole financial market, or a sector of it, is an 'index'. A figure derived from the price or other measure, of a large or small sample of transactions. An index figure is only of value by comparison with a baseline figure, the immediately preceding one being the most revealing of the current trend. If the FT 30 index was set at 2000 in 1990 and it is now 3000, then the sample's price has increased by 50% over the period. However, because of the effects of inflation and of changes in the sample from time to time, the value of the index is in indicating changes on a much smaller time-scale. It is much more significant if a single stock or a portfolio has increased perhaps 4 pence, while over the same week the market as a whole has increased 6 pence.

Although for less frequently recalculated indices, sample sizes are impressive, for the purposes of judging the performance of a small number of stocks they always have to be treated with caution. A sample should really be weighted according to both volume of trading in the market and proportion of a financial commodity traded – for instance, the number of shares traded, in relation to the market capitalisation of the company. The famous Financial Times Ordinary Share Index (FT Index, or FT 30) is based on an industry spread of 30 heavily traded 'blue chip' shares, unweighted for market capitalisation. The small sample and simplicity means it is possible to recalculate the FT 30 about every 25 seconds, making it the earliest and most sensitive indicator of London equity market trends.

The Financial Times-Stock Exchange 100 Share Index (FTSE 100, or Footsie) is also constantly updated, and with a sample of the 100 biggest UK PLCs is a better measure of the state of the London stock market. For this reason FTSE 100 normally appears on the *FT*'s front page in the World Markets summary, along with the FTSE All-Share and indices of USA and European markets.

In conjunction with the Faculty and Institute of Actuaries, the *Financial Times* calculates and publishes many more equities indices, as 'UK Series' and 'European Series'. Each index concentrates on either a specific sample size, or sub-markets and companies of a particular size or status. For the UK the FTSE All-Share is based on the largest sample - more than 800 shares, and necessarily calculated less frequently than others. Most significantly, the FTSE All-Share also appears as FTSE Actuaries Industry Sectors, where separate indices are calculated for approximately 8 broad industry sectors (resources, industrials, consumer goods, etc.), and 35 narrower sectors (Alcoholic beverages, food producers, etc.). The breadth of this index, its weighting for market capitalisation, and the separate figures for industry sectors, allows the all-important comparison of a company's performance against its industry peers.Versions also exist for Europe, and for worldwide performance there are FT S&P Actuaries World Indices.

One or more recognised indices exist for other financial markets, in other countries, and as illustrated above, sometimes for a number of markets and countries at once. They are devised and calculated by a combination of authoritative financial publishers, respected independent professional bodies, and exchange authorities themselves. Most are permanently available via the real-time information providers and, like price listings, selectively and occasional available via the near real-time and intermediate currency sources; examples follow.

Examples of financial market indices

Equities

United Kingdom
> *FT Ordinary Share Index (FT 30)*
> *FTSE 100 (Footsie)*
> *FT-SE Mid 250 Index*
> *FT SE Actuaries 350 Index*
> *FT All Share-Index*
> *FT-SE Actuaries Fledgling Index*
> *FT-SE Higher Yield Index*
> *FT-SE Lower Yield Index*

Australia
> *Sydney All Ordinaries*

Belgium
> *Brussels BEL 20*

Canada
> *Toronto TSE 300 composite*

France
> *Paris CAC 40*

Germany
> *Frankfurt DAX*

Hong Kong
> *Hang Seng*

Ireland
> *ISEQ Overall*

Japan
> *Nikkei 225*
> *Nikkei 500*

Netherlands
> *Amsterdam AEX*

Singapore
> *Singapore Straits Times*

Switzerland
> *Zurich Swiss Market*

USA
> *Dow Jones Index*
> *Standard & Poors*

International
> *FTSE Gold Mines Index* (World and regional indices)
> *FT S&P Actuaries World Indices* (World, and separate countries)

Capital

> *FTSE Actuaries Gov't Securities*
> *Nikkei Bond Index (Japan)*

Commodities

> *Reuters Commodities Index*
> *CRB Futures*
> *GSCI Spot*
> *Nikkei Commodity Index* (Japan)

Other Numerical Analyses

As well as price and price change figures for certain individual instruments, calculations such as yield and price/earnings ratios are not only sometimes given in the share and bond listings above, but also included with a price index figure. Thus on the front page of the *Financial Times* of February 26th 1999 an FT 30 Index figure of '6206.5 (-101.1)' was accompanied by a mean yield ratio of '2.57'. Another desirable complement to price and index figures, already referred to, is data on trading volume. Turnover figures are often therefore also sometimes given side by side with indices, and since December 1997 the *FT* gives volume data for individual stocks in its daily 'London Share Service' listing.

A variety of other calculations may also be unpredictably found within editorial material, graphically illustrating some news or development concerning a particular market or instrument, or broader financial or economic point. Many show the movement of a price or index figure over time, or show the relationship between several other variables. This is potentially valuable investment research data which may be available to subscribers to Bloomberg or Datastream, or may be unique to a particular financial periodical. The *Financial Times'* pages are sprinkled with such graphs and charts, and although retrospective sources of such data do exist (see later section), they are difficult data to retrieve via either *The Financial Times Index* (published monthly by Primary Source Media), or online news databases such as *Reuters Textline*.

Editorial Material

The editorial matter in business and financial periodicals expresses what cannot easily be expressed by figures, especially the reporting of non-financial facts, and discussing or analysing events. By virtue of its role and coverage, most of the textual material falls into one of three categories:

- News and analysis of the *external environment*, for the longer term effect on the financial markets
- *Reports* on short-term developments in financial markets
- *Analyses* of the financial markets, short-term or over a longer period.

News and Analysis of the Environments Affecting the Markets

In sophisticated printed and electronic financial periodicals, news and analysis of the markets themselves is complemented by at least as much news and analysis of the environments which affect them, emphasising the role of these organs in longer term research. In its first or main section, the *Financial Times* extensively reports and discusses market sensitive issues relating to companies, market sectors, the economy, the geopolitical environment and so on. Only brief examples of these are given below, since sources covering these environments are dealt with in separate chapters; these headlines represent news on the legal, economic, geopolitical and competitive environments.

- 'Water Industry – Regulator indicates scope to impose lower prices'
- 'Indonesian crisis – Jakarta claims economy is over the worst'
- 'Chile general tries to calm army tensions'
- 'BSkyB moves to boost cable goup margins'

Reports on Short-term Developments in Financial Markets

Text and pictures are a high impact, effective way of communicating complex issues to those who can or must make the time available to consider them. Although text is also used by the real-time providers for instant notification of certain events, organs like daily newspapers normally have the opportunity to incorporate a certain amount of verification, enlargement and discussion in their editorial matter.

Real-time financial news services are available to a wider pay-per-view clientele also, either as components of the quotes/trading services mentioned in earlier sections, or as separate services. Even dial-up or web sites of pay-per-view hosts such as Dialog allow 'alerts' to be set up; though the results are not usually as instantly visible as via flat-fee services such as Bloomberg, Reuters, or even the less specialised Dialog Corporation's *Profound*. *Reuters Business Briefing* is that firm's dial-up, PC- and Windows-based host for the less specialised user. Its *News Wires* and *News Search* gives access to the same *Reuters News* received by subscribers to Reuters' terminals, including the searchable ten-year archive. *Dowvision, Dowvision on Demand*, and *Business News Stand* are the text of Dow Jones' news wires and *The Wall Street Journal*, either as a continuous 'broadcast feed', dialed into when required, or as a subscription-based web version.

Analyses of the Financial Markets

In the *Financial Times* and other daily newspapers with significant financial coverage, major analytical pieces are less common than reports and comments on the previous day's events. Although the the *Financial Times'* much respected Lex column does every day venture an analysis of significant events, weeklies, including *Investors Chronicle*, are a more obvious source of research and analysis. Nevertheless, the *Financial Times* has almost daily supplements, each of which focusses on a particular country, region or industry, constituting a valuable piece of research on the environments of the relevant financial commodities and of business in general.

Financial editorial matter is found in the mainly international news wire or agency services, covered in the 'News and Analysis . . .' section above, and in a less immediate but more refined form in a country's business and financial periodicals. Some of the latter issue their own indexes for retrospective retrieval (such as *The Financial Times Index*, published monthly by Primary Source Media), and the full text of most are searchable via their publisher's or others' retrospective business or financial news sources such as the *Financial Times* et al's *World Reporter*, or via general business news databases such as Reuters *Textline*. The general online hosts also offer databases with same-day, searchable financial and business newspapers in full text, such as on *Dialog Knight Ridder/Tribune Business*, containing about 80 newspapers and other periodicals. FT Profile hosts several relevant newswires (included in the 'Summary of Examples of Online Hosts . . .' above) and full text newspapers including articles (not tables) from all editions of the *Financial Times* itself, from approximately 0300 hrs on the day of publication.

Financial Instruments Performance Guides; Ratings Services; 'Tip Sheets'; Monitoring Services

Performance Guides

A number of directories and other reference services may appear to be general company sources, but actually relate specifically to financial instruments. The following examples present the data necessary for investors to 'study form', including time series of financial and share performance data, and often the publishers and or others rating of the invesment. The manuals and handbooks established by Moody's are now published by the Financial Communications Company (USA) division Financial Information Services (or FIS and FIS Online *http://www.fisonline.com/*):

> Moody's:
>
> *Industrial Manual and News Reports*
> *Municipal & Government Manual and News Reports*
> *Handbook of Common Stocks*
> *Handbook of Dividend Achievers*
> *Bond Record*
> *Dividend Record*
> *Industry Review*
> *Company Data*
> *International Company Data*
> *Company Data Direct*

Essentially the above printed or electronic services rate the shares and bonds of US companies and other issuers, providing investors with a 'simple system of gradation by which the relevant investment qualities of a bond may be noted'. Examples of other performance guides – some investors' reference services are a specialised form of company directory:

BondCall Notes/BondCall Direct. First Call Corporation; direct via the Internet (*http://www.firstcall.com/*), etc. 'Source of commingled fixed income research notes, providing institutional investment firms with electronic access to real-time analysis from major bond houses, rating agencies and other third parties.'

Emerging Markets Desk Reference. Capital Access International; regularly republished Profiles of 'over 400 buyside institutions and 70 top sellside firms active in the multi-billion dollar fixed-income emerging markets.'

Mortgage and Asset-backed Desk Reference; Derivatives Desk Reference; Corporate Bond Desk Reference. Capital Access International; regularly republished. Relevant data on companies and their financial instruments, and active buyers in the market.

Ratings Services
(See also the 'Stockbroker Research' section of the 'Company Information' chapter, for sources of expert estimates and recommendations on stocks and shares)

A version of personal and company credit assessments is commonly applied to financial instruments by respected independent assessors as a guide to their underlying investment quality. As Europe's capital markets expand, so does the business of rating bonds. Large ratings agencies like Standard & Poor's, Moody's and Fitch IBCA, are gearing up to increase the proportion of European 'investment grade' companies with ratings, from about 10% to the USA norm of more like 100%. In their *Risk Management Service* the London Business School distinguishes the two types of risk which ratings systems reflect, to protect their users from. 'Market risk' is the financial instrument's sensitivity to general market movements, and 'specific risk' concerns factors peculiar to the company. The U.S. based information providers Standard and Poor's, and Moody's are major players in this area of risk management. S&P's ratings for corporate and government bonds can be seen in a separate column of the *Financial Times* listing of US and other bonds. With the experience of the 1997/8 Far East financial markets crash, S&P's have recently added a 'contingent liability rating' for governments, that is a measure of their exposure to the liabilities of their private sector banks.

Example of Moody's ratings (Money Market Funds, United Kingdom, 12th October 1998):

Advisor	Fund	Credit Risk	Market Risk
CCLA Investment IManagement Limited	CBF Deposit Fund	Aaa	MR1+
CCLA Investment Management Limited	COIF Charities Deposit Fd	Aaa	MR1+
Fidelity Investments Services Ltd	Fidelity Cash Unit Trust	Aaa	MR1+
Schroder Investment Management Ltd.	SIM CMR Cash Pool	Aaa	MR1+

Moody's styles itself as the leading provider of independent credit ratings, research and financial information to the capital markets. It maintains independent rating opinions on nearly $14 trillion of debt securities, including on 3,000 issuers of bonds globally, and the other financial institutions and instruments listed immediately below; their explanation of one of the ratings systems follows. This data is based on that given in the Moody's Investors Service web site, from which current ratings are freely available (*http://www.moodys.com/*)

Moody's ratings

> LONG-TERM RATINGS
> Debt Ratings – Taxable Debt & Deposits Globally
> Debt Ratings – U.S. Tax Exempt Municipal
> Counterparty Ratings
> Bank Financial Strength Ratings
> Insurance Financial Strength Ratings
> Managed Fund Ratings
> Preferred Stock Ratings
>
> SHORT-TERM RATINGS
> Prime Rating System – Taxable Debt & Deposits Globally

Definition of one of Moody's ratings – taxable debt and deposits globally (i.e. bonds):

Aaa   Bonds which are rated Aaa are judged to be of the best quality. They carry the smallest degree of investment risk and are generally referred to as 'gilt edged.' Interest payments are protected by a large or by an exceptionally stable margin and principal is secure. While the various protective elements are likely to change, such changes as can be visualized are most unlikely to impair the fundamentally strong position of such issues.

Aa   Bonds which are rated Aa are judged to be of high quality by all standards. Together with the Aaa group they comprise what are generally known as high-grade bonds. They are rated lower than the best bonds because margins of protection may not be as large as in Aaa securities or fluctuation of protective elements may be of greater amplitude or there may be other elements present which make the long-term risk appear somewhat larger than the Aaa securities.

A Bonds which are rated A possess many favorable investment attributes and are to be considered as uppermedium-grade obligations. Factors giving security to principal and interest are considered adequate, but elements may be present which suggest a susceptibility to impairment some time in the future.

Baa Bonds which are rated Baa are considered as medium-grade obligations (i.e. they are neither highly protected nor poorly secured). Interest payments and principal security appear adequate for the present but certain protective elements may be lacking or may be characteristically unreliable over any great length of time. Such bonds lack outstanding investment characteristics and in fact have speculative characteristics as well.

Ba Bonds which are rated Ba are judged to have speculative elements; their future cannot be considered as well-assured. Often the protection of interest and principal payments may be very moderate, and thereby not well safeguarded during both good and bad times over the future. Uncertainty of position characterizes bonds in this class.

B Bonds which are rated B generally lack characteristics of the desirable investment. Assurance of interest and principal payments or of maintenance of other terms of the contract over any long period of time may be small.

Caa Bonds which are rated Caa are of poor standing. Such issues may be in default or there may be present elements of danger with respect to principal or interest. Ca Bonds which are rated Ca represent obligations which are speculative in a high degree. Such issues are often in default or have other marked shortcomings.

C Bonds which are rated C are the lowest rated class of bonds, and issues so rated can be regarded as having extremely poor prospects of ever attaining any real investment standing.

Moody's applies numerical modifiers 1, 2, and 3 in each generic rating classification from Aa through Caa. The modifier 1 indicates that the obligation ranks in the higher end of its generic rating category; the modifier 2 indicates a mid-range ranking; and the modifier 3 indicates a ranking in the lower end of that generic rating category.

Other examples of ratings services:

Risk Measurement Service (RMS) – London Business School; quarterly. 'Risk measures and other key data for some 2,000 British shares for all industry sectors'. A considerable amount of numerical data, including tables of shares ranked by various criteria, and several risk ratings for each.

Credit Ratings International – Financial Times; published serially. 'The only regularly updated comparative listing of international credit ratings, produced in co-operation with the world's most influential credit rating agencies'. Up to 12 different ratings for each company, plus the *Financial Times'* own composite rating. Each rater and rating system is explained in detail.

'Tip Sheets'

'Tip sheets', such as *Analyst*, are serials which try to assist their subscribers' 'stock picking' efforts. Each employs a particular systematic method of identifying good investment opportunities, providing and evaluating other investment aids, profiling and rating listed companies, and reporting on their portfolios. *Tiptracker* provides a quarterly assessment of the effectiveness of such investment newsletters, and the financial pages of newspapers.

Monitoring Services

In addition to the many sources of news on the markets and the events affecting them, there is a need for systematic monitoring and cumulation of events relating to financial instruments themselves. Events include the creation of new instruments, and changes to instruments, individually announced in special statutory documents and the notifications in newspapers sometimes referred to as 'tombstones'. Regular listings like the London Recent Issues: Equities listing in the *Financial Times* has already been cited in the context of shares. Certain other sources provide an even more systematic source for investors, potfolio managers and others, of such 'capital events':

> *Takeovers, Offers and New Issues* – Extel Financial; monthly looseleaf and other formats.
> Listing of capital events relating to London Stock Exchange listed companies.

Specialised Retrospective Sources

As mentioned when discussing them, retrospective numerical data is a necessary complement to the real-time data feed services, and some of the services of a less current and comprehensive level. One of the main uses of it is as past evidence of patterns which may repeat themselves in the future, for example to predict the effect on the UK stock market of a sudden decline in the US or Japanese market. Past price and index data is also used for the more mundane purpose of retrospective valuations; for instance, for calculating how much sterling a certain number of dollars was worth in 1945, and what those pounds would buy today. It is comparatively easy for the creators and providers of current financial information to archive that data for future use. However, decisions have to be made about which method of calculation or figure is the most authoritative, how much detail should be recorded, and how often. Just as important as the data itself, appropriate software has to be provided for its retrieval and analysis over chosen periods, in relation to other chosen factors. As in the case of current numerical data, the leading financial information providers offer the widest range and longest time series, while smaller providers, and providers of information of intermediate currency, are more selective in both respects. The *Financial Times*'s data constitutes a huge resource when cumulated, and has long been purchasable in microform as *FT Stats Fiche*. It is now more usefully available as *FT Prices on CD-ROM*: 14 years of the newspaper's price and index data, in monthly instalments cumulating annually. Thus a share price or an exchange rate can be tracked over a period, and displayed graphically.

Examples

Various

International Financial Statistics – International Monetary Fund. Economic indicators and financial statistics for most countries.

FT Prices on CD-ROM – FT Electronic Publishing. 13 year archive of prices and indices from the *Financial Times*.

Securities

IFR Securities Data – division of Thomson Financial Services. Services include online databases of complete historical transaction data for Eurobonds, foreign bonds, global mergers and acquisitions, US and international equities (as well as company merger, acquisition and joint venture data).

Currency

Foreign Exchange Rates Calculator – Financial Times. 5 years' exchange rates history for 130 countries, updated monthly, cross calculation software.

Further Sources

R. Bashford (ed.). *Guide to Financial Times Statistics*, 3rd edn. FT Business Information, 1991. A very useful companion to financial market data in the *FT* and any other source.

M. Brett. *How to Read the Financial Pages*, 4th edn. Century Business, 1995. A user-friendly, British guide to financial data and jargon.

W. M. Clarke *How the City of London Works: An Introduction to its Financial Markets*, 4th edn. Sweet & Maxwell, 1995. Includes a glossary of City terms.

A Glossary of Stock Market Terms. London Stock Exchange (web site – *http://www.stockex.co.uk*). A good and detailed glossary among the many free ones on financial web sites.

R. G. Lester (ed.). *Information Sources in Finance and Banking*. Bowker-Saur, 1995.

5

Product Information

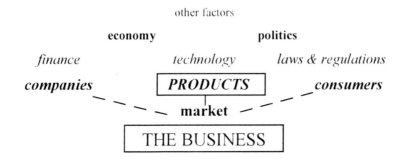

Introduction

This chapter is concerned with the aspects of products which come within the definition of business information used throughout the book. The content is from the point of view of the person making decisions with direct commercial implications, rather than from the point of view of a product designer or technologist. Information for sourcing is covered, partly because purchases can have important commercial implications for the purchaser, and partly because the related sources are considered as 'business information'. The documentation of technology and industrial property (sometimes 'intellectual property') is treated very selectively; only types of source with a vital role in commercial decision making are considered. Although the term 'products' is normally used for the sake of brevity, it is almost always intended to include services also.

Products and services constitute part of the 'immediate external environment' of any commercial enterprise. By definition all businesses exist to sell their product or service, while the profitability of most depends also on the competitiveness of their purchasing. Products and services are also part of any given business' 'market', along with other businesses as competitors, suppliers and purchasers, and private consumers. Perhaps the most important commercial decision that private consumers themselves make is major purchases. Products and services are the visible result of manufacturing and service industries, and are the very centre of the market and therefore of business and the economy.

The aspects of products which are inextricably associated with 'the market' are considered in the 'Market Information' chapter and are not repeated here. This includes current and future volume of production, sales, and consumption, the concerns of market research, and advertising expenditure. Similarly, products were inevitably treated as an attribute of companies in the 'Company Information' chapter, so certain source types covered there will be referred to, rather than repeated here. As the following outline shows, the chapter discusses the remaining needs for finding out about products, in each case considering what information would satisfy the need. Following that, the relevant source types are examined one by one. The structure is:

Needs –

> To:
> Select and acquire ('source') products and services
> Be aware of existing competitive and substitute products
> Be aware of changes – new and future competitive and substitute products
> Monitor technological developments which could affect products
> Protect own, and use others' industrial property legally

Sources types –

> Primary descriptive data
>> Trade literature
>> Product pick-up services
> Secondary sources of descriptive data
>> Trade directories
>> 'Package libraries'
> Tests and evaluations
> New products monitoring services
> Technology monitoring services
> Patents documentation
> Trade marks documentation

Needs for Information on Products and Services

Selecting and Acquiring ('Sourcing') Products and Services

Sourcing is the business activity which most obviously requires information on products and services. Although purchasing (or 'procuring') can be a common and mundane process, supported by a plethora of more or less systematic information sources, it can also involve very difficult and significant decisions. Everything a business owns and depends on involves selection and purchase, including human resources, raw materials, plant, components, and information systems. Many purchases involve huge and long term financial and strategic commitments, and a commercial dependence on the acquisition performing as expected. It is hard enough to draw up specifications to meet the organisation's strategic and more specific needs, let alone to match those with the specifications of available products and services. It can be necessary to match needs and products on a surprisingly large number of criteria (below), some of which are easily defined and satisfied, others not. As so often in business, information is just as necessary when it can only reduce uncertainty as when it can give definite answers:

Criteria Which May Need to be Matched with Available Products

Alternatives

What alternatives solutions are available; of those, who supplies what, with which mix of the criteria below.

Performance

In relation to needed and claimed specifications, initial and long term; in comparison with alternatives.

Cost

Overall, initial, terms of payment, costs of maintenance, parts, updates, in comparison with alternatives.

Ethics and legality

Ethical soundness of item's materials, processes, effects, appearance, perception, suppliers, advertising, packaging.

Current and future legality of the item and its purpose, including dangerous or polluting, components, operation or outputs.

Conditions of purchase or contract

Inclusions and exclusions, including coverage in relation to materials, failure, dissatisfaction, maintenance, updates, consequences of breaking contract on either side. Record of manufacturer, supplier and others.

A considerable level of detail can obviously be necessary, in a spectrum from written data on the range of alternatives and their suppliers, to illustrations or models, to examination of the product or service itself, to the reports of independent users and evaluators. The table at the beginning of the 'Source Types' section below shows that a wide range of information source types is relevant to answer some or all of these questions, though such a wide range can be difficult to systematically exploit. It is most unfortunate for businesses and private consumers alike that so many important purchasing decisions are taken without the benefit of a systematic search in independent compilations of product details and comparisons.

Awareness of Existing Competitive and Substitute Products

A very similar wide range of details, and therefore sources, is necessary for this very different objective. Everything needs to be known about competitor products or services, including as discussed in the 'Market Information' chapter, how they are advertised, who acquires them and how they are perceived by actual and potential purchasers. Competitors' interests differ somewhat from potential purchasers', in that a competitor also wants to actually or figuratively take the item apart, to know what it was made of, how and where, and see how it compares and whether there is anything to learn.

Awareness of Changes – New Competitive and Substitute Products

It is probably *changes* in products in the market which have the greatest strategic and commercial significance. Existing competitive products may cause problems, which can be responded to and survived, but greater anxiety attaches to the product just around the corner, because its effect may be earth shattering. Naturally, products which do not yet officially exist are the hardest to discover the existence of, let alone details; their suppliers take great care to ensure secrecy and disinformation. Naturally also, therefore, business' information needs in this area are matched by a considerable range of sources, all attempting to make the unknown manageable and reduce uncertainty.

Figure 17. Headline from Construction News 22.10.98, p. 19

While the next section addresses product developments which are even further back on the production line, this one concerns itself with the need shared by purchasers and competitors, to monitor what changes are on the production line (or the services equivalent), or newly launched onto the market. Suppliers certainly ensure that maximum detail is available once the product is ready for delivery, but they often also release certain performance and perhaps cost details in advance, in order to market test or to market the item. Other than that, specific information is usually withheld and becomes the object of surmise and even industrial espionage, legal or otherwise. Dealing here just with the surmise, information sources appropriate for reading between the lines include companies' annual reports and house journals, and the conclusions of journalists and other analysts, sometimes based additionally on interviews and privileged information. Systematically exploiting developments gleaned from such sources is dealt with in the 'News Sources and Industry Sources' chapter.

The information required about new products is potentially the same as on established products; the important consideration is getting as much information as possible, as early as possible. Seekers must either trawl a range of primary sources, including firms' press releases, advertisements, and those mentioned above and in the table below, or hope to achieve dedicated and sufficiently current coverage from 'new products sources'.

Monitor Technological Developments Which Could Affect Products

This need is related to monitoring actual new products and services. The difference is that the changes are probably further into the future, less specifically relatable to products, and therefore more difficult to research and to have any certainty about. There is in fact both bad news and good news about discovering relevant scientific and technical developments. It is also a problem that much of the research is carried out or sponsored by companies, and so highly secretive. However, much parallel and unique work is also done in the public domain by research establishments and universities, and therefore traceable by those who use the scientific and technical bibliographical apparatus. Further good news is that even commercial discoveries have to be patented in order to protect them, and that the patents literature is as yet underexploited by business as an indicator of the way that large companies' product development is going. The European Patent Office challenges business in this way on its web site (*http://www.european-patent-office.org/index.htm*):

> 'Each year, about a million patent documents are published, 200,000 of them in Europe. Patent information products give the public access to this huge collection of technical and scientific knowledge by organising and indexing the data to make it easy to use.
>
> Because of a lack of information, existing inventions are reinvented, problems that have already be solved are solved again, and products that already are on the market are redeveloped. Duplication of efforts in this way costs European industry:
>
> US$ 20,000,000,000 every year – simply because of the lack of information.
>
> Only 59,000 companies in Europe have made use of the patent system in the last five years, leaving another 111,000 companies that should have the patent system, but have not.
>
> 80% of technical information is published in patent documentation – and often nowhere else.'

Even more value is added to known scientific and technical developments, by a whole range of secondary 'technology monitoring services'. These, detailed in a section below, trawl for potentially relevant innovations, and consider their significance for products and industries.

Protect Own, and Use Others' Industrial Property Legally

Needs for information relating to industrial property range from the routine and factual, to the more complex and strategic. Industrial property includes both the ownership of inventions, and ownership of the names and marks associated with businesses and brands. Patents can be applied for by organisations or individuals, granted by a national or multinational patents organisation and kept in force by the payment of modest fees. A patent protects the inventor's rights to benefit exclusively from a unique device, process and even drug, plant, chemical compound or genetic material. In return for exclusive benefit, an inventor is encouraged to invest in research and to reveal the results. In Britain as in most countries, either the national patents office or the World Intellectual Property Organisation also registers trade marks and names (under the Madrid Agreement and Madrid Protocol), in this case almost entirely for the benefit of the applicant.

Inventions and trade names or marks are often of enormous financial value to their owners, so there is a great incentive both to get them registered, and once that is done, to prevent deliberate or accidental infringement by other businesses. Thus, even a business without any patents or registered trade names needs industrial property information, to exploit available technology legally, and use names and marks without expensively contravening the owners' rights.

Searches of patents which are both applied for and in force are necessary for a variety of reasons, other than, as covered above, as indicators of strategic product development. That is: to discover the ownership of a technology, to trace needed technology, to avoid unnecessary research, to avoid infringement of others' registered inventions, and to check for infringement of a firm's own patents. All these cases require searching by the technology involved, a much more difficult approach than by owner's name or nationality. It is almost as difficult, but of course necessary to use competitors' products themselves as evidence of infringement of a firm's own patents.

The range of needs for information on registered names and marks are similar: it is often necessary to discover the origin of a product or services from its brand name or trade mark – searching by a mark or device presenting particular challenges to any retrieval system. Searches are also necessary before designing, applying to register, and using a mark, and afterwards to ensure there is no infringement by others.

Source Types

The table on page 192 equates needs for product information with the types of information source available. Some types of source are valuable for a number of purposes while others have a more specialised role. Not listed here is the range of general purpose secondary sources which combines information from any of these primary types.

Trade Literature

'Trade literature' or 'product literature' is the term used to describe the disparate documentation produced by businesses to describe and at the same time market their products and services. It may be a single illustrated sheet or a brochure about a single product, or a brochure on a company's product range. There may be separate sheets of technical data, more detailed information, prices; installation, instruction and maintenance manuals; and in some cases samples of materials. Agents, suppliers or retailers may additionally produce more systematic catalogues, and samples collections, with integral or separate price lists. Some of these become standard reference tools in specific trades, such as the Whitaker catalogues of British books in print. Unfortunately, few other products are as systematically documented.

Trade literature is usually attractively printed, and available with or without the products it relates to at relevant exhibition sites and outlets; the most up-to- date and detailed version is often available at the supplier's web site. It is usually the most comprehensive published source of information on any given product. For direct competitors and those involved in specialist sourcing, secondary sources are no substitute for immediate access to this primary literature, if possible complemented by product samples. This is despite the fact that product literature is so unruly in shape, size, frequency and coverage, making it difficult to systematically acquire, store and access. A notable attempt to standardise and aid the handling of construction industry product literature is visible in the 'CI/SfB' code printed prominently on the front of much of it, representing the filing position in an agreed classification system. Sfb is currently being superceded by the Uniclass system, for both construction and quantity surveying; *Uniclass: Unified Classification for the Construction Industry* was published by RIBA in 1997. For all but essential sourcing and competitor monitoring purposes, businesses appreciate the advantages of secondary sources such as the 'package libraries' and trade directories detailed in following sections.

Product Pick-up Services

As has already been said, there are occasions where more information, or at least the particular information required, has to be obtained from the product itself. A number of information providers, particularly in market research and consultancy, do include 'product pick-up' in their range of services. For example, the UK based Mintel associate IIS Ltd calls itself 'The leading product pick-up and product watch service for the world's packaged goods industries'. With 450 field representatives in 130 countries, the worldwide pick-up service aims to obtain samples for 'competitive evaluation, trade age analysis and quality assurance. IIS can have a product from say Brazil, in your hands, within a matter of days, for as little as £150. You can then touch it; examine it; smell it; take it apart; use it; adapt it; make it better – it's a supply service that can become almost addictive ... '. (Latter quote from IIS literature, 1997.)

Purpose	Relevant Source Type								
	Trade lit.	Product pick-up	Trade direct.	Package libraries	Test & evals.	New product services	Technol. monit. services	Patents doc.	Trade marks doc.
Select and acquire ("source") products and services	X	X	X	X	X	X			
Know existing competitive and substitute products	X	X	X	X	X	X			
Monitor changes – new and future competitive and substitute products	X	X	X	X	X	X			
Monitor technological developments which could affect products			X				X	X	
Protect own, and use others' industrial property legally	X	X	X			X	X	X	X

Table 3. Needs for product information cross-referenced with available sources

Trade Directories

Role and Scope

The thousands of trade directories are the long established, standard secondary source of basic product information. As subject-searchable compilations of product and supplier data, they are the first resource for day to day sourcing purposes, and as the table above shows, they also have a role in product intelligence for other purposes. Trade directories may be the very same directories as described in chapter 2 as sources of basic company information, and in chapter 3 as sources of marketing opportunities – the reciprocal of sourcing. To help discover and select a required product or service a directory must not only give sufficient details of firms' activities, but also provide effective access by product or service.

Trade directories today may still be monolithic bound volumes, or more often online or CD-ROM databases; hundreds appear as supplements to relevant trade journals. More and more free but less quality-controlled 'virtual' trade directories are appearing, in the form of classified business telephone or fax directories and web search gateways which link product names to the web sites of supplying companies. Trade directories usually cover all trades in a particular country or even town, or cover a specific trade or industry in a country. A smaller number concentrate on specific functions in relation to a particular product and/or area; for example, listing importers, or distributors. More information, and examples of local and national general directories, and directories of specific trades, are given in the chapter 2 section 'Sources of Basic Company Details'. The following paragraphs add information on using trade directories for product information purposes.

Selectivity of Compilation

For sourcing purposes, editorial selectivity on grounds of reliability of companies and products is desirable, as well as authentification of details given, and appropriate assignment of product classifications. However, conflicting with that, comprehensiveness can also be desirable for the person looking for a specialist, or locally available product or service, or who prefers to do his or her own quality control. From the variety of types of trade directory in existence, the user is able to choose one to suit each objective. The free or cheap yellow pages and web-based type of product directories tend to cover countries or wider geographical areas, and give unlimited access to participating companies. Street by street local business directories, such as Thomsons, and those based on business telephone directorie,s are both comprehensive and unselective, while those based on automatic inclusion of companies' web sites, self-registration or payment for inclusion, are often just unselective.

A distinguishing feature of the comparatively expensive national trades directories, such as *Kelly's*, *Kompass* or *Key British Enterprises*, is the standard and uniformity of data, quality of indexing, and selectiveness. Selectiveness is partly imposed for reasons of size, quality control and commercial viability of printed and CD-ROM versions. Information from public sources is usually complemented by details obtained directly from businesses. Directories which originated in electronic form can cover more companies, but rarely collect much information from the smaller ones. In the case for ICC's *British Company Directory*, all 1 million plus registered firms are included, at varying levels of detail.

Whereas directories of particular trades may also be compiled with the varying levels of selectivity seen above, a 'buyers' guide' implies the substantial independent information which a buyer would hope for, and which not every supplier would volunteer. The Design Council invites its chosen manufacturers to provide details for a series of buyers' guides, on product areas such as furnishing, and tableware and cookware. Dialog hosts *Buyer's Guide to Micro Software*, described in the database catalogue as providing far more than a basic trade directory:

> 'It provides directory, product, technical and bibliographic information on leading software packages, integrating this information into one succinct composite record. Review information is also included.
>
> The file is highly selective, listing packages rated at least "good" by the technical press, all packages from major software producers – even if negatively reviewed – and packages unique to specific business segments...'

Whether called directories or buyers' guides, there is scope in electronic versions of product selection tools for considerable detail, including possibly multimedia illustrations. Directories of some high volume and complex product lines are now available on the web or CD-ROM, and some even via the large generalist hosts. For example, the *DataPro Information Services* files hosted by Dialog, which are for computer, telecommunications, information systems and related products, are a combined source of product specifications, reviews and software directory.

Access Methods

The access methods used by printed and electronic trade directories reflect the whole range of subject retrieval approaches. All those of any quality use a method of assigned index terms to achieve search precision, while electronic directories usually also offer a free-text approach. Nevertheless, it is rarely possible to specify in a search anything more than a product's broad or precise function. This is a list of the different subject approaches, showing examples of trade directories which use them:

- *Controlled Vocabulary/Assigned Index Terms*
  Alphabetical
    1. Alphabetical classified sequences such as in UK *Yellow Pages*.
    2. Databases indexed by product names from a standardised list or thesaurus, such as ICC's company information databases and IAC's *PROMT*, though most such systems are also searchable by the code equivalent of terms (as below).

  Codes
    1. Databases indexed by standard product codes (usually indexed and searchable by the equivalent standard name also), such as SIC (Standard Industrial Classification, separate UK and US systems), as below, Harmonised Commodity Description and Coding System, and Harmonised Tariff codes, used in TradStat's *UK Importers* database on DataStar.

       Morland PLC
       UK SIC codes – as given in ICC Directory of UK Companies *database*
       15960 Manufacture of beer
       51340 Wholesale of alcoholic and other beverages
       52250 Retail sale of alcoholic and other beverages

       Morland PLC
       US SIC codes – as given in Who Owns Whom *database*
       2082 Malt beverage manufacturers
       2086 Soft drink manufacturers
       5813 Alcoholic drink establishments
       3599 Miscellaneous non-electrical machinery manufacturers

  Systematic, browsable sequences
    1. Non-alphabetical classified arrangements, such as the proprietary classification used in the products sequence of the printed *Kompass* editions, and the NACE or SIC classification systems (described under Industrial Classification Systems in chapter 8) used in many publications and databases where a product/service approach or arrangement is necessary.

- *Natural Language/Free Text*
  In most electronic databases the software allows the user's own terms to matched with all terms in records. This makes for simple and specific subject searching, and in many full-text databases is the only retrieval method available. It is preferrable that a free-text system is complemented by one of the above controlled vocabulary systems, for times when high relevance and low recall is needed.

The UK Business Directory, on the Yahoo! UK & Ireland web site, has alternative free-text and browsable classified sequence approaches. It begins by presenting an empty box labelled 'I need (e.g. a plumber) in (e.g. Oxford)' then presents the first level of classified headings, any of which can be selected to eventually discover relevant services.

Level of Detail

The level of and type of detail about products in buyers' guides, such as *Buyer's Guide to Micro Software* described above, is exceptional. Typical printed and electronic general trades directories give little more information about the product than is revealed by the index term the company's name appears under. This is true of *Kompass*, where whether the company is a manufacturer, distributor or importer of the product is also recorded, and trade marks and names are often reproduced. If a firm is invited to also place an advertisement in the directory, as in the *Yellow Pages*, and commonly in directories of specific trades, then there is scope for more product information. Some directories incorporate both the advantages of the directory, and of the original product literature – the Catalog File of the American *Thomas Register* includes reproductions of selected firms' catalogues:

Thomas Register Catalog File (CD-ROM)

'Pop in one of the seven catalog disks to view over 5,100 company catalogs. Negotiate with the complete company catalog in front of you without wasting time for catalogs to arrive in the mail.' (From Thomas' description of the CD-ROM; the 8 volume printed equivalent has fewer catalogues.)

Such efforts have largely been superceded by the more compact and easily maintained 'package libraries' treated in the section below. Also much more efficient are directories on CD-ROM, and the more recently established web-based services. These may include multimedia product descriptions, and even links to the suppliers' own web sites, as in the *UK Web Directory* (*http://www.ukdirectory.com/*).

Tracing Directories

Because there are so many national, regional, industry-specific and other trade directories, all with different scope, contents, access methods and costs, finding the right one systematically becomes important. As well as guides to business information sources in general, guides to databases, online hosts' own finding tools and so on, specialised bibliographies do exist, some specifically covering trade directories and other directories in general. Just a few examples follow:

Current British Directories. C.A.P. Henderson, revised by S. Murphy. CBD Research, 1993. Not limited to business directories. Also: *Current European Directories*.

> *Trade Directory Information in Journals*, 6th edn. British
> Library Business Information Service, 1986. Covers hun-
> dreds of highly specialised and otherwise hard to trace
> directories, buyers' guides and similar, appearing regu-
> larly or occasionally, in or with trade journals.

Package Libraries

This is the name often given to ready-made alternatives to in-house collections of trade literature. The advantages to subscribers are several and considerable: not only is the difficult task of acquiring and storing a paper
collection removed, but so is the job of indexing, and what is more, the
whole collection is reduced onto microform. Package libraries are not available for all product or service types, only for industries which are large and
have a high volume of sourcing which is dependent on access to the original product literature.

The construction and engineering industries are well provided for; the firm
Barbour Index has for many years provided their construction materials
literature service to architects and others, originally by physically visiting
subscribers to maintain files. Technical Indexes Ltd also provided microform
collections of product and other literature, but today offer Construction Product Library and Engineering Product Library on CD-ROM:

> 'The Construction Product Library provides the solution.
> Original full-text information is included from around
> 5,000 construction manufacturers and suppliers, making
> this the most comprehensive reference source on the mar-
> ket. Regular updates ensure information is accurate and
> current and advanced search software takes you to ex-
> actly what you need at exactly the moment you need it.
> Every three months, new update CD-ROMs are supplied
> to ensure the validity of your information.'(From the TI
> web site at *http://www.techindex.co.uk/*)

Tests and Evaluations

Purchasers and others welcome further testing of products than that carried out to qualify for appropriate national or industry standards. Additional tests and evaluations, of varying degrees of independence and
reliability, exist for a considerable proportion of expensive, mainly consumer
products. They typically assess performance, value for money, and reliability, in relation either to comparable products, or to some meaningful benchmark. Where they exist, can be traced and are sufficiently current, test reports
are obviously valuable both to potential buyers and to market competitors.

In the UK the Consumers' Association is responsible for a large body of
authoritative comparative tests aimed at private buyers which has a high

profile and is easily traceable via the excellent *Which?* cumulative indexes. Consumer Reports is a 60 year old non-profit making American equivalent, whose often free ratings, test results and recommendations are available from Consumer reports Online (*http://www.consumerreports.com/*). Many other bodies, from industry associations to trade journal publishers, carry out tests and evaluations which may be well known in the industry, but are more difficult to trace systematically. Examples include the bench testing of new microcomputers and computer software by computer journal publishers, test drives of cars by motor magazines, and reviews of business information products in relevant periodicals.

Performance Data Compilations

Related to testing is the systematic recording of detailed specifications and performance data for certain devices and components. Data on matters such as operating characteristics and reliability are placed in databanks by competent testing authorities, where it is sometimes made directly available to enquirers for sourcing, design, engineering or manufacturing purposes. A few such databases are sufficiently often needed to be available via generalist online hosts, such as:

> *Plaspec Materials Selection Database* – IFI/Plenum for D&S Data Resources; on Dialog
>
> '... detailed engineering and design data, chemical descriptions, and trade names for over 11,500 grades of plastic materials. Records may contain up to 65 properties and characteristics for each grade. Data ... is provided for thermoset, thermoplastic, and elastomeric materials in more than 60 generic families. References to plastic materials include chemical type; manufacturer name; trade name; price; and electrical, mechanical, optical, physical, processing, and thermal properties.' (From Knight Ridder *Complete Database Catalogue*, 1997.)

New Products Monitoring Services

Because of the significance, already discussed, of new products for both sourcing and competitive purposes, a considerable number of secondary sources and services exist to monitor and report them. These range from the familiar new products or product review sections in journals, through bespoke monitoring services, to databases where evidence from a wide range of sources is available for ad hoc searching. Primary evidence of new or changed products in the market includes of course the products themselves, in exhibitions or shops, but also in printed form as advertisements, press releases, trade literature and so on.

Specialist Monitoring Services

As mentioned under 'Product Pick-Up Services' above, IIS Ltd. also offers a subscription 'product watch service' covering the world's packaged goods industries. They use printed as well as physical evidence of new products, or products newly launched in a particular area, to report back on subscribers' product and geographical areas of interest. IIS's monthly research journal *New Product Development News* gives worldwide coverage of 'Marketing News: product developments, packaging/labelling developments ... ; Launch Reviews: backgrounds on companies/brands, brand status, brand and product strategy, trade reaction ... '

Databases

International New Product Report is itself a new CD-ROM product from IIS, using Lotus Notes software. A major attraction is the depth of data included, including fast-loading colour pictures of the products. This, or the printed equivalent, fortnightly records around 300 worldwide food, drink, cosmetic and household products launches. Alternatively customers can search on the web, search their own CD-ROM copy, or order searches in the related *International New Product Database*. This contains country and manufacturer's names, and product descriptions, including colour pictures, packaging and price information, for tens of thousands of consumer products.

The *IAC New Product Announcements/Plus* database was described in the Dialog Database Catalogue as follows:

> '... provides the complete unedited text of product-related corporate press releases, often well before the news appears in print. There is a focus on product and service introductions, and although all products and services are covered, particular emphasis is placed on high technology and emerging industries. In addition to product announcements, NPA/Plus typically contains key details about new products and technologies, including technical specifications, availability, uses, licensing agreements, distribution channels and prices'.

Services for Specific Industries

IMSworld Product Launches (Dialog database) monitors the introduction of pharmaceutical products around the world, including generic drugs. It is the equivalent of two printed publications, one of which records manufacturer, trade name, product type, dose, price, indications, local market details, and other details of new products; the other records similar information on product line extensions.

IIS currently offer approximately 75 different Case histories and World development briefings, which are studies of the development of particular food and drink products, brands, companies, or markets – such as *Bottled sauces – new usage opportunities wanted, Feb. 1997*. They offer some 25 Launch reviews, detailed analyses of the launch of new food and drink products (two per month) including research into consumer awareness, purchasing and repur-chasing, and interviews with retail buyers to assess trade reaction – e.g. *Persil Power – Lever Brothers, Feb. 1995*.

Technology Monitoring Services

Like most of the subjects with the greatest strategic implications for busi-ness, the future impact of technological developments is very difficult to be precise about. Nevertheless, even if only to reduce uncertainty, there are sources which aim to detect relevant technology, sometimes specifically from overseas; sources dedicated to the analysis of business significance; and others which collate both technology and analyses from diverse primary sources. Investext's *Markintel* online service includes all of the following technology implications analysis series:

> *Decision Resources*
> Reports evaluate the commercial implications of technologies.
>
> *Richard K. Miller & Associates*
> 'Research reports designed to provide an understand-ing of applications for technology, competitive ben-efits and new market opportunities.'
>
> *TechMonitoring – SRI Consulting*
> 'Reports evaluate technology breakthroughs, alliances, new ventures and R&D funding, as well as provide vital data and discussion on 41 technology areas.'
>
> *Teltech Resource Network*
> 'Specialised dossiers provide in-depth, one-year analy-sis of individual technologies, including objective assessment of each technology's current limits, recent developments, market strategies, and future outlook.'
>
> *Theta Reports*
> 'Studies assess the impact of rapidly changing tech-nologies and include forecasts for emerging and established markets, profiles of public and private companies, and analysis of competitors' products.'

BioBusiness, from BIOSIS and currently on DataStar, is an example of a data-base collecting items from any point in the product development spectrum between potentially relevant sciences and a particular industry. It still may not be easy for a strategic decision maker to handle the contents of such a database and draw definite conclusions from it, but it would be far harder to discover and acquire such a wide range of material oneself:

> 'Provides current and retrospective information to business executives, financial analysts, product development and marketing professionals ... about the business applications of biological and bio-medical research.... Approximately 600 technical and business journals, magazines, newsletters, meeting proceedings, patents, and books from all over the world are scanned for relevant articles.'
> (Knight Ridder *Complete Database Catalogue*, 1997.)

The Overseas Technical Information Service (OTIS) is the result of the scientific and technical intelligence work of British embassies in the world's major industrial nations (OTIS's separate existence could not be confirmed at the time of writing); it is assumed to have been incorporated into the TradeUK Export Sales Leads database and service, currently operated for the DTI by Dialog (described in the 'Sources of Market Opportunities' section of the 'Market Information' chapter):

> 'From the regular flow of information on overseas scientific and technological developments and policies reaching Whitehall, OTIS makes available reports, articles, official reviews and surveys which are not easily accessible outside government.... Subscribers to OTIS receive brief summaries of the incoming data relevant to their interests. Fields of interest are selected from the OTIS subject index and may be revised by the subscriber at any time.... Where a subscriber wishes to have more detailed information, a photocopy or loan of the source document held at PERA can normally be provided.... OTISLINE – OTIS summaries are also available on a database at PERA.' (From publicity material.)

Technological news sources can be coveniently monitored using the web-based news aggregator *NewsLinx* (*http://www.newslinx.com*). The site provides 'real-time' headlines from a wide range of web sources.

Patents Documentation

Since patents relate to technology which is by definition in the public domain, at a national if not international level, it is not surprising that they are well documented. In fact complementary official and commercial documentation systems exist in many Western industrialised countries – correctly suggesting that providing the necessary access is not in fact straightforward.

An important selling point of commercial patents databases is their role in satisfying two difficult search needs – both arising from commercial as much as technical motives. One is to trace technology which could be transferred to a required application, regardless of the application it was patented and documented in connection with. The other, more clearly a commercial need, is to deduce companies' or even countries' strategic directions from their patents and patenting behaviour. A further advantage to global trading is that commercial patents databases make it possible to search across the boundaries of official national and even European patents indexes, and disparate national and international subject classification systems.

Searching by technology requires a level of indexing and/or retrieval system not usually present in the official patents documentation, and analysing patenting behaviour requires search software with sophisticated pattern recognition and analysis capabilities. Unless otherwise specified in the examples below, databases normally include the patent 'abstract' rather than the full text; that is the 'front page' where the invention is succinctly described, and all the identifying details are given.

Official Patents Documentation

Individual countries' patents offices typically publish both patents applied for and patents granted, in periodic official gazettes or journals. Granted patents are also made available individually, and their details included in cumulating official indexes, accessible by various names and dates, and a subject classification system. The International Patents Documentation Centre's *INPADOC* documentation, whose databases are available via the European Patent Office, Dialog and other commercial hosts, is the official centralised bibliographic source for the patents of 65 countries. Its records are bibliographic rather than full-text, but for either monitoring or retrospective purposes, allow a single search, rather than searches in many separate and varying national systems.

Although copies of patents are still normally obtained from a patents office or documentation centre, certain databases are now including the full text.The European Patent Office's *European Patents Fulltext*, available on Dialog, contains the full text of European patents since the EPO's opening in 1978, and these patents have been available via the Internet since 1998. The U.S. Patent and Trademark Office also produces a full-text database, *US Patents Fulltext*, in conjunction with the Dialog Corporation. The British Government's patent promotion efforts include support for the Patents Information Network of participating libraries throughout the country. All the designated centres hold at least the official indexes, and, depending on their PIN status and own holdings, some have and supply copies of all UK and many other countries' patents.

Commercial Patents Documentation

The British specialist Derwent Information provides the leading international patents documentation services. Its *World Patents Index* (on Dialog and other hosts), and *Patent Explorer* on the web (*http://www.derwent.com/*) contains over 7 million inventions from over 14 million patents documents issued by 40 different national authorities. Patents on all subjects have been included since 1974, including Japanese unexamined patents (JP-A series) since 1996. Image copies of electrical, mechanical and chemical structure drawings are now also included with the abstract. The complete 'patent family' is given with any record, and a separate *Patents Citation Index* enables the patents whose examiners have cited a given patent, to be traced also.

Sophisticated Search Facilities

Because of the complexity of patents documentation, and the unfamiliarity of technical enquirers with the available solutions, it is common for patents offices and information providers to undertake searching and monitoring on the user's behalf. The European Patents Office, for example, through its Vienna sub-office, offers inventor's and applicant's name searches and monitoring. As noted below, patents' legal status can be monitored, and through the EPO's *WATCH* service, subscribers can be notified of worldwide additions to specified patents families. Derwent's software, especially with the help of their staff, is capable of very sophisticated searching for commercial intelligence purposes. It is possible for instance to chart the change over time of an individual companies' or countries' patenting in a particular technology. Pie charts can also show the breakdown by technologies of companies' or countries' patent ownership or activities.

Examples of Specific Subjects

IFI/Plenum provides *CLAIMS* publications (for example a number of databases via Dialog) for sophisticated retrieval of U.S. patents in the commercially important area of chemical compounds:

> *CLAIMS/Compound Registry*, the electronic equivalent of several printed lists, is the IFI thesaurus of chemical compounds. It enables identification of the unique term name and number for a specific compound, for searching in the *CLAIMS/UNITERM* patent files. *CLAIMS/Reference* enables identification of the subject classifications used in the substantive *CLAIMS* patents databases. Thus it is an alphabetical index to both the official U.S. Patent Classification Codes, and the IFI/Plenum terms. *CLAIMS Citation* (Dialog) enables a searcher to trace the patents whose examiner's reports cited a given patent, thus like a citation index, linking the records on related subjects. The records of the substantive databases such as *CLAIMS/U.S. Patents Abstracts* include references to the 'patent family', that is coverage of the invention in other countries, in most European countries.

IMSworld Patents International (IMS Global Services, Dilaog and DataStar) allows users to monitor the status of the patents associated with competitors' pharmaceutical products, with a view to exploiting the industrial property if and when it becomes available:

> '... provides an analysis of the product patent position of more than 1,000 commercially significant pharmaceutical compounds, either marketed or in active R&D... Each entry contains an evaluated entry for all international patents, estimated patent expiration dates by country ...' (and much more). (Knight Ridder *Complete Database Catalogue*, 1997.)

Infringement Litigation; Changes in Patents' Status

The IFI/Plenum Data Corporation *CLAIMS/Reassignment & Re-examination* database as hosted by Dialog '... provides information on the current status of U.S. patents, including reassignments [transfers to other owners], requests for re-examination [i.e. possible retrospective alteration, or withdrawal of patent status], re-examination results, extensions [i.e. renewals], expirations, reinstatements, adverse decisions on interference actions, disclaimers and dedications'. The Patent Register Service of the European Patent Office provides access to multi-country legal status data, in online or other format.

A smaller number of commercial sources and services specifically monitor successful and unsuccessful infringement lawsuits. One such is Derwent's *Litalert* database on Dialog, which via the Commissioner of the United States Patent and Trademark office collates information on relevant litigation, relating it to specific registered patents and trademarks:

> 'Records include bibliographic information about the patent or trademark; classification titles and codes; names of the plaintiff and defendant; the court in which the action is taking place; the docket number; the filing date of the lawsuit; and the judgement action and date, if applicable.'

Trade Names/Marks Documentation

For various purposes outlined under 'Needs for Information ... ' above, it is necessary to discover which names and marks an organisation owns, and what products or services they use them for; or the more demanding reciprocal of this, to trace the owner of a given name or mark. As in the case of patents, registered names and marks are comprehensively documented, most at a national level, so the main problem is meeting a variety of retrieval needs. However, another problem is that many brand names and marks are not formally registered though they may have the protection of custom and practice.

Here also, the available sources are a combination of official and private sector contributions, more sophisticated needs again being met by commercial publishers adding elaborate search software to officially provided basic data. Commercial publishers also step in to provide the international approach, interested particularly in the high volume usage area of consumer brand names. Since marks and names, especially those relating to brands, are an attribute of products and services, many trade directories record them alongside other company and product information, and sometimes also allow access by trade names.

In parallel to its patents documentation system, the UK's Patents Office publishes notices in official journals of trade marks and names applied for and granted. The standard retrospective retrieval tool is the semi-commercial *UK Trade Names* printed directory from Reed Information. However, a printed directory with access by product type, trade name and company, even if trade marks are reproduced in one of the sequences, is inadequate for some purposes. Electronic databases are necessary if users are to be able to find names which look and especially sound similar to the one they are interested in, and especially to be able to search for a trade mark, that is a graphic device. The following examples illustrate the spectrum of trade names and marks sources, from inclusion in trade directories, to dedicated basic alphabetic matching tools, to much more sophisticated search 'functionality'.

Inclusion in Trade Directories

> *UK Kompass.* Reed Information Services. Printed and CD Plus versions include trade names, and reproductions of marks The *UK Kompass* file hosted by Dialog also incorporates data from the *UK Trade Names* sister publication. *Industrial Trade Names* is the title of one of the separately purchasable CD-ROM 'volume'.

> *Key British Enterprises* 1997. Dun & Bradstreet, 1997. Annual printed version includes a separate sequence in alphabetical trade name order, giving owner's name and contact details, and a reference to the company's main entry.

> *Thomas Register.* Thomas Publishing. Includes trade names and marks data for many companies, which are searchable in electronic versions, such as the CD-ROM and *Thomas Register Online* on Dialog.

Basic Dedicated Sources

> *Brands and Their Companies/International Brands and their Companies.* Gale Research. The former is the Dialog database equivalent of separate print versions. 'Worldwide

directory of over 340,000 consumer brand names and their owners ... Each record provides a brand/trade name, a brief product description, and the company name ... About half of the brand names have been supplied by the companies themselves, providing information not generally available in other sources. Many of the brand names in the file are not registered, but may be protected by common law usage.'

European Directory of Consumer Brands and Their Owners/ International Directory of Consumer Brands and Their Owners/World Directory of Consumer Brands and Their Owners. Euromonitor, 1996. *World Directory* ... on CD-ROM, 1997; includes 'a packshot library of photographic images' and allows searching by region or country and market sectors, and by brand or company name. Claimed as the largest single brand names compilation, covering 86 countries, 8,584 companies and 55,945 brands.

More Sophisticated Data and Search Interfaces

Trademarkscan is a series of country-specific databases, provided by Compu-Mark, Belgium and others, and hosted by Dialog. Files for certain countries also available from Dialog on CD-ROM. On Dialog there are separate files for Austria, Benelux, Canada, Denmark, France, Germany, Ireland, Italy, Liechtenstein, Monaco, Switzerland,UK, USA (separate federal and state files), and for trademarks registered through WIPO for simultaneous protection in a number of separate countries. Indexing includes entries under conventional words for trade names which intentionally corrupt them (e.g. 'Boys' for the name 'Boyz'). The Rotated Trademark Index allows searchers to discover words or parts of words, whether they constitute the whole name or just part of it (e.g. 'Girl' might find 'GIRL', 'Supergurl' and 'Powergirlplus'. Trade mark images are stored in records, though not displayed with conventional retrieval interfaces. Descriptive words are allocated for a simplistic form of retrieval, but with appropriate software, 'design element searching' can be performed, for instance, by sketching the sought design ordesign element with a light pen.

Tracing Trademark Litigation

Derwent's *Litalert* database on Dialog, referred to under 'Patents documentation' above, collates both patents and trademarks litigation information from US courts.

General Purpose Secondary Sources

For the person searching for a range of information, or generally monitoring a particular raw material, manufactured product or service, there is the convenient alternative of one of a number of broad spectrum secondary sources.

The task of collating and disseminating relevant information from a potentially infinite number of primary sources, even if only bibliographic citations or abstracts, is only really feasible for online databases. Several are prominent sources of product information, despite the fact that they may also provide other types of business information. The descriptions, taken from online hosts' catalogues, reveal the scope of major examples:

> *PROMT* – Information Access Company; also via Dialog, DataStar, FT Profile etc. Standing for Predicasts Overviews of Markets and Technology, *PROMT* is a combination of indexed full text and abstracts of a great number of more than 1500 trade journals, and other industry sources. As such, one of its five stated focuses is 'Technology – new products, processes, resources and trends. Free text searches can be made, but a controlled vocabulary allows the specification of precise products, geographical area, and of the type of information sought; including the "event code" E3 for information on products, and E33 on new products'.

> *Business and Industry* – Responsive Database Services; also via major hosts. More recent than *PROMT* though aiming for similar scope and quality of indexing, for which it has already gained a wide usage. For product information purposes, broad or specific SIC code searching is valuable, as is the ability to search by assigned 'concept terms' such as 'Distribution license', 'Franchising', Product development', 'Price trends', 'Product discontinued', and 'Trademarks'; or 'All product and service information'.

Tracing Information Sources on Specific Product Types

Where substantial general guides to business information sources have sufficiently specific subject arrangements or indexes, it is possible to discover sources on specific product areas. Such as in, for instance, the *MacMillan Directory of UK Business Information Sources* (further details in the 'Bibliographical Apparatus' section of the final chapter), where entries are arranged by NACE economic activity nomenclature. *Dialog Product Code Finder* is a 'Search aid database' breaking the barriers of diverse databases and product retrieval methods. It matches the searchers' name for a product line with the product name fields in all the records of all the relevant databases. The search results in a list for each database of the product name and code, and the number of records relating to that product. Any items selected from the list can be selected to be saved and automatically executed as a search in the databases concerned.

6

Country Information

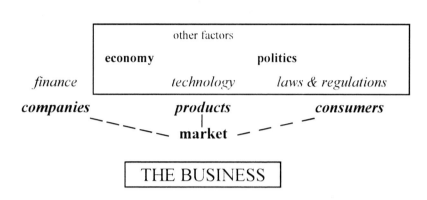

Introduction

The term 'country information' is not used widely to describe this aspect of business information, and by no means satisfactorily describes it. A still inadequate, but slightly more descriptive alternative is 'economic and geo-political information'. What 'country information' attempts to embrace in this book is: matters on a national scale which affect business, other than those in the more immediate external environment. This most obviously includes politics and the economy; but also any other subject not separately identified as a domain. The term is made appropriate by the fact that such information is more often needed in relation to countries other than a company's own, and is almost inevitably country-specific. A business often needs to be briefed on everything about a country which could affect a business venture in it, other than the core 'business information' topics which would be researched in greater depth. A typical list of subjects appears below. Although hard to name and define, country information is a coherent area of many business' information needs, and does coincide with an identifiable range of sources.

Information Needs

The reason is often to identify lucrative yet safe opportunities in the 'emerging markets' of the world, and once involved in such markets, to keep a weather-eye on all aspects of an unfamiliar environment. Although a wide and dedicated 'literature' may exist for each aspect, for most commercial purposes it is simply not appropriate to use it. It may not be appropriate because the information is needed on a foreign and perhaps 'unknown' geographical area, so the standard information sources are not available or accessible. Also the standard information sources on the economy, politics, climate and so on, can be unnecessarily many and detailed for the purpose; furthermore, they are not oriented to the needs of the business decision maker. So when it comes to routine monitoring of the wider environment, or even ad hoc research into the general business conditions in a specific country or region, there is a need for business-oriented secondary sources.

Specific questions involving the remoter areas of the business environment, may well draw upon the normal information sources appropriate to the subject, but even here, a general or specialised business-oriented source may have advantages of point of view, convenience, and accessibility to the business person. If a business is contemplating a significant involvement in a country which is little known to it, information may be simultaneously needed on all of the following aspects:

Political

>Form of government; constitution.
>
>Nature & colour of political regime.
>
>Stability of current regime; future possibilities.
>
>Administrative and decision making system, centres of power and influence.

Economic

>General state of the economy; macro- and microeconomic indicators.
>
>Creditworthiness – balance and liquidity of national accounts; availability of foreign currency.
>
>Economic trends and forecasts – affecting above and consumer standard of living and expenditure.

Business environment

>Laws and regulations and business practices affecting:
>
>>employment, training, payment, working conditions of staff;
>>
>>business premises and equipment;
>>
>>import and export, of people, financial assets, products, components, equipment etc.;
>>
>>foreign owners, employers and employees;
>>
>>taxation of business operations, products, profits etc.;
>>
>>other business operations, including additives, emissions.
>
>Availability and cost of necessary human and energy resources, raw materials and equipment.
>
>Business customs and practices, including entertaining and negociating, financial inducements.

Import, export, distribution and retail systems and patterns.

General environment

Security and other risks to expatriate business people.

Living conditions, including medical, housing, shopping, education and leisure, for expatriates.

Climate, weather, altitude; state of air and water; hazards of disease; flora and fauna.

Physical infrastructure

Availability, reliability and costs of electricity, fuels, telecommunications etc.

Routes, cost and reliability of road, rail and air transport systems.

Relevant geographical and geological factors.

Cultural

Implications for employment, products, marketing etc. of:

language(s);

religions;

customs;

education and training.

Population numbers, locations and socio-economic groups.

Earning, buying, spending and saving patterns.

If the business already has an involvement with a less known country, only a watching brief is required, reporting changes in the topics relevant to the country's involvement. As will be seen, sources exist both to provide basic information on all these factors and to monitor them. Naturally there are also sources which specialise in certain aspects of countries, and some which specialise in either basic data or monitoring.

In relation to the home country the basic information is well enough known or can easily be discovered from specialist sources. Business news sources, and industry-specific sources (the subject of another chapter) can be monitored for changes anywhere in the business environment which may affect any or all business activities. Sources such as market surveys monitor and discuss changes which may affect the market for goods and services, as does the financial and investment press for changes which may affect the City. Certain of the 'less immediate' areas of the environment are complex and important enough to have a body of business-oriented monitoring and interpreting sources dedicated to them. Just as 'technology monitoring' sources were discussed in the 'Product Information' chapter, a section below is dedicated to sources which conveniently interpret the economy for business purposes.

Information Sources

Business-oriented country information sources are divided below into identifiable groups, according to their scope. General purpose reference sources for people doing business in, exporting to, or otherwise visiting foreign countries are obviously also relevant, but not discussed here beyond listing the following:

Doing Business in Eastern Europe. Kogan Page. Series of 8 titles; also Latin America, Germany, China etc.

Doing Business Guide: ... series. PricewaterhouseCoopers

A Guide for Businessmen and Investors: ... series. PricewaterhouseCoopers.

Anglo-American Trade Directory. Kogan Page. Also *Anglo-Spanish Trade Directory.*

CBI European Business Handbook. Kogan Page. Business prospects and conditions in 26 countries.

The Export Handbook. Kogan Page. Guide to exporting, including opportunities, contacts and advice.

Business Africa. Economist Intelligence Unit. Also Asia, China, Eastern Europe, Europe, Latin America, Middle East, Russia.

Export Intelligence Service of overseas trade leads, run for the DTI by the Export Network Group, and an online version of Hints to exporters. Other sources on the Export Network online service provide country-specific exporting guidance.

Hints to Exporters guides to countries. UK Department of Trade and Industry.

Setting up Business in . . . series. UK Department of Trade and Industry.

Europa World Yearbook. Gale, 1998. Standard annual directory of current social, political and economic data for all countries; and direcory of international organisations.

Croner's Europe. Croner. An updated reference source on legal and business developments within the EU; package includes loose-leaf volumes, disk version, bulletins and updated pages, annual pocketbook, and monthly newsletters.

CIA World Factbook. Central Intelligence Agency, US Government, 1997. Also available on CIA web site *(http://www.odci.gov/cia/publications/factbook/index.html).* Entries for all countries.

As shown below, a source like PRS' *Country Report Service* incorporates at least one basic directory of countries series, and one visitors' briefing series.

Country Briefings

A number of different series aim to brief the business person on all the aspects listed above, for many of the countries of the world. The quality of data collection and analysis in the Economist Intelligence Unit's series equals the best available gathered by the governments of certain of the developing countries covered. As is apparent from the examples detailed below, series differ in geographical coverage and in the range and type of information provided. It is common for a background report or profile to be published separately from a more frequently updated survey of economic, political and other indicators. It is now also common to be able to view selected extracts via online or CD-ROM databases, saving high costs and other overheads of subscribing to the printed reports on one or more countries. Most of the established series produce snapshot risk assessments for various aspects of countries (more information under 'Risk Services' section below), which can be checked online comparatively cheaply and conveniently on a regular basis, to be built into insurance calculations and other strategic business decisions.

Economist Intelligence Unit

Specialist gatherer and publisher of business-oriented intelligence on countries of the world. Non-industry specific publications include: *Country Profiles, Country Reports, European Policy Analyst, Licensing and Trading Conditions Abroad, World Outlook, World Trade Report* (regulatory and risk related publications are referred to in the relevant sections below). *Country Profiles* provide the whole range of necessary topics in relation to approximately 180 individual countries, updated approximately every year, while *Country Reports* are the more frequently published updates on the economic, political and other conditions of greatest concern to business. The EIU's publications are distributed directly via their web site and on CD-ROM, and selectively through providers and hosts including FT Profile, Bloomberg, Datastream, Profound, LEXIS-NEXIS, MarkIntel, and the Dialog Corporation. *EIU ViewsWire* is a web-based interface to the data on 195 countries, intended as a 'decision support tool for corporate executives'.

EIU ViewsWire is presented as three 'Country' series. *Country Views* – the latest analysis, which includes monthly Country Updates, and Consensus Forecasts (various authorities' forecasts on currencies, equities and interest rates), and quarterly Country Forecast Summary (extracts from EIU's *Country Forecasts*), Five-year Forecast Table, and Country Risk Summary. *Country Background* – profiles of current conditions organised as Country Fact Sheet, Quarterly Economic Indicators, Trade, Tax and Foreign Exchange Regulations (continuously updated), and Weekly Interest Rates. *Country Alerts* – daily news briefings on events particularly relevant to businesses, including company strategies, economy, finance, industry trends, investment, labour, politics, regulations, trade. *EIU Viewswire* is available direct, via some of the generalist hosts, and certain of the more specialist ones including Reuters Business Briefing and NewsEDGE.

MarketLine International

Similarly structured *CountryLine* reports provide a markets and industries oriented overview of over 100 countries. Sections of each include Executive summary, GDP and interest rates, GDP by industry sector, Employment by industry, Current account, Population by gender, Population by age, Advertising and media, Retailing, etc. Available via FT Profile and DataStar.

Eurofi European Business Reports

'When you want to find your way around Europe . . . health and safety, legislation, commercial law, employment law, taxation, trading in the single market . . .'

Arthur Andersen, EIU and Craighead Publications

These firms jointly provide the subscription-based web site *CountryNet*, to answer business people's social, political, cultural and tax questions about approximately 84 foreign countries (*http://www.countrynet.com*).

Barclays Bank

Barclays' quarterly *Economic Review* includes medium-term assessments of the economic prospects of the UK and elsewhere.

Business Monitor International

Producer of standard format annual Reports on 22 'emerging markets' countries, and frequent region by region newsletters. The former give a political overview, with asessments of future risk, and coverage of legislative and economic issues. The newsletters are aimed at those who need to monitor risk and exposure. *Business Monitor International* is available on FT Profile.

PRS Group, a division of International Business Communications

> The *Country Report Service* database (as hosted by DataStar) comprises country-specific data from a variety of the PRS publications, including *Country Report*, *Executive Report* and *International Country Risk Guide*, which includes extensive statistics. It includes facts, data, background, and commentary on every geopolitical entity in the world, plus the provider's own series of in-depth political and economic forecasts, covering 147 countries. PRS Group's own network of country risk analysts monitor the climate for business, and rate the risks to long range political, economic, and financial outlooks for business, as well as tax laws and changes. The database also includes the U.S. government publications *World Factbook, Background Notes, Foreign Economic Trends* (extracted from Dialog Complete Database Catalogue).

World of Information

> Wide-ranging basic briefing appropriate for visiting or otherwise involved business people. For over 200 countries, similarly structured reports include: Review (recent social, political and economic events), Key facts (government, languages, currency), Key indicators (population, economy, trade), Country profile (political system, media, industrial production), Business guide (includes travel and communications infrastructure, visa requirements), Business directory (hotels, business advice facilities). Available as the printed directory *The World Business and Economic Review*, and as the *World of Information* database on FT Profile.

UK Department of Trade and Industry

> The DTI draws on its considerable intelligence on countries' markets, trade, economy and other relevant conditions, to publish a low-priced *Country Profiles* series.

BBC Worldwide Monitoring

> *International Reports* contain the political and economic news gleaned by the BBC from 3,000 TV, radio, news agency and press sources on 140 countries, in 70 languages. Subscriptions can be for specific countries, re-

gions or topics; the reports can be emailed or faxed as
created, or batched.

US Federal Document Clearinghouse

> *World Sources Online* is a news service on FT Profile con-
> sisting of full-text articles on emerging markets and de-
> veloping countries, selected from a variety of English
> language publications.

Country Risk Services; Monitoring Services

Whereas the emphasis of some providers and their publications is on producing broad and detailed reports, certain others style themselves as monitoring services, or even specifically as country risk services. Typical details
of both types of source follow the example of a risk analysis, extracted from
the *Country Report Service* database, provided for DataStar by the PRS Group:

Text
1 OF 1.
KENYA UPDATE
June 1, 1998

MOST LIKELY REGIMES AND THEIR PROBABILITIES
18-Month: Moi 75%
Five-Year: *Moi/Kanu 60%

FORECASTS OF RISK TO INTERNATIONAL BUSINESS

	Financial Transfer	Direct Investment	Export Market
Turmoil			
18-Month: High	B-	B+	B-
Five-Year: High	C	B-	C+

* Indicates forecast of a new regime.

Financial Times East European 'newsletters'

> *Financial Times Business Reports: Business/Finance* (via FT
> Profile) includes the *FT*'s East European series of news-
> letters, providing news and commentary on political and
> economic developments throughout that region. There
> is analysis of political and economic restructuring, in-
> cluding financial services, banking, debt and financial
> regulation, and their implications for trade in the West.

Economist Intelligence Unit's 'newsletters'

> In addition to the basic country data compilations, the
> EIU publishes a number of newsletters containing just

the latest news and analysis of developments which might concern a foreign business or investor. *Crossborder Monitor* is international in scope, while *Business Asia, Business China* and others cover regions, and titles such as *Business Russia* cover individual countries. All these newsletters are combined in databases such as *EIU: Business Newsletters*, on Dialog.

Economist Intelligence Unit's Country Risk and Forecasting Services

The EIU's *Country Risk Service* analyses the short and medium term economic creditworthiness of at least 90 countries. Each report includes an analysis of local financial markets, credit risk ratings, economic growth and financial indicators, international financial flows, pointers for lenders and investors, and a two-year projection of external finances. Their *Country Forecasts* give a medium term outlook on economic, political, and business trends in around 58 countries. Each country forecast gives information on environmental issues, exchange controls, external debt, foreign investment, foreign trade and payments, GDP growth, industrial policy, infrastructure, interest and exchange rates, political scene, tax regimes, ten year growth, and wages and prices. Both of these services are also available as a database, such as *EIU: Country Risk and Forecasts*, from Dialog (from which this information is taken).

Control Risks Group, a division of Control Risks Information Services

The company 'analyses risk to foreign business from political change and instability, and assesses the impact of crime and political violence upon all forms of international operations, ranging from large investment projects to the travel plans of an individual executive'. The work of analysts in London and advisers around the world results in:

Security Forecast – daily updated online assessment of relevant issues in over 70 countries;

Country Risk Service – printed briefing equivalent of the above, issued monthly;

Travel Security Guide – continuously updated online assessment, with advice, for travellers;

Special Reports – commissioned as required by clients, according to particular needs.

Internet Securities (http://www.securities.co.uk/)

> Continually updated news, company, financial and other
> information, branded as the *ISI Emerging Markets* series
> of databases, available via dial-up or web. Covers spe-
> cific Eastern and Central European countries, the Baltic
> States, eight Latin American countries, China and In-
> dia. Includes macroeconomic data, legal databases and
> privatisation information, supplied by major 'country
> information' providers and translated from the local
> general and business press. '*ISI Emerging Markets* deliv-
> ers news, company and financial data direct from emerg-
> ing markets to thousands of emerging markets specialists
> around the world, providing them with the local intelli-
> gence they need for global advantage'.

Dun & Bradstreet

> The monthly *International Risk and Payment Review* is also
> available as an online database or disk of the same name,
> and as individual country reports. This complements
> D&B's company risk services by indicating stability and
> trading conditions at a national level in more than 120
> markets worldwide. For each country there is informa-
> tion on typical payment terms, the payment transfer situ-
> ation, export and credit insurance, plus an assessment
> of overall risk to trading and investment, in the form of
> a score. Socio-political and economic issues are also con-
> sidered, in each of the major regions of the world.

Specialised Information on Countries

The chapter covering news sources refers to various self-help ways of watching developments on a broad front in foreign countries. Included there, and
very relevant here, is monitoring the broadcast media via the *BBC Summary
of World Broadcasts* (via FT Profile, DataStar, or direct in printed form), and
monitoring governments from their press releases, such as via the UK Central Office of Information's faxed, mailed or electronic daily index and text
delivery service. The examples below are of other sources which provide a
particular view of a country's business environment, rather than a comprehensive survey. Legislation and regulation affecting business and investment abroad has significant and wide-ranging implications, and is constantly
evolving; a number of information providers monitor it via an imaginative
range of primary sources. FT Profile's *EU Policy and Legislation* 'Data collection' allows relevant information to be simultaneously retrieved from 6 otherwise separate databases.

Legislative and Regulatory Information

Business Monitor

> The London firm collects commentary and analysis from 150 of the world's leading banks, tax advisors, corporate financiers, law firms, accountants and others on legislative, regulatory, and business issues. Much is otherwise unpublished information on the legislative and regulatory framework affecting business and investment in Europe, Asia, Africa and offshore centres. The *Business Monitor* database is available via DataStar and FT Profile.

Economist Intelligence Unit

> The product *Worldwide Regulatory Update* is either available separately or included in some of the EIU databases available via hosts – such as Dialog. The EIU provides Tax Regulations for the financial information provider Bloomberg, quarterly briefings on issues affecting tax policies in 41 countries, including recently approved and proposed changes.

DRT Europe Services

> *DRT European Business* reports, available on DataStar, comprises reports provided by DRT Europe Services on current business, industry, and legislation within the European Union, and country-specific information on all aspects of business development and expansion in Eastern Europe. The continually updated reports include data taken from EU official publications, newspapers, journals, legislative and policy documents, and unpublished sources within the EU and Eastern European countries.

Consultancy Europe Associates Ltd.

> Their *Spicers Centre for Europe* is a well indexed file of abstracts relating to EU legislation at its different stages. Data is taken from the Official Journal, and entries refer to the full text of the legislation in the official *CELEX* database. Spicers, together with *CELEX*, Europe Information Service's *European Report* newsletter, and the DTI's *Spearhead* database of single market information, are all relevant to doing business in the EU, and can be separately accessed as databases on FT Profile.

World Bank

> The World Bank's periodic print and CD-ROM *World Development Indicators* presents life in nearly 50 developing countries primarily through statistics – more than 80 tables with some 600 indicators, complemented by commentaries.

Economic Information

If 'country information' is a distillation for business people of the infinity of factors in a country which could affect them, then economic indicators are the appropriately concise way of representing an economy. As the examples showed, many of the broad scope country briefing and risk services incorporate economic indicators for just that purpose. The EIU derives from its other products *Economic Overviews* – analyses of the economic conditions in 81 countries, in the context of the political and wider landscape, especially to complement the financial information available on Bloomberg. Some secondary sources specialise in the collection and dissemination of economic indicators, for the person who needs to research or monitor the home country's, or even a foreign economy in greater depth.

Macroeconomic Indicators

Macroeconomic indicators are statistics which concisely reveal the state of an economy as a whole. They are supposedly meaningful measures of the economy, calculated in a standard and accurate way, and therefore comparable over time and between one country and another. The statistics which have gained this status are issued by governments themselves, but also by international authorities such as the IMF, World Bank and OECD. Just as company financial performance ratios, in practice a particular statistic has a role in describing a particular aspect of the entity at a particular point in time, and the best picture is obtained from a number of complementary measures. For example, the 'UK economy at a glance' in the *Sunday Times* Business section, which lists current, previous month's and year-to-date figures under the headings Sales and Output, Prices and Pay, Unemployment, and Government Finances Balance of Payments, shows a typical range of the familiar macroeconomic indicators used to give a snapshot of the British economy.

Microeconomic Indicators; Surveys of Business Activity

Many other statistics, either regularly or rarely quoted, are valuable as measures of specific aspects of the economy but are too specific to be taken as a reliable indicator of the whole. Such statistics emerge from a more diverse range of non-official bodies, on a diverse range of subjects. Sometimes microeconomic indicators attract brief attention in the national news media, especially if newly released by an authoritative body, and coinciding with topical public concerns. On these occasions a headline statistic has usually been extracted from a regular survey of a particular aspect of industry activity, from a particular viewpoint. The *Sunday Times* business supplement's 'Indicator of the week' is an example, others include headline pay rises from the reports of Incomes Data Services or the Reward Group, company start-ups or failures calculated by business information providers such as Dun & Bradstreet, consumption and sales data from market researchers like Mintel. Other bodies with specialist or inside knowledge of factors which indicate or will affect the future economy, include large retailers, employers organisations, and those who make purchasing decisions in manufacturing or service sectors. The Confederation of British Industry has, via its wide national membership, privileged knowledge of the activities and even the mood of 'UK PLC'. As such it is a producer of authoritative, high profile surveys on a considerable range of activities and sectors, including those detailed below (some of which are produced jointly with other bodies). Examples of surveys follow, by type of organisation, web addresses are included, from which further information and often free data can be obtained:

Industry Organisations
CBI (*http://www.cbi.org.uk/cbi/htdocs/standard/trend_surveys/*)

CBI Industrial Trends Survey

> Quarterly (more detailed) and monthly analysis of trends and expectations of UK manufacturers; the best known and most cited CBI survey, which includes questions on employment, investment and export orders.

Distributive Trades Survey

> Quarterly and monthly; includes information on volume of sales, orders placed, stocks, employment, business confidence and investment.

Financial Services Survey

> Quarterly; trends revealed by the responses of a large proportion of the UK financial services industry.

Business Strategies Regional Trends Survey

> Quarterly; a regional approach to the manufacturing data in Industrial Trends Survey.

Small & Medium Enterprise (SME) Trends Report
> Quarterly; drawn from the quarterly Industrial Trends Survey

Economic Situation Report

> Eight per year – analysis of data from other CBI surveys and official statistics to produce a snap-shot of UK and international macroeconomics.

Property Trends Survey

> Biannual; claims to be a unique source of short and long-term private sector property requirement trends.

Major Companies

John Lewis Weekly Retail Sales Report

> John Lewis Partnership, mixed retails stores. Figures for the following week appear in the weekly periodical for partners *The Gazette*; available on subscription to the outside subscribers by telephoning 0171 592 5243.

DHL Asia-Pacific Quarterly Export Indicator

> Survey carried out by Gallup for DHL Worldwide Express, international couriers to measure the level of business confidence in 15 (named) Asia-Pacific countries. Over 75 senior executives from top manufacturing export companies in each market are interviewed and asked about their expectations for export orders over the next 12 months, and over the next five years. Reports are published periodically in *DHL News* (*http://www.dhl.com/info/news/index.htm*). Excerpt:
>
> EXPECTATIONS FOR EXPORT ORDERS – SHORT TERM (12 MONTHS)
>
> > 10 of the 15 countries surveyed were more optimistic about export orders over the next 12 months than one year ago. More than half indicated that they had 'Good' or 'Excellent' expectations.
>
> EXPECTATIONS FOR EXPORT ORDERS – LONG TERM (FIVE YEARS)
>
> > The majority of respondents (11 of the 15 markets) were more optimistic about export orders over the next five years than over the next 12 months. More than half indicated that they had 'Good' or 'Excellent' expectations.

3i's Enterprise Barometer

> For ten years the venture capital firm 3i (formerly Investors In Industry) has sought the views of the companies it invest in, on a variety of management and business/economic climate issues. Summarised data is freely available on the web site *http://www.3i.co.uk/market.htm*.

Business information publishers

UK Business Expectations
> *http://www.dunandbrad.co.uk/FailExp/failexp.htm*
> Based on a quarterly questionnaire sent to managing directors by Dun & Bradstreet; typically responses from over 1,400 managing directors in all regions and sectors of British business. The same survey model is applied in over 15 countries. Results, detailing business failures and expectations, are freely available on the web site.

Purchasing managers

Report on Business and Report on Services
 http://www.kellys.co.uk/Kellys/KP1.htm
 Monthly measure of increase or decrease in orders, employment etc.,
 by the Chartered Institute of Purchasing and Supply.

Management consultants

Trendsetter Barometers series

 http://www.pwcglobal.com/extweb/ncovrvw.nsf/docidserv/
 Reports from PricewaterhouseCoopers on topical issues, based on surveys of a panel of leading US companies; available on the PwC's web site:

> 'Each quarter, PricewaterhouseCooper's Trendsetter Ba-
> rometer interviews more than 400 CEOs of companies
> identified in the media as the fastest-growing U.S. busi-
> nesses over the last five years. The surveyed companies
> range in size from approximately $1 million to $50 mil-
> lion in revenues.'

Examples of titles:

8/13/98 – Citing Concerns About Future Benefits, Growth Company
   CEOs Favor Refinancing Social Security Before Any New Tax Cuts

8/4/98 – More Fast Growth Companies Forsake BankBorrowing As
   Margins Continue To Improve But High Tech Firms Go Their
   Own Way

6/18/98 – Optimism And Margins Among Fast-Growth Firms At A
   Record High; Barriers To Growth Retreating

Forecasts

Finding out about the past or present state of the economy is usually only a
means to predict the future. Not surprisingly then, experts' forecasts are a
popular direct source of that valuable commodity. Individuals and organisations with the necessary information resources, expertise, computer models and proven success rate commonly sell their updated forecasts for
business and other strategic purposes. All the following are well-known
publishers of economic forecasts; their headline predictions also make the
national news from time to time:

* HM Treasury
* Oxford Economic Forecasting
* Hoare Govett
* Barclays Bank (in *Barclay's Bank Economic Review*)
* Henley Centre for Forecasting
* London Business School, Centre for Economic Forecasting

- National Institute of Economic and Social Research
  (in *National Institute Economic Review*)
- OECD (in *OECD Economic Outlook*)
- Economist Intelligence Unit's Eastern Europe and Former Soviet Union Forecasting Service

A less obvious source for many countries is the US government's *Foreign Economic Trends,* sometimes incorporated in commercial information providers' online country reports services. *FETs* are reports prepared by U.S. embassies abroad to describe foreign country economic and commercial trends and trade and investment climates.

A number of services aid the tracing and comparison of required economic (and sometimes other) forecasts. These include *Forecasts of the UK Economy: Comparisons of Independent Forecasts* published monthly by the British government's Treasury and freely available on their web site (*http://www.hm-treasury.gov.uk/pub/html/forc/comp/f981014.pdf*) and Gower Publishing's *World Index to Economic Forecasts*. Information Access Company's *IAC Forecasts* is a highly searchable database of forecasts on all subjects, gathered from predictable and less predictable sources.

Economics Secondary Sources

Although indicators succinctly inform businesses about countries' economies, there are advantages in obtaining them from sources which gather many together, perhaps with related information. A number of databases are well known and used in business information because they do gather economic data from many primary sources, on all countries and regions. For example:

WEFA
> *http://www.wefa.com/index.html*
> A leading economic information and consulting firm, now merged with Chase Econometrics, and part of the Primark Group. Collects data from around the globe, monitoring developments in over 152 countries and forecasts 94 economies in depth. WEFA's global, national, regional, subregional and industry forecasts, and other data are delivered via a range of databases.

Quest Economics
> (Janet Matthews Information Services; online direct, CD, FT Profile & DataStar)
> A collection of country or industry-specific macroeconomic research, forecasts and analysis, from leading banks and financial and economic research institutions. Basic data is complemented by weekly bulletins, monthly or quarterly research reports, and economic, political and investment risk profiles from the contributing institutions. There are in-depth profiles on 240 countries, and regularly updated forecasts for 80

countries. The publisher also monitors the international press daily for economics news and editorial matter.

Statistical Data Locators

http://www.ntu.edu.sg/library/statdata.htm

This has been mentioned elsewhere in the present work as both a source of and gateway to diverse statistical series on most countries – especially strong on Singapore and the Far East. These include many macro- and microeconomic indicators, for example:

Hong Kong

Statistical Resources HK

Hong Kong Statistics (Census and Statistics Department, Hong Kong)

It comprises three sections: A. Hong Kong in Figures; B. Frequently Asked Statistics provides time-series data for selected statistics; C. Press Releases on Statistical Data provides updated figures with analysis and commentary for selected statistics.

Hong Kong Trade Statistics (HKTDC)
Monetary & Banking Statistics (HKMA)
Country Risk Report (PERC)
Major Economic Indicators (PERC)
Fact Sheet (CIA)

Economic Trends

The Office of National Statistics' monthly printed *Economic Trends* is an accessible source of the figures and commentary for indicators appearing in a wide range of UK official sources. The regular Economic Update feature is an overview of the most topical economic statistics and forecasts.

Handbook of International Economic Statistics

U.S. Govt., 1997, at *http://www.odci.gov/cia/publications/hies97/toc.htm*

New Cronos and *REGIO*

Eurostat databases available through the European Commission, comprising time series of economic and related data from various providers, including in the areas of general statistics (the most important economic indicators for member states, and significant others), and macroeconomic indicators for developing countries (105,000 series covering demographics, social factors, national accounts etc.).

World Economic Factbook, 1997/8

Euromonitor directory which provides economic and wider profiles of 207 countries. There is detailed statistical coverage for 33 indicators, with three-year time series and league tables. Coverage of profiles is from birth and death rates, GDP and inflation, to adult literacy, tourism receipts – 'an immediate guide to the economic health of a nation'. For each country, the statistics are complemented by 13 point written analyses.

World Marketing Forecasts

Euromonitor, 1997 (CD-ROM), is a compilation of social, demographic and economic forecasts, as forecasts of sizes of markets for specific products and services.

World Competitiveness Yearbook

This International Thomson publication is compiled by the International Institute for Management Development in Lausanne. Each of 46 countries is measured by 224 relevant criteria, concerning domestic economy, internationalisation, government, finance, infrastructure, management, science and technology, and people. Data are presented by country, and countries are also ranked under many of the indicators.

Japan News and Retrieval/Nikkei Economic Electronic Databank System

This Nikkei online business information host includes the *Nikkei Economic File* of 18,000 series economic indicators on Japanese GNP, public finance, trade, balance of payments etc. The Nikkei Macro Model uses 50 equations to make quarterly forecasts of the economy.

Primark Decision Economics (PDE)

Interpretation of global economic and financial market events for decision makers. A large number of publications, represented by their sample list web services (*http://www.pde.primark.com/*):

> *The Daily Comment*
>
> *Allen Sinai's Weekly Executive Summary of the Financial Markets*
>
> *Bulletin Series*
>
> *Comments on Current Economic Indicators*
>
> *Prospects*
>
> *U.S. Economic Forecast*

Subscribers Only

> *The Daily Comment (Every Weekday)*
>
> *Allen Sinai's Executive Summary of the Financial Markets*
>
> *Bulletin Series*
>
> *Comments on Current U.S. Economic Indicators*
>
> *Comments on World Economic Indicators*
>
> *Comments on World Economic Events*
>
> *Economic Studies and Economic Outlooks*
>
> *Forecast Calendars*
>
> *Global Economic Developments in Review*
>
> *Prospects*
>
> *U.S. Economic Forecast*

7

Business News Sources;
Industry Sources

Introduction

The Context

News Sources

Changes

companies products consumers city economy etc. EXTERNAL
ENVIRONMENT

Information

industry x   industry y   industry z

Industry Sources

This chapter deals with two categories of business information which, unlike all the others, report not on a particular 'domain', but on the external
environment as a whole. The large and prominent group of 'business news
sources' trawls the environment for significant changes, while the smaller
group of industry sources trawls for business information of relevance to
particular industries. These two categories of business information have
little else in common and will be treated separately here. It is difficult to
know which of these groups to allocate the minority of sources which report only *news* for a particular *industry*; however, the following definitions
clarify the way the terms are used in this chapter:

Definitions

Business News Sources
Sources reporting or recording commercially significant news on the
external environment.

Industry Sources
Sources reporting or recording information on the external environment which is of commercial significance to a particular industry.

Part 1: Business News Sources

The Importance of News to Business

A word of explanation is desirable – perhaps only as a reminder of the obvious relationship between business and news. Business' need to know what is current, new, what has changed, stems from the crucial relationship between an enterprise and the external factors which affect it and which it must affect. If, as asserted in the first chapter, information is the means of sensing these factors, it follows that the sooner a new or altered circumstance is detected, the sooner strategy can be adjusted to take advantage of it. In most situations the advantage is one of efficiency – preparation for a new regulation, acting on the news of a weather or travel problem, buying something while it is available, or marketing something while a fad for it lasts.

But in most cases there is also a direct competitive reason to have the latest knowledge – perhaps to snap up a buying/selling opportunity before the competition does, to establish a promotion idea or a product ahead of others, or to be the first to take advantage of a technical development to improve production efficiency.

Problems of News Information

Just as business information as a whole is information selected from everything known about the infinity of external factors, so business news is at least as diverse and unpredictable in terms of subject and medium. This feature of news presents great management challenges to suppliers and users, steering between the horrors of too much of too little relevance, and missing information through filtering. Further problems relate to the ephemeral nature of news, where potentially valuable information appears in diverse, often informal formats, sometimes not committed to print, not disseminated widely, or not thereafter systematically traceable. Added to which is the notorious factual unreliability of news, where the penalty for immediacy is the lack of corroboration and the testing of time.

Despite all the problems of acquisition management and use of such a welter of dubious facts – or more likely because of these problems, business people find news vital, a fruitful area for competitive advantage. Armed with their own knowledge, experience and scepticism, business people willingly wade into the news morass, feeling more confident to have information than not to have it, because it reduces the risks of decision making. They know also that among the millions of words, some topics will get attention never to be repeated in any other source.

Business' burning desire for the news, both at the time of creation and retrospectively, and the difficulties in exploiting it, explains the current high profile of business news sources and services. Huge investments of space and time in periodicals and press cuttings collections and circulation are giving way to the use of commercially produced full text databases, and systems selectively channelling news from journalist to user's desktop. If competitive advantage goes to the person who manages the unmanageable, then controlling news information is a strong motivation for commercial 'aggregators' and software providers. The self-defeating result could be that business people shift their attention to another information problem-area, where there is still scope for competitive advantage.

Types of Business News Source

As in the chapters covering source types which relate to specific environmental domains, the following sections will address the primary and secondary sources which a business person might use. The role and types of documentary news sources can be represented as follows:

companies products consumers city economy etc.	EXTERNAL ENVIRONMENT
press releases electronic journals & newsgroups newswires newspapers broadcasts newsletters trade press etc.	PRIMARY NEWS SOURCES
indexes databases redistribution services	SECONDARY BUSINESS NEWS SOURCES

As in other areas of business information, primary sources may be used directly, because of the level of specialisation, detail and currency they offer. Alternatively, secondary sources offer convenient, selective control over the complex primary 'literature'. However, unlike most other areas of business information, few of the primary news information types are identifiably about business or for business, leaving vital value-adding potential for secondary sources – as implied by the diagram above. The following sections will consider the sources under these headings:

How the Relevant News Arises

'News' can be taken to be new knowledge which is anomalous or otherwise has potential repercussions for a recipient. As such it is information on new occurences, and updates on existing ones. News of potential interest to business comes into being in one of a number of ways:

> First dissemination of new knowledge, in sources which make it identifiable as such – e.g. informal and formal news organs.

Information from routine reporting sources selected for presentation in news organs – for example, anomalous financial market figures, company accounts figures, or research findings.

Events observed or investigated, and reported as news if considered significant – for example by journalists through attending events, doing interviews or other research.

It is apparent that news is 'in the eye of the beholder', and methods exist both at the level of ordinary individual business information sources and at the level of business information services to identify what is anomalous or otherwise significant. Nevertheless, the following sections deal only with known and dedicated sources of news.

Primary News Sources

News of potential relevance to a few businesses or many is disseminated through an ever-widening range of media, constituting millions of serial titles. All physical media are involved, and types of news sources range from the specialised and limited reach to the more general and mass audience; and from the raw, wholesale news to polished end products:

> *Specialised scope and/or circulation*
> Press releases
> House journals; organisations' official documents and web sites
> Local newspapers and broadcasts
> Trade journals
> Industry newsletters

> *Broader scope and/or circulation*
> National general newspapers
> Financial/business newspapers
> Weekly/monthly periodicals
> Broadcasts
> National, international and business oriented news agencies

At least some of these primary source types are exploited by most businesses because they can or must do their own monitoring of the topics central to their interests. Thus they monitor a limited range of subjects in the limited range of sources of known high relevance – the trade journal, the national and local newspapers, the suppliers', buyers' and competitors' publications. The only practicable way to monitor the many more peripheral subjects, and the many other sources which less predictably include relevant material, is to use secondary sources. Some of these categories of primary source need more explanation than others.

Press Releases

Larger businesses, government departments and agencies, trade associations and many other types of organisation issue new information as a formal press release, either when they believe it to be of interest to the news media, or they would like it to be. Thus businesses tend to do so when there is something favourable to report, or to emphasise the positive element in another recent release of information. Although press releases are offers of material to journalists, others obtaining them may benefit from timeliness as well as information which does not go on to be formally published. It is often possible to be put on a mailing list for a relevant organisation's releases, and the same information can usually be found on their web site. The many and important releases of governments are more conveniently obtained. *US Newswire* is the Dialog equivalent of press releases distributed by *US Newswire* for the US federal government and other national level bodies. It has long been possible to subscribe to the Central Office of Information's consolidated list of UK Government press releases, and now the releases themselves are available freely on the Central Office of Informations site (*http://www.nds.coi.gov.uk*), where the list with links to the full text on the issuers sites is are updated several times daily. A random sample of titles follows, showing obvious business information potential:

> Department of the Environment, Transport and the Regions
>
> 22-10-98 GOVERNMENT RESPONDS TO ROYAL COMMISSION REPORT
>
> 22-10-98 MANAGING ENERGY SAVES – REPORT THE SAVINGS – MEACHER
>
> 22-10-98 UPDATING & REVISING THE INDEX OF LOCAL DEPRIVATION
>
> 22-10-98 IMPLEMENTING NEW POLLUTION PREVENTION
>
> Countryside Commission
>
> 22-10-98 MOTORISTS SHOULD REPAIR DAMAGE DONE BY EMISSIONS

FT Profile hosts the past and present UK government press releases, dividing them into three separate *Hermes files*, according to currency. *Today's Hermes* begins a working day empty; incoming releases are added at four points during a working day. As stated in FT Profile's catalogue:

> 'UK government press releases are of interest to a wide
> range of customers – including the legal community, the
> media, accountants and the financial services sector . . .
> for all those with a need to keep up to date with the
> details of UK government policies and the plans for their
> implementation.'

House Journals; Organisations' Official Documents and Web Sites

Many large and prominent companies and other organisations freely distribute new and mainly advantageous information about themselves, in the form of an attractive periodical. Some of the information is similar nature to that in press releases, though articles usually provide much more detail, and much of the information is not truly novel. News, including illustrations, on a company's personnel, plant, products, performance and strategy may be found, which when enhanced by 'reading between the lines' may be unique to this source. Dissemination of information by business and other organisations, including of news, is being greatly increased by the use of web sites. Web directories may be necessary to find a site, but once found the software can be used to 'bookmark' it, or to alert the user to an update of a web page. Although business news and other secondary business sources systematically cover press releases, it is much harder for them to identify and package news from companies' own documents and web sites. The *Standard and Poor's Daily News* database (the Dialog equivalent of *Standard and Poor's Corporation Records, Daily News* section) cumulates a great variety of information from the official releases of PLCs.

Local Newspapers and Broadcasts

Local newspapers in particular are used to disseminate and record commercial and official announcements. Businesses are particularly interested in planning applications, and advertisements. Although rarely searchable in electronic full-text, and rarely indexed, they are more systematic sources of information than broadcasts in that print stores information for use and reuse as required. Most businesses do formally or informally monitor their local news media, though as detailed in the 'Advertising and Media Monitoring' section of the 'Market Information' chapter, intermediaries can be paid to undertake the task. The business news secondary sources cannot be relied upon for anything but highly selective coverage of local news media.

Trade Journals

Unlike most of the other news media which businesses might monitor, trade journals are a concentrated and obvious source of information on developments in a particular industry. Since a single weekly or monthly title may for many managers be the main means of scanning the external environment, it is fortunate that many publications also trawl more diverse sources for material relevant to readers. *The Grocer* and *Construction News* are typical and comparatively large circulation weeklies, which the trade uses both to assess itself and to inform itself of environmental changes it may need to act upon. An example of potentially valuable market, company and other information follows, from *The Bookseller*, published weekly for the book trade by Whitaker.

Bookseller headlines for the issue of 23rd October 1998 (from the web site *http://www.thebookseller.com/*)

> Cassell fortifies defences
>
> Sixth year of growth for RH
>
> Marginal growth for books'
>
> Premier Direct beats expectations
>
> Golden Books fails interest payments

Heads roll at Daisy & Tom

Metro rescues Richard Cohen

Independent sells Delia at £5.99

Global Site for HC

E-commerce and the bookshop

The role of the trade press is very much one of updating all levels of practitioner in a trade or industry, and allowing them to keep an eye on partners and competitors – what amounts to communication in an industry. As such, their content typically includes short editorials and reports on developments concerning companies, products, markets, and personalities in the industry; and matters in the less immediate environments, such as laws and regulations, technical advances. They are an effective dissemination channel for public and private sector industry organisations, including trade associations and research associations. There may be systematic coverage of new products, and of meetings and training opportunities, and of course advertisements for jobs, products and services. Their revenue depends on the indispensability of their current awareness service and very much also on advertising the services and products consumed by the industry. Nevertheless, exploiting them directly is not simple; they contain a diversity of types of material of value, much of it appearing insubstantial, relating both to the industry and to the environments which affect it. Trade journals are rarely indexed, so this information is only systematically accessible via news and other business databases. Some of it is picked up by secondary sources covering particular business information domains, such as the company, market, or product news sources, which are discussed in other chapters.

Industry Newsletters

Often referred to simply as 'newsletters', these differ from trade journals in that they analyse an industry and matters which affect it in a much more 'scientific' way. They usually cover more specialised industry areas, and are aimed at strategic decision makers in the industry, and those outside it such as investment analysts and strategic consultants. Newsletters cannot attract the volume of advertising of a trade journal, and so are much more expensive. In many industries, one or more newsletter has the status of an important source of research and expert analysis on the industry and its environment. Industry newsletters are used to track strategic and competitive developments, as well as analyse the significance of new technologies, industry trends, government regulations, international trade opportunities, and so on. Typical titles are:

Aerospace Daily

Space Exploration Technology

Toxic Chemicals Litigation Reporter

Semiconductor Industry & Business Survey

International Coal Report

Product Safety Letter

European Media Business & Finance

Ice Cream Reporter

Multimedia Business Analyst (fortnightly; one of circa 42 industry newsletters from Financial Times Information)

National General Newspapers

Taken as a group, newspapers still have no equal for the communication of new and soft information on unlimited subjects. What they lack in speed and mode of delivery is made up for in exhaustiveness and specificity in treatment of topics, their wide circulation and public influence. For a business person scanning the less direct environments, they are a necessary source of unexpected, unpredictable facts, and an unmatched source of dubio-facts, rumour and speculation. It is useful even to know what serious or frivolous matters are being discussed currently, and what images the popular media are presenting and reflecting. A business person interested in a foreign country can usually identify one or more newspapers as a convenient way of remotely monitoring the business, economy, government and society. Broadsheets are valuable for the quantity and quality of their reporting and analysis, several dedicating up to 30% of available space to business pages, and substantial business supplements in the Sunday papers. Tabloids at least reveal popular tastes and preoccupations, the current image of companies, people and products, and cannot be ignored as business information sources.

Whether on paper or web sites, newspapers' print medium gives them a greater capacity than the broadcast media, and greater flexibility of use, both for current and retrospective purposes. Newspapers' availability in electronic form has greatly increased their value for systematic monitoring and searching for information on specific topics. While free web sites, such as the *Electronic Telegraph* version of the *Daily Telegraph* are proving very popular for current awareness, systematic and retrospective searching is usually best carried out on the full versions available from online hosts soon after publication. Here the current issue or a specified run of a single newspaper or specified group can searched, using sophisticated retrieval and output software. FT Profile is a specialist in news media, currently hosting 'almost all UK national newspapers' in full text, searchable individually or in country groupings. Apart from the convenience of on-demand access to so many newspapers, they are often online before they are on the street. The *Financial Times* for example is added to Profile's *Today's Financial Times* at 0.00 hours every morning, though the tables and listings are excluded for reasons of format. More often now, periodical publishers and hosts offer the text in the original image version, so that the format, including listings, illustrations and advertisements, is preserved on the user's screen.

Financial/Business Newspapers

The comparatively few daily and weekly newspapers specifically about and for business are rich sources of news on the more obvious environments. Newspapers such as *The Financial Times* also provide a thorough companies and financial markets news service, but also report on the wider events which inevitably affect business. Their role and content is examined in more detail in the 'Financial Information' chapter. Much of what has been said about general newspapers is also true; *Financial Times* articles are available in full text on FT Profile from the moment of publication. The *Financial Times'* value as a current and retrospective business news source is reflected in the fact that an index is published (by Primary Source Media), and that its publisher does not generally allow it to be included in news databases, such as Reuter's *Textline* or even their own *World Reporter*, except when they are hosted by FT Profile or FT Discovery.

Weekly/Monthly Periodicals

News of relevance to business is obviously likely to appear in general or business periodicals other than newspapers. Much of what has been said above in relation to newspapers is true here, though less frequently published periodicals tend to have less news and more analysis. This makes their direct use for new information less rewarding, leaving another role for secondary business news sources. As this sample from the huge *World Reporter* source list shows, a wide range of periodicals have business news value compatible with newspapers and newswires:

Eastern Economist Daily	Fulltext	USA	English	Newswire
Egypt Today	Fulltext	Egypt	English	National newspaper
El Cronista	Abstracts	Argentina	Spanish	National newspaper
El Mundo (Spain)	Abstracts	Spain	Spanish	National newspaper
El Pais	Abstracts	Spain	Spanish	National newspaper
El Wekalah	Fulltext	UK	English	Magazine
Electrical Review	Fulltext	UK	English	Magazine
Electronics Times	Fulltext	UK	English	Trade journal
Elsevier	Abstract	Netherlands	Dutch	National newspaper
Evening Standard	Fulltext	UK	English	Regional newspaper
Exchange Telecom. Newsl.	Fulltext	Australia	English	Newsletter
Expansion	Abstracts	Spain	Spanish	National newspaper
Extel Company News	Fulltext	UK	English	Newswire
Financial Director	Fulltext	UK	English	Journal
Financial Express	Fulltext	India	English	National newspaper
Financial Mail	Fulltext	South Africa	English	Magazine
Financial Post	Fulltext	Canada	English	National newspaper
Financiel Econ. Magazine	Abstract	Netherlands	Dutch	Magazine

Broadcasts

Although broadcasts have the advantage of currency over print media, problems of systematically exploiting them are compounded by their comparative lack of factual content. As detailed in the 'Media . . . Monitoring' section of the 'Market Information' chapter, specialist firms do undertake monitoring and recording of UK broadcasting, according to specified subject and other criteria. The Broadcast Monitoring Company (of the Financial Times Group) is one such, which from its scanning of over 60 regional titles for mainly business news, publishes the general purpose *Regional Press Summaries*, also available on FT Profile. Broadcasts assume greater news value in countries where the print media are for some reason inadequate, though it requires technical, linguistic and other skills to interpret their significance. For the foreign user, the only feasible way to exploit news broadcasts in a number of countries at once is via the monitoring work of the BBC and the US Government's Foreign Broadcast Information Service. The combined result *BBC Summary of World Broadcasts* is published by BBC Worlwide Monitoring as daily political reports and weekly economic reports, for each of five regions of the world. The majority of items are editorial accounts based on one or more original piece, highlighting or summarising main points; the remainder are verbatim translations of the original. Weekly editions have a detailed subject guide to contents and subject arrangement. *SWB* can be subscribed to directly in printed form, or the data accessed on the day of issue in databases on FT Profile or DataStar.

Excerpt from *BBC Summary of World Broadcasts, Weekly Economic Report: Part 1 Former USSR*

From Contents list:

> *Russia – Defence Industry.*
>
> *Kamov company to bid in Finnish combat helicopter tender*　　*p. ...*
>
> *Russia, France poised for mass production of Grad missile*　　*p. ...*
>
> *France acquires Russian military laser technology*　　*p. ...*

From classified order main sequence:

> *Russia – Transport: Railways.*
>
> *First fast container train leaves Far East for Europe*
>
> *The first fast rail container service has left Nakhodka in the Russian far East for Brest in western Belarus via the Trans-Siberian Railway, Radio Russia reported on 16th April.*
>
> *The train, which is fitted with a satellite navigation system, intends to shave five days off previous journey times and reach Brest in nine days. It will deliver containers with cargo from Japan, South Korea and the Philippines to Europe.*

The new fast rail route via Russia and Belarus 'is designed to create serious competition with the international southern transoceanic container route' the radio said.

Source: *Radio Russia, Moscow, in Russian 0400 gmt 16 Apr 98.*

National, International and Business Oriented News Agencies

News agencies are important as the originators of much of the foreign information presented in the home news media. It is their journalists who observe and attend events worldwide, and wire reports and photographs to their centres. Individual reports are compiled into wire services fed continuously through dedicated lines to subscribing news publishers and others. Publishers select and pay for what they need, and present it alongside their own journalists' material. As exemplified below, there is a small number of market-leading international news agencies and a greater number of regional and subject specialists:

Africa News

Comtex Scientific Corporation's newswire file (on Dialog) of material from African newspapers, agencies and other sources.

Agence France-Presse

Worldwide – 1,100 journalists in 170 countries.

AFX News

Financial and economic news – worldwide.

Associated Press

1,600 journalists & 212 bureaux worldwide.

Asahi News Service

Daily English language wire on Japanese topics.

Antara

Indonesian national news agency.

Business Wire

Media relations wire service that carries full-text corporate news releases for 12,000 U.S. companies representing primarily the high-tech, Fortune 1000, and Nasdaq sectors.

Futures World News (FWN)

News and information that relates to, or has an impact on commodities traded at the world's commodity futures exchanges.

ITAR/TASS

The Russian state news agency, covering also the CIS countries and beyond. *ITAR/TASS News* is Comtex Scientific Corporation's English language version on Dialog.

UPI

United Press International News Agency. *UPI News* is the version on Dialog.

Xinhua News

Comtex Scientific Corporation's English version of the output of the Chinese state news agency.

Happily the rest of us can subscribe to the wire services also, and the news agencies offer dial-up, web sites, and access via online hosts as an alternative to the more expensive continuous-feed option – such as via Profound's *Wireline* combined database of around 30 newswire services. Nevertheless, it is still very difficult to identify the material of relevance to a given business, and a business oriented secondary service is often the first resort.

Ways of Managing Primary Sources

Short of using secondary sources and services, there are certain ways of mitigating some of the problems of primary news sources. Some of the solutions assist in the control of individual sources, others of groups of them.

Individual Titles

The content of the few news periodicals which have associated indexes can be exploited conveniently and systematically, albeit very much retrospectively. The content of the increasing number either delivered electronically or available concurrently in that form is even more exhaustively and selectively accessible via accompanying search software. As already mentioned, FT Profile hosts many separate newspapers and periodicals, most of which are available there within a day or so of publication. Hosts also allow 'alerts' to be set up, the user specifying the criteria to be matched against material as it is added to one file or a group of files. Dialog and DataStar *Alerts* can send relevant data to users by mail, email or fax, either at the time of its addition to the database or at specified times.

Groups of Titles – Indexes

The increasing availability of the full text of publications in machine readable and searchable form, makes conventional printed indexing and abstracting services less necessary. Business-oriented news indexes, such as the *Company Data Supplement* to the *Clover Newspaper Index*, are rare. However, even general indexes covering one nation's major newspapers have obvious advantages of scope, if not of exhaustivity or currency, over an index to any *single* newspaper. *Clover Newspaper Index* covers the UK broadsheets, their colour and other supplements, including *Observer, Sunday Times, European, Economist* and *Financial Times. British Newspaper Index*, on CD-ROM and via Primary Source Media's web site, indexes a similar range of titles. For the USA *National Newspaper Index* (available via Dialog) exhaustively indexes several important titles, including *The Wall Street Journal. Research Index*, although mentioned in another chapter in the context of market information, is now searchable as a web site, and is current and broad enough in scope to control the UK-oriented news appearing in a significant range of periodicals.

News Index is an impressive free resource offered by the authoritative British NISS web information gateway service (*http://www.niss.ac.uk/news/index.html*). It provides simultaneous searching of over 300 online newspapers, as well as links to their sites. The freely available meta search engine *WebTrawler* allows searching and retrieval of free and charged for articles from the archives of hundreds of news organs worldwide, including the *Financial Times* from the UK and *The Gleaner* from Jamaica. Like *News Index*, it is not business oriented, and *WebTrawler* is not appropriate as a current awareness service; nevertheless, these services are a cheap partial alternative to the commercial services exemplified under 'Secondary Business News Sources and Systems', below.

News Digests

A less selectively disseminated version of 'daily me' and 'push technology' services is frequently distributed digests of the news relating to particular industries. These survive in the form of published lists of titles and/or abstracts, 'tear sheet' or press cuttings services, often delivered daily by mail fax or courier to subscribers.

Hosts' Solutions

One of the main advantages of online hosts is the unified access they provide to diverse sources. Most allow files to be specified for joint searching, or designate collections in advance. FT Profile's News 'Data Collection' allows simultaneous searching of the hundreds of full-text news wires and individual periodicals hosted. Searches can alternatively be carried out in sub-sets, including *UK News*, *International News*, *European News* and *French News*. FT Profile's superfile *World News* gives simultaneous coverage of two major news databases as well as the *Financial Times* in full text. The individual newspaper files on Dialog can searched together under the superfile *Papers*. Thus stored or ad hoc searches can be used to monitor or retrospectively check a group of news sources at a stroke. Certain databases are themselves the full text of collections of individual titles, similarly gathered together to facilitate simultaneous exploitation. Examples are IAC's *Magazine* and *Newsletter* databases; the latter constituting a worldwide source of 650 of the industry newsletters and trade periodicals described in sections above, albeit not available until two to four weeks after publication. FT's *Asia Intelligence Wire* and *Middle East Intelligence Wire* are not so much news wires as agglomerations of existing newswires, newspapers, trade journals and other publications on and from those regions. Dialog hosts Comtex Scientific Corporation's news wires *Africa News*, *ITAR/TASS* (Russia) and *Xinhua News* (China).

Hosts' alerting software has already been discussed, whereby additions to many of the databases can be channelled to users according to personal profiles. In addition, both Profound and Financial Times Electronic Business Information connect their real-time news providers with users' intranets like any other 'push-technology' service. Profound's NewsNow and FT's News Alert are therefore described among the more comprehensive solutions to managing the collection and redistribution of news from primary (and secondary) below.

Secondary Business News Sources and Systems

Needs for Secondary Sources

The above strategies do little to reduce the need for sources or services giving both broad coverage of primary titles and selective treatment of their content. All the following are particularly important tasks, in the case of business' need for news, for secondary sources:

> Discovery and acquisition of primary material
>
> Identification and selection of items of business significance
>
> Presentation of diverse items in standard, convenient form and in English
>
> Provision of systems for current and retrospective retrieval by sought criteria
>
> Provision of selective dissemination and in-house news management systems

These attributes, formerly only possible through expensive scanning, circulation and filing systems, are indeed offered by a considerable number of competing services. These are divisible into two categories, the first more traditionally involving user-initiated access to aggregations – that is, databases of news items; the second based on the active distribution of incoming items to users – 'push technology'. A third strategy is possible, however, and outlined below: using proprietary software to select and distribute news imported from chosen primary and secondary sources within an organisation.

Databases

Although 'push-technology' products have been introduced since, many business news users are reasonably well served by databases which include appropriate searching and alerting software. Reuters' *Textline* has for many years been perhaps the best known of all business databases. In the 'Annual Business Information Resources Survey, 1998', four of the seven most used databases were essentially news sources, with *Textline* still the clear leader among specialist business news databases (*Business Information Review* 15(1), 1998, pp. 5-21). Financial Times Information, Knight Ridder and Dow Jones have only recently jointly introduced *World Reporter* to challenge its market position. Such databases are great pools of the news items selected as of potential relevance to business from a huge range of worldwide news media. Most items are in full-text, though not held as graphical images, so the original format, photographs and illustrations such as graphs are usually omitted. They combine the latest items and an archive, and add further value in the form of translation and often abstracting of non-English items, and indexing items by subject and other criteria. Some, like *World Reporter*, maximise their scope and avoid duplication of effort by selectively including material from more specialised databases. In 1998 FT Profile launched *World News* as an 'exclusive, unbeatable combination of news sources' – namely a combination of the databases they already host: *Textline*, *World Reporter* and *Financial Times Full Text*. It is for the user to decide how to employ the supplier's or the host's, or proprietary software (as covered in the next section) to exploit the content for retrospective searching or alerting purposes, for ad hoc individual access or selective re-distribution through an organisation's intranet.

The following details give an impression of the scope and facilities of the most used of the Western-oriented international business news databases:

Of broad scope:

World Reporter

Joint venture between Financial Times Information, Knight Ridder and Dow Jones, based at FTI in London; available via the major hosts. Coverage: approximately 500 general and business newspapers and newswires worldwide trade press items from *PROMT* and *Business & Industry* databases.
Features: pay-per-view basis; English items full-text, English abstracts of others; 'high quality indexing' including US SIC codes for subjects.

Textline

Produced by Reuters, currently available via FT Profile and no longer updated on Dialog Corporation hosts.
Coverage: International, national & regional newspapers, journals & wire services.
Features: European emphasis; translations into English from 17 languages 85% articles full-text; others abstracts; updated daily.

Globalbase

Known as *BIS Infomat* before it was owned by Information Access Company; available directly through IAC's InSite interfaces, as well as via other hosts. A database of abstracts of items of mainly European and Asia/Pacific Rim business relevance, from a wide range of daily papers and industry journals in many languages. Some similarities to IAC's *PROMT*, including the same sophisticated indexing, though the geographical emphases are distinctive.

LEXIS/NEXIS
NEXIS is the non-legal, news information side of this huge US-based Mead Data Central operation. The source base includes many news and other types of business sources, and there are separately searchable databases, including the general business news ASAP and Business Dateline.

Northern Light (http://sirocco.northernlight.com/search.html)
A web search engine ('research engine') which can also be used to search its own two million item current and retrospective news and business publications database.
Coverage: The Special Collection includes content licensed from a wide variety of sources, including news wires, other news aggregators, and business information providers.
Features: Retrieval and document summaries are free; some documents can be viewed free, the cost of others compares well with alternative providers.

Of limited or specialised scope:

FT McCarthy Company & Industry Information
Available on CD-ROM or as a database on FT Profile.
Coverage: articles (or translated abstracts) selected from over 70 of the most significant, predominantly European, business and general newspapers and periodicals; thoroughly indexed.

Business Dateline
Provided by UMI International, USA; available on Dialog.
Coverage: 350+ US local & regional business publications including wire services, daily papers, business journals. Full-text of 2,000 articles added per week.

Infomart Online (http://www.infomart.ca/iopage.htm)
Provides and hosts Canadian business news databases, collected from daily newspapers, business weeklies and Canadian wire services.

Press Rover (http://www.russianstory.com)
A search engine available to search Russian Story Inc.'s archives of Russian newspapers and periodicals. Searching by Cyrillic and other characters retrieves full text and image originals with relevance rankings. Searching is free but a fee is required to retrieve documents.

Redistribution Services

This group can be considered services as much as sources, because their role is to aggregate and redistribute existing news source material. Services range from those which are primarily gateways to diverse electronic news, to those which collect and if necessary translate the primary material themselves, perhaps selectively distributing it to subscribers from a central database by low-tech means ('Daily me' services, below), and to those where the emphasis is on channelling original electronic formats directly to networked users ('Push-technology' services).

Web News Gateways

A considerable number of the major web browsers, search engines (notably Yahoo!) and directories, and information gateways, include business news options. These usually consist of links to a useful group providers of free information; though sometimes news is already selectively aggregated, and presented as a scrolling headlines service. The British universities' NISS service on the JANET network offers links to sites including Financial Times Information, Bank of England press releases, *Business Day* interactive, BBC News business page and *The Scotsman*'s business pages. Details of these and other examples follow:

> *FT.com (http://www.FT.com/)* is Financial Times Electronic Publishing's web gateway to its own huge range of products. By way of an inducement it also includes much news and other data which are free in return for registration. Quoting from it:
>
>> 'FT.com is Europe's number-one news site, delivering global business and financial news, comment and analysis to nearly a million registered users in some 160 countries . . . combines the editorial values of *The Financial Times* . . . with the immediacy, depth and interactivity of the web. The site is updated 11 or more times throughout the day. Its offerings include:
>> *Business and financial news*
>> *Free search* [past 30 days *FT.com* content; small charge for downloading]
>> *Special reports* [i.e. *Financial Times* supplements]
>> *Financial Times archive* . . .'
>
> *TotalNEWS (http://totalnews.com/)* is a web news gateway rather than a true aggregator. Relevant options include World News, and Business, in the latter links under sub-headings Finance, Business, Marketing and Advertising, and Trade, Industry and Professions are provided, to an impressive range of sites, some free and some charged. Alternatively, a search facility allows all the available stories to be searched by keyword.
>
> *Newshub (http://www.newshub.com/summary.html)* probably originated news aggregation on the web. Free news, mainly from business-oriented U.S. sources, is updated every fifteen minutes. Headlines can be viewed under a choice of subject categories, and lead to articles' text. A search engine provides access to full-text articles from a range of international sources. Financial markets quotes, personal stock portfolio, and ticker bar news and prices options are available.

InfoBeat (*http://www.infobeat.com/*) (formerly *Mercury Mail*) is a popular free web-based news service. It allows a choice of seven subjects, each yielding a daily emailed collection of items edited from a number of free sources. If required, the full text can be obtained via the *InfoBeat* web site. The Finance option delivers US closing prices and edited news matching the user's portfolio of companies and other investments, alerts can optionally be set up for topics where daily mailings are insufficient.

NISS Services, News area (*http://www.niss.ac.uk/news/index.html*). Part of the information gateway service provided by the UK joint academic project NISS. Mentioned above as an index to many news sources, its 'Business and financial news' option also provides links to authoritative individual news providers' sites.

NewsNow (*http://www.newsnow.co.uk/*) was launched in 1998 as probably the first UK news aggregator. It is a convenient and impressive free one-stop-shop for news from sources, its Business and Finance section includes *Money World*, *Sky News* (Business), *VNU Newswire*, *Yahoo! UK* (Business) and *Wired* (Business). It includes side-by-side presentation of alternative stories on a topic, and a real-time feed updated every five minutes. An example of a NewsNow display follows; each headline leads to the full article:

5 to 10 minutes old
> UK's Friends' Provident to Buy London & Manchester for 744 Mln Pounds Bloomberg 10:35

10 to 15 minutes old
> Mersey Docks sees slower spending
>
> Sky News 10:30

15 to 30 minutes old
> Ciba SC 1st-Half Profit Rises Less Than Expected; 1,100 Jobs Will Be Cut
>
> Bloomberg 10:20
>
> European Equity Movers: London & Manchester, Ciba, OMV
>
> Bloomberg 10:20
>
> UK repaid £5.4bn debt in July
>
> Sky News 10:15

30 minutes to 1 hour old
> [etc.]

UK Business Park (*http://www.ukbusinesspark.co.uk/*) is an attractively presented, British-oriented, database of brief news items organised by company and industry sector. Though the full, chargeable service is intended as a corporate competitive monitoring service, the free search level is a very convenient source of company or industry news.

'Daily-me' Services

Esmerk Information's products exemplify high input and added value business-oriented news gathering and redistribution. Representatives around the world select, translate (from and into 20 languages) and abstract current publications, to provide tailored reports to subscribers. This Finnish firm has the advantage of 20 years experience, geographical and linguistic specialisms, and a claimed 800 corporate clients and 30,000 individual users. Products include daily or weekly personalised printed or electronic briefings on user-defined topics, briefs on selected countries, and tailored distribution via corporate executive or management information systems, or access to the whole database as the CD-ROM marketed as '12 months of international market intelligence'.

Push Technology Services

The term 'push technology' is applied to this comparatively recently developed group of sources or services, because the emphasis is on uninterrupted channelling of news from its creator to its end user. The services are offered by established online hosts, and other information 'aggregators', 'integrators' or 'redistributors', each of which provides the software, and contracts with news agencies and others to supply of the news. The dual selling points are speed of access to news, and the ability to process and distribute it 'within the corporate firewall' according to company, department or individual profiles. Although, or even because, most services are unlimited in subject scope, they can be tailored for general or very specific business information purposes. Such services are particularly aimed at organisations with developed 'executive information systems', an intranet linked to the Internet, and a proliferation of desktop computers. This technology allows the graphic image of news items to be received, including the original columns and colour pictures.

Although the information industry has great expectations for this new product line, it was alarmed when the demise of the well-established NewsNet Inc. in 1997 suggested that pricing was already too competitive to cover costs, or that there were too many players in such an immature market. *Business Information Review*'s '1998 Annual Business Information Resources Survey' found very little take-up of the considerable range of 'filtered/push news alerting services' by either organisations' end-users or information services. NewsNet's impressive source range included 20 newswire services, 750 business newsletters, trade journals, extending beyond business news to real-time stock quotes, and company financial and credit data and news contracted from providers including TRW, Dun & Bradstreet and Standard and Poor's. Building on their systems rather than information-providing experience, even IBM have joined the business news redistribution market – verging on general business information online hosting. Their *InfoSage* (*http://www.infosage.ibm.com*) service filters and redistributes via the Internet,

US-oriented news and company information from providers similar to those just mentioned. Information on the news redistribution services of Nikkei's *Japan News and Retrieval*, *Dow Jones Interactive* and Reuter's *Business Briefing* can be found in the 'Financial Information' chapter.

The examples following the quotes on the former NewsNet, and the Livewire services illustrate the aims and the scope of news redistribution services.

> [NewsNet's] '*NewsFlash* is an automatic, offline retrieval application that works continuously in the background, while you work on something else. NewsFlash watches for news that fits your needs. It lets you know when it finds something. Just check in anytime during the day. It can search for as many topics defined as broadly or narrowly as you like. And you pay only for your "hits", not for your search of the 17,000+ stories available on NewsNet every day. . . . Only NewsNet offers such a flexible array of delivery options . . . directly through your computer, via e-mail, from your fax machine or through your company's group-ware.' (NewsNet brochure, 1996.)

> 'Today's technology has no problem in pushing the latest news to you. But "push" rapidly turns to "shove" and important information is lost in an overwhelming tide of irrelevant data. *LiveWire* is perhaps the first truly intelligent use of "push" technology for news broadcast.' (LiveWire brochure, 1997.)

> **LiveWire** – a service of the Profound online host.
> Coverage: 25 global newswires, 10,000 stories a day.
> Features: articles are fed to Profound continuously; automatically indexed by subject and other criteria in real-time using Profound's InfoSort system, and are automatically matched with users' personal profiles. Matching articles are pushed via networks to users; users are alerted by scrolling ticker or icon on screen, and access the articles by clicking on the ticker or icon. Unlimited access is provided for fixed monthly fee.

> **FT News Alert** (*http://www.ftep.ft.com/ftna.htm*)
> Coverage: continuous newswire feeds e.g. AFX, Universal News Services; newspapers (at time of 'going to bed' e.g. the *Financial Times*, *The Times*, *European*, *El Pais*; News databases (as updated) e.g. *World Reporter*, *Business & Industry*.
> Features: delivered via Internet and/or corporate intranets; uses leased telecoms line or ISDN line; articles

and alerts can be delivered via web browser or email; payment via subscription.

NewsEdge Corporation (*http://www.newsedge.com*)
A quoted company and major player in the aggregation and redistribution of (US oriented) news, formed by the merger of Desktop Data, Individual, and ADP/ISS, NewsEdge, calling itself the world's largest independent news aggregator. The NewsPage, delivers personalised information over the web, the features of which include:

- daily issue on the web, tailored to the individual user;

- articles from over 450 of the world's business trade journals, newswires, newspapers and newsletters;

- 1,000 industry topic briefings monitored by NewsEdge Corporation's vertical industry specialists;

- news on 65,000 public and private companies, including from news articles, press releases, stock quotes and charts, SEC filings, corporate profiles from Hoover's, Corptech and others;

- daily email news summary of the 20 most personally relevant news articles;

- five-day news archive;

- saved news searches enabling ongoing tracking of people and issues.

NewsEdge Insight-Web delivers real-time news to intranets 'empowering end-users with value-added, editorially enhanced news and information, enabling them to "read less but know more."' This product line offers great customisation at enterprise, group and individual levels, enabling end-users to receive highly focused news, editorially organized by topic, in order to meet particular requirements. *Insight First!* delivers concise personalized news briefings through a web browser. Some 20,000 stories daily are categorised into over 2,000 topic areas focusing on market segments, strategic competitive issues, enabling technologies, legislative and regulatory issues, and global or regional updates. These are also sorted by company name and grouped according to the client's organisational structure or lines of business. Details of *NewsEdge NewsTools* products appear in the 'Stand-alone Redistribution Software' section below.

News Circle (Jacobs Software, The Netherlands; *http://www.newscircle.com/*)
Independent from any particular news provider, *News Circle* aggregates, manipulates and redistributes news from a wide range of sources, in a variety of services. Sources include: 'Dow Jones News Retrieval and Dow Jones Premier Publications for non-dealer floor use, including the *Wall Street Journal* and the *New York Times*. Other sources range from general business news publications such as the *Financial Times*, the *Economist*, and the *Het Financieele Dagblad* to specialized information published in *Platt's Oilgram News*, *Business Week*, FDC *Pink Sheets*, and others.'
Services include:
'A complete network of startegic information products, including:
Full-Text Publications – access to publications and their archives.
Industry monitor – industry trends for a wide range of sectors, such as the pharmaceutical industry, banking, telecom and insurance, among many others.
Company Briefing Report – inmediate and complete company profiles.
Same Time News – same time wire service news updates.'

Reuters News Explorer
A sophisticated free-text search engine which matches individual profiles with the news resources on the Reuters Business Briefing host, to deliver via an intranet. Coverage: Reuters' news base of national and international newspapers, newswires and trade press, including news-feeds such as Reuters IPTC picture and text wires, and Reuters *Business Alert*.
Features: user's profile, including free text search terms and country, topic, date, industry etc. topic filters, is matched using Muscat search engine relevance algorithms on the intranet with the incoming news. Notification can either be via email or on the browser screen as an alert or live scrolling headlines.

WavePhore Newscast (*http://www.newscast.com/*)
A family of web-based general business intelligence services – using patented filtering and pattern matching technology: 'The news and information is customized by
user-defined profiles and seemlessly integrated into
intranet, email and groupware applications, including
Lotus Notes& trade . . .'
Coverage: 'over 2,500 data sources', including
newswires, Usenet postings, direct links to companies'
announcements, and data selected from other providers, such as IAC and FT Extel.
Features: services include on demand access via web
browser, or via a range of corporate customising filtering and 'push technology' software; includes 180 day
archive. Worldwide, but emphasis on USA. Products include Newscast Today: 'This turnkey service delivers
custom-filtered business intelligence to corporate knowledge workers throughout the enterprise. Access *Newscast Today* via your favorite internet browser or a private
connection with one of Newscast's extranet partners.'
Newscast for Lotus Notes: 'Using the power of Lotus Notes,
Newscast delivers custom-filtered news and business
intelligence on-demand. You control the replication cy-
cle, how often you replicate and when.'

Stand-alone Redistribution Software

Already operating for nine years, US based NewsEDGE Corporation's products are prominent among several specialists in 'enterprise-wide news delivery' software. The *NewsEDGE NewsTool* products include a server to
receive news from third party providers, and to 'push it out to the corporate knowledge workers'. *NewsObjects* software works with the server to
format the in-house feeds to the various formats needed, and within the
various existing systems in use. Thus, a company's financial managers might
be provided with City news headlines continuously scrolling across their
accounting systems screens, or each employee might get an alerting icon
when using any Windows software on the local area network, prompting
them to click to receive national or corporate news of relevance to them.
NewsEdge also offers news feeds for incorporation in other providers' redistribution systems.

Part 2: Industry Sources

Information sources which report on the external environment from the point
of view of an industry sector are rarer than those which cover individual domains of the environment, regardless of industry. 'Industry sources' are either

of general purpose, in that they collate *any* information of commercial signifi-cance to a particular industry, or, they specialise in the collation of *news*.

General Purpose Industry Sources

This is a comparatively small group of sources, not even one source for each industry sector. They are usually online electronic databases, a format suitable for holding a large archive of relevant material, as well as adding to and searching on demand. As the following catalogue description of the Dialog and DataStar database *Chemical Industry Notes* indicates, such sources are intended as one-stop information repositories for the business decision makers in the industry. Although such a database may not be able to com-pete with domain-specific sources for a profile of a company, or even a survey of a market, its value is in recognising and collating diverse items with implications for the industry.

> *Chemical Industry Notes*
> 'Indexes and abstracts over 80 important worldwide journals, newspapers and periodicals that are business oriented . . . directed at decision makers who are inter-ested in the management, investment, marketing & pro-duction aspects of the chemical industry. Principal coverage of CIN includes government and society, mar-ket data, resources and resource use, people, products and processes, organisations and institutions, and unit cost and price information'.

Extracts from Bowker-Saur's description of the *Chemical News and Intelligence* web site show how it is a combined 'reference' and industry news service:

> *Chemical News and Intelligence (http://www.CNIonline.com)*
> '24 hour news coverage . . . Extensive reference library containing more than 40,000 articles from leading chemi-cals magazines . . . A Who's Who containing informa-tion about key players in the industry. Detailed chemical events calendar and a gatway to the best sites on the Internet, including a link to ICIS-LOR service for exist-ing subscribers.'

Though not as rounded in scope, 'virtual' one-stop industry databases can be created combining and simultaneously searching the relevant databases on online hosts. Notable is the *Industries* option on FT Profile which gives a choice of 'Data collections', each of them including whole relevant databases, and relevant records from others. Separate collections are Accountancy, Ad-vertising and Marketing, Aerospace and Defence, Chemicals, Civil Engi-neering, Computing and Telecoms, Energy, Finance and Banking, Insurance, Management, Media & Public Relations, Property, Retailing.

News-Oriented Industry Sources

Industry-oriented digests of news are more common than general purpose industry sources, and obviously coincide in their selective dissemination and current awareness aims with the news redistribution services and software discussed in the 'News Sources' section of this chapter – see also especially under 'News Digests'. Just as in broad scope business news sources, the provider either cumulates current and retrospective items in a database (such as *Chemical Business Newsbase*, below), or continuously distributes new items to the subscriber by printed or electronic means, such as Business International's *East European Monitoring Service* series, below. The possible advantage of the latter over big systems like *NewsAlert* or *Livewire* is the provider's subject specialisation. Such a service constitutes a kind of industry newsletter or trade journal itself, but its advantage is that it combines relevant information from these and less obvious sources. The quote below indicates the breadth of source material, and of the external environment which industry-specific news sources may cover.

> *Chemical Business Newsbase* (on Dialog, DataStar [updated twice-weekly] and CD-ROM)
> '... offers fast and consistent coverage of news, views, facts and figures for the chemical industry worldwide. . . . Records contained in the database summarize items from journals, press releases, company reports, advertisements . . . and other sources that are appropriate to covering chemical business news. . . . CBNB provides information affecting chemical markets or products, and covers a variety of topics, including legislation, environmental aspects, merger information, markets, sales, new products, production, trading, and company results.' (From Knight Ridder catalogue.)
>
> *BioView Today*
> Industry specific version of the former service, now *WavePhore Newscast*.
> Coverage: data relevant to the pharmaceutical and biotechnology industry filtered from the same source base as the former generic service, plus 'over 100 additional industry-specific sources' – a mixture of individual primary sources and established secondary sources such as *Biotechnology Abstracts*.
> Features: can be accessed on demand via web browser, or via a range of corporate customising filtering and 'push technology' software; includes 180 day archive.

East European Monitoring Service series
Approximately seven printed periodicals covering different chemical industry sectors, and 13 other industrial sectors. These 'Industrial monitors' are published by Business International, a member of the Economist group.

Further sources

D. Nicholas and G. Erbach. *Online Information Sources for Business and Current Affairs: an evaluation.* Mansell, 1989.

N. Spencer (compiler). *News Information: Online, CD-ROM and Internet Resources.* British Library, 1997. An aid to the identification of online and CD-ROM versions of news serials, guidance on the scope of news databases, and details of news aggregators and distributors; worldwide coverage.

8

Accessing Business Information

Introduction

As its title suggests, this chapter aims to be a bridge between the business person or the intermediary, and all the information introduced in the previous chapters. In fact it concerns the bridge, the interface between the user and the potentially available information; an interface which includes barriers of different kinds, including the sheer number and variety of sources, and the lack of obvious congruence between a typical business problem and the sources, but an interface which also includes aids to overcome the problems, to ensure the right information gets to the right person at the right time. Direct use of sources involves knowledge of and decisions about delivery formats, costs and alternative providers including hosts. It also involves the identification of the appropriate source or sources for a particular purpose. Indirect use, that is using intermediary services, involves decisions on when it is appropriate to use library and information services, and which offers what. The chapter breaks down these information interface factors under the following headings, and provides guidance on each. Although current issues in in-house information management are briefly discussed, this is the aspect of the interface covered in the least detail here, but very well documented elsewhere.

Current Information Management Issues

Many business people and IT people have recently become very excited about information sources and their exploitation, and talk about it with the zeal of the convert. Its association with the computer has done wonders for the image of information in the eyes of business, giving it an air of modernity, efficiency and availability which was not associated with the book and the librarian. The Internet is bringing the sum of the hitherto unimagined published output to any humble desk. It is hardly surprising if business end-users and the IT people who mediate their web access do not always see the association with librarians and their profession – even when they are called 'information managers' and 'information management'. The initial tendency has been to leave the information professional to manage their traditional sources, and independently to invent new ways of managing access to what are most of the time the same sources, delivered in a new way.

Although there are obvious disadvantages in independently rediscovering information management problems and solutions, including the development of a parallel vocabulary, converts should always be a cause for rejoicing, and turning new eyes on timeless problems does produce fresh solutions. The availability to each and every business person of so much data and so much software – 'information overload' no less – does call for new solutions, and does at least imply changes in the role of the information professional. Topics, whether justifiably or not thrust onto today's information management agenda are discussed in the following sections. One is the 'disintermediation' debate, the suggestion that the imposition of an intermediary between end-user and sources is no longer necessary. Another is the concept of 'knowledge management', arising from organisations' acknowledgement not only of the value of information on both internal and external environments, but also that the value of information is only realised when it becomes knowledge.

Information Overload

There has hardly been time to celebrate the wealth of information now available before it is being decried for its volume – at least by those who sell ways of making it more manageable. Although Reuters may seem to be part of the problem rather than the solution, they have been identifying their products with the antedotes to information overload. Reuters commissioned the report *Dying for Information: An Investigation into the Effects of Information Overload in the UK and Worldwide* (London: Reuters, 1996), and subsequently the widely publicised *Glued to the Screen?: An Investigation into Information Addiction Worldwide* (London: Reuters, 1997). The latter includes statistics such as that 61% of British and American managers already suffer information overload, and 80% believed it would get worse. More alarming for business, but promising for an enterprising information industry, is that the reaction of half of the sufferers is to ignore the surplus information, and the other half to store it with the intention of later use – 55% worry about making poor decisions in spite of all the information at their disposal. It appears that the majority of managers already believe that the cost of gathering and using information outweighs its value. They feel they should be taught information management at school and university level, and employers should organise training courses.

When information, or at least data is plentiful, as well as expensive and time consuming to sift and incorporate in existing knowledge, value does need to be added to ensure the right information gets through at the right time to the right person. The different strands of the day-to-day solution to this problem are as follows, as addressed by different sections of this chapter.

Task	*Solution*
Tracing the right source	Bibliographical control Choice between formats, host and direct access
Effective extraction of information from sources	Software such as intelligent agents, search interfaces, controlled vocabularies
Incorporation of available data into information and knowledge	Knowledge management, intranets
Ensuring all of the above components	Information services – in-house or external. Choice between end-user and intermediary access

Knowledge Management

'Knowledge management' has recently emerged from 'information management', itself a variously-defined interpretation of 'librarianship' intended to distance itself from images of collections of printed works and free public libraries. In information management, the emphasis is on *information*, on organising and acquiring it from wherever necessary, usually to support the aims of an organisation. The concept of knowledge management rightly emphasises the difference between information, the raw material, and knowledge, which is information applied, an even more valuable but less tangible corporate asset. The term therefore acknowledges the role of individuals and teams in creating, holding and sharing knowledge, and implies its effective nurturing and exchange to fulfil the needs of an organisation.The development of this concept, leading to the appointment of Knowledge Managers within some companies, is in part a response to the rapid turnover of knowledge, due to speed of change, shorter employment tenures, and the availability of information. It represents also management's acknowledgement of the true value of information and knowledge, not just in the interests of efficiency, but as a new opportunity to gain of competitive advantage.

Corporate Intranets

The 'intranet' is often cited in conjunction with knowledge management, as technology complementing an appropriate corporate strategy, and as 'knowledge management software'. An intranet carries out within an organisation the information storage and communication functions of the Internet outside it, while interrelating seamlessly with the Internet. It is a tool which can help implement the principles of knowledge management, including integrating different information stores and flows; it can bridge the potentially fatal gap between external ('business') information and internal information. As a system which adds value to information rather than simply transmitting it, the intranet may have a greater impact on both the information industry and its corporate customers than the Internet itself.

In, for instance, the sections on 'News Sources' and on 'Online Hosts' below, it is apparent that direct and third party information providers are gearing their delivery to corporate intranets, expecting increased usage by reaching more end-users.

Intelligent Agents, Data-mining, Push Technology and Other Software

Coincident with the exponential growth of the Internet, and the awareness of information overload, is the development of software promising to bring the vast information resource back under control, or even convert it into knowledge. Areas of information science ripe for further attention include indexing itself, or rather the matching of natural language search terms with the natural language text of documents. Although standardised labelling ('metadata') of web pages by their creators promises increased 'precision' in searches, the text of the document itself is the most fertile target for search engines. Effective free-text retrieval depends on good codification of the syntax and semantics of languages, which is also necessary for another research priority: translation and summarisation software. As in the case of 'push technology' described in another chapter in relation to business news sources, the emphasis of many information management developments is necessarily on personalised solutions. For commercial and more altruistic reasons, source and software providers wish to empower the 'end-user', but realise that doing so depends on preventing the negative attitudes reported above by Reuters in relation to information overload. Thus there is also much research and development in the creation of corporate and personal profiles which can be translated into algorithms, either to optimise 'recall' and 'precision' in searching a vast range of sources, or to facilitate the exchange and sharing of information within groups of people.

Even the first point of contact with the web – browsers and search engines – invite a certain amount of customisation, so that parameters such as language, country and preferred sites and subjects can be set as defaults. Advanced searching options optimise precision through for example targeting specific fields of web pages (such as the title, or host's name or domain), or through Boolean and word proximity operators to specify compound concepts, and the inclusion or exclusion of terms. Searches can be limited to, for example, British sites by taking the appropriate options on the UK versions of worlwide search services, such as these options on the Yahoo! home page (*http://search.yahoo.com/search/options*):

World Yahoo!s

Asia – Australia & NZ – Canada – Chinese – Denmark – France – Germany – Italy – Japan – Korea – Norway – Spanish – Sweden – UK & Ireland

Choosing UK currently leads to the following hypertext link options:

Search: All sites   UK & Ireland sites only

Accommodation – Football – Email Search – News – Stock Quotes – Pager – New: Sport – My Yahoo! – Weather – Yahoo! Mail – Yahoo! UK Business Directory – more

and the display of the top level of the classified directory of web sites (only partially shown below). Alternatively keywords can be entered in a box provided, if a search engine type search is preferred.

Arts and Humanities
Photography, Theatre, Literature

Business and Economy [Xtra!]
Companies, Investments, Classifieds, Taxes

Computers and Internet
Internet, WWW, Software, Multimedia

. . .

Country-specific searching can alternatively be done using dedicated services like SearchUK (*http://www.searchuk.com/*). Though limited in coverage of cyberspace, search *directories* such as Yahoo! above, as opposed to search engines like Alta Vista (*http://www.altavista.telia.com/*) can be chosen for the advantage of selection and indexing done by humans rather than by 'web crawler' software, and the option of retrieval via a classified sequence. Free 'meta' search engines such as Dogpile (*http://www.dogpile.com/*)and Metacrawler (*http://www.metacrawler.com/*) not only simultaneously search a variety of other search engines, but Ask Jeeves (*http://aj.com/*) attempts to translate a query expressed in natural language into the various appropriate search statements, to deliver an answer and also suggest refinements.

However, much greater sophistication is offered by commercial software already available and in development, some of which aims to do the searching for the user, and others the management of the information found. ProSearch is one such intelligent search agent (or knowbot, WebBot or just bot), developed and licensed for commercial testing by British Telecom (described by John Davies at the UKOLUG Conference, Manchester, 14-16 July 1998). It translates a user-defined subject profile into appropriate search strategies for existing search engines, to trawl the web and any intranet and directly accessed news sources for hits. Further value is added by processing the results, eliminating duplicates, and scoring and sorting them according to various algorithms – including by citation analysis based on hypertext links. Even further value is added by the delivery of results in the form of summaries of the retrieved documents. BT's ProSum is available specifically for the creation of summaries of electronic documents. Armed with the user's personal preferences, it identifies key sentences, and delivers summaries of the size specified – such as 5% or 20% of the original. ProSum can be linked with a web browser to summarise all results, or invoked as required for a particular document.

Software like BT's Jasper is very much in the spirit of 'knowledge management'. It assists the sharing of information within a community of users, such as all or some of the users of a corporate intranet. A Jasper 'agent' works with each user's information retrieval software, holding their personal profile and 'observing' their information usage. As in the case of ProSearch, the user can comment on the relevance and value of documents they 'handle', so that the profile and software evolves. Group profiles result from the coincidence of individual profiles. This information is used by the agent to tip-off (by email) individuals or groups whenever a colleague consults a new Internet or intranet source. Records consist of the name and summary of the page, the original user's name, plus a hypertext link to the page, star-rated according to the match with the recipient's profile. Knowledge created by the user's interaction with the document is preserved, in that annotations can be added to records, where they influence routing to colleagues.

Other research and development assists in the exploitation of relevant documents by representing them in more tangible ways. For instance, choices between documents may be facilitated if the relationships between their subjects are shown in three dimensions, perhaps as items in rooms in virtual reality buildings, or leaves, branches and plants in a virtual reality 'information garden'.

Disintermediation

Although business people and others with information needs have always both accessed information independently, and via intermediary services, the term 'disintermediation' is a response to the nearly simultaneous explosion of electronic sources, with the growth of 'point and click' graphical user interfaces (GUIs) and 'intelligent' retrieval software, and the widespread take-up of the Internet and intranets. By no means for the first time, some publishers and even librarians envisage the disappearance of the information intermediary over one horizon as the enabled end-user rises over the other. It is true that if so many sources of business information are both electronic and networked, and so many people use the Internet, any one of them has more resources at their fingertips than contained in all the business libraries in the world. Headland Press' '1998 Business Information Resources Survey' found that the Internet is already used by far more end-users than dial-up online or CD-ROM ever was (*Business Information Review* 15, March 1998, pp. 5-21). In a quarter of the sample, more than half of end-users had desktop access, a trebling in just over a year.

This makes it necessary to try to explain why professional information intermediaries are actually used more and more, not less and less. There are several reasons, encompassed by the fact that the effective and efficient translation of business problems into information solutions remains a specialist task. Certainly more business people are accessing more information directly for themselves, but rather than satisfying demand, this leads to further and more complex expectations. Furthermore, while information as knowledge is better appreciated, and the available information may now seem infinite, money and time remains finite, so professional management of the information resource is paramount. Reasons for and against 'disintermediation' are spelled out in the list below.

Business people may access sources directly because:
- it can be faster, more convenient, cheaper;
- the end-user is the subject expert;
- much information is a couple of key strokes away from many business people;
- many sources are user-friendly, targeted at end-users;
- web browsers, search engines, hosts' interfaces, push-technology and agent software etc., facilitate selective information gathering from a wide range of sources.

Information intermediaries may be used to:
- carry out tasks requiring specialised information skills rather than business or management skills;
- achieve advantages of scale and of division of labour in carrying out processes;
- translate problems into information solutions;
- identify appropriate sources from the vast range available, and evaluate alternatives;
- effectively retrieve information from complex, variable and diverse sources;
- synthesise information from various sources, and repackage it in the form required;
- plan and co-ordinate an organisation's overall information and knowledge exchange;
- manage an organisation's relevant expenditure;
- select, install and maintain sources and systems;
- promote information sources and services to the organisation and its members;
- assist and train individuals in their direct use of sources and systems;
- execute ongoing tasks, including monitoring and proactive selective dissemination.

In practice middle management business people can and should use all the advantages of agent software, push-technology and user-friendly interfaces to networked sources, where they are confident of a reasonable result. The role of a business' 'librarian', 'information manager' or 'researcher' is no longer centred on an in-house collection, but on a far wider and potentially harder-to-manage pool of information resources. In this situation their skills in identifying and selecting appropriate sources are just as important, as well as skills of interpreting problems and queries, retrieving information from complex sources in diverse formats, and synthesising it into a form readily used in decision making. Most of these are rightly considered specialist tasks, most efficiently and effectively performed by designated and appropriately qualified persons. Even the management of relevant budgets, the selection of hosts, source subscriptions, and information management software, the design and maintenance of information storage, access and distribution networks, the promotion of information use and the training of end-users for direct access to selective sources and systems, requires specialist attention. Increased availability of sources and appreciation of the value of information and knowledge places increased expectations on performance in all aspects of information use.

Sources

Sources and their attendant problems were introduced in the opening chapter. It is very obvious by now that business information sources are numerous, ever-changing, and represent every physical format – including non-documentary sources such as persons and organisations. Their internal format, arrangement and method of access is equally diverse, and in scope they represent all possible combinations of subject, geographical, time period and any other parameter of the subject concerned. Although a very large number of the most-used documentary sources are now available in electronic form via any networked PC, the whole range still has to be considered when identifying the only source for the purpose, or the best, the cheapest or the most convenient. The whole range of formats inevitably has to be exploited for in-depth and specialised enquiries.

There is no point here in discussing the pros and cons of the different external and internal formats of business information sources; they have to be accepted, and they all have their role. There is certainly a trend away from printed versions of directories, reports and periodicals alike, towards more rapidly updatable and more flexibly usable electronic forms. While the CD-ROM format holds its own as a medium for large amounts of less time-sensitive data and software, most business information is also, or exclusively, delivered online in World Wide Web format.

Cost Considerations

It is not only the advent of the web and user-friendly interfaces that has 'democratised' information use, but also charging policies. Whereas a copy of an expensive printed or CD-ROM source was held centrally in an organisation's library, or even a public collection, online databases and even CD-ROMs are available in a variety of payment packages including fixed-cost agreements for whole organisations, and pay-per-view alternatives. As the Appendix demonstrates, the most useful sources are still expensive, and therefore continue to be accessed within businesses via information professionals, who either hold the appropriate budget for the firm or charge expenditure to departmental cost centres. Free business information is easily found by business users of the web, via for instance business gateways on search directories like Yahoo! or subject-specific gateways. Although free sites are of limited value on their own, there is a danger of end-users regarding them as their total and adequate information resource, and foregoing the rewards to be gained from further effort.

Online Hosts

Choice Between Direct or Host Access

> 'Search the world's largest business database . . . Find the facts instantly . . . Get updated immediately . . . Track your competitors . . . Follow the markets . . . Get the essential facts fast . . . Get an instant view of current affairs . . . A global resource that doesn't cost the earth. Profound can . . . scour over 45,000 market research reports, 250,000 analyst reports . . . ecomonic forecasts and analyses for 192 countries and 4.5 million country reports. It can look through archived news from over 4,000 newspapers, magazines and trade journals from around the world and 27 global newswires . . .'
> (From a Profound brochure, 1998.)

Whether an electronic source is used directly by the business person, or by an information professional, the user often has a bewildering choice of routes to it. The example of ICC's company information products, in the 'Comprehensive Company Information Databases' section of chapter 2 shows how the same basic data is available in different forms, under different database names, direct from the publisher and via a number of hosts. Information intermediaries have favoured the use of hosts because the large ones are the nearest thing to the 'one stop shop' concept claimed even for the sites of single specialist providers. Hosts offer a standard interface and single contract and invoicing for many of the databases which heavy searchers need.

Since the late 1980s business information sources have ever-increasingly predominated on the hosts, such that in the 1990s Profound and FT Profile, two of the largest, are identified entirely with business information. There are other advantages in using hosts, including their ready-made selections of complementary databases, all accessible via a choice of common search interfaces. Additional search features compensate for and capitalise on the wide range of databases offered, such as:

Bibliographical aids

Where hosts' resources are effectively separate databases as opposed to commonly indexed documents, file descriptions such as DataStar's *Datasheets* and Dialog's *Bluesheets* are necessary. DataStar's *BASE* is an example of far more detail on individual databases, which may include lists of sources, and company- or industry-controlled vocabulary codes. Thus, searching the 'Description' field of *BASE* could show for instance which database covers Italian companies and gives directors' names. The free database selection aids on DialogWeb and DatastarWeb are a useful preliminary, even if you are going on to do a dial-up, command search. These take the form of hierarchical subject trees, where the last stage is a list of databases matching the desired criteria.

Multiple database indexes

Similarly, where there are separate databases, which the user must or may choose between, devices like Dialog's *DIALINDEX* and *DataStar's Cross Database Search* check the indexes of predetermined groups of databases or user-specified groups, for a searcher's term and report the number of hits per database.

Dialog Product Code Finder matches the searcher's name for a product line with the product name fields in all the records of all the relevant databases. It reports for each database of the product name and code, and the number of records relating to that product. *Company Name Finder* is an equivalent which works similarly.

Simultaneous searching of multiple databases

FT Profile's Data Collections – e.g. *Market Research*: simultaneous searching of the full text market surveys held in approximately 30 separate databases. Dialog's OneSearch and DataStar's StarSearch are similar, allowing seemless searching of pre-defined or user-defined sets of databases, including eliminating duplicate records from results. In very user-friendly approaches characterised by Profound's AutoSearch or WorldSearch interfaces, the software uses a sophisticated index to relate the query directly to the ultimate documents, eliminating the concept of intervening proprietary databases.

The other features offered by hosts capitalise less upon their range of databases, and are now widely found in the search interfaces of individual online information providers also. Prominent are:

Commands and facilities valuable in retrieving business information
Command language interfaces, sometimes marketed as 'Classic' interfaces, are even now favoured by experienced information professionals as the most direct way of extracting data from field-structured databases. Unlike 'user-friendly' devices, such as responding to prompts, or leaving the software to make generalised assumptions about syntax and semantics, command searching requires knowledge of the particular host's command language, the database's field structure and indexing and their combination into effective search strategies. The following syntax devices can be used separately or in combination, in for instance *ICC British Company Financial Datasheets*:

Syntax	Result – finds company records where
MORTGAGE=YES	A mortgage register document is available
ICAC=YES	Full text accounts are available in ICC's ICAC file
ICBR=YES	A broker's report available in ICC's ICBR file
SUBSID=YES	Records for subsidiaries of the company exist
PP=NEGATIVE	There is a negative figure in the Pretax profit field
SA>1000000	There is a figure greater than 1,000,000 in the sales field
EM WL 100,1000	The employees are within the limits 100 and 1000

Example of a search statement to find all the quoted companies in Manchester with ICC scores greater than 60, not advised by Coopers and Lybrand:

(QU=YES AND RO=MANCHESTER AND CS<60) NOT COOPERS ADJ LYBRAND.PR.

As graphical user interfaces improve in effectiveness, and hosts give the less experienced end-user a high priority, the future for command languages is uncertain. Especially in their newer web versions, FT Profile, Dialog and DataStar give a low profile to their command languages by comparison with their more user-friendly alternatives. The comparatively-recently launched Profound host has never had a command interface. In common with Dow Jones Interactive and many other of the latest GUIs, Profound 'conceals' what in practice may be diverse source databases behind a limited number of subject or format-oriented virtual databases. Once a query is entered, it is up to the software to identify and present the relevant data in relevant formats; in Profound's case this is InfoSort, their 'powerful proprietary indexing technology'. The InfoSort concept is to allocate every source record with standard terms for market sector, company, title, publication date, country, publisher and scope as appropriate, as well as allowing free text retrieval. Thus in the more advanced *WorldSearch*, terms can be typed into a search form for some or all these fields, to be matched against all the documents and databases in the six virtual data collections. In the Profound Worldsearch screen-shot below, the Wireline 'database' has been selected, and the user is invited to enter search values in any of the eight InfoSort criteria:

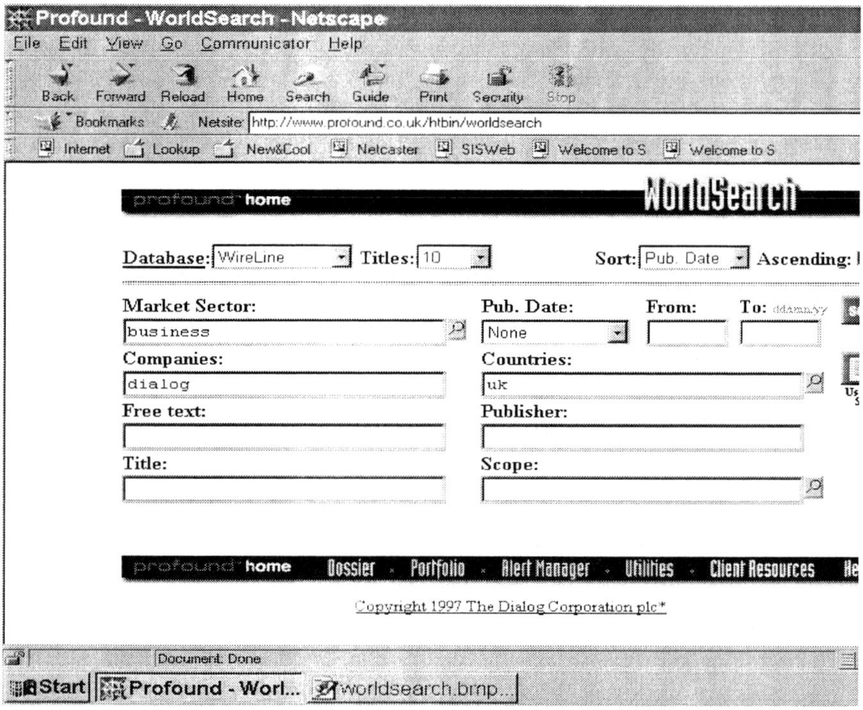

Figure 18. Worldsearch – Wireline search using Infosort categories

In *EasySearch* mode, users can instead select from a limited number of terms offered on search screens, such as one offering a search for all kinds of information relating to any of about 30 different industry sectors.

The bulk of Profound's searchable resources are represented by the six simple one word 'databases' options given below, with other information services under 'buttons' such as *GlobalNews Plus*, *Quotes* and *Custom Alert*. Further explanations are linked to each, from which the notes below are taken; a list of ultimate sources is normally available, but by virtue of *InfoSort*, and in common with the trend in interfaces for business end-users, Profound does not present its service in terms of named proprietary databases. Thus it is difficult to compare the scope of Profound with competitors, which since its convergence with Dialog and DataStar are few other than FT Profile anyway. Nevertheless it appears that Profound uses fewer and less diverse provider's and source databases, concentrating on the standard subjects, data types and record structures which the software and the end-user are comfortable with. All the details on Profound, Dialog and DataStar in the following sections are very much subject to change resulting from the convergence.

Researchline
Current and archived market surveys from over 70 (named) worldwide market research companies, many of which are exclusive to Profound.

Brokerline
Thousands of analysts' reports from hundreds of named, mainly UK and USA brokers.

Newsline
Newspapers magazines and trade journals from over 190 countries, translated from 17 languages. Includes up to ten years' archive.

Wireline
Real-time wire articles from approximately 30 of the world's best known news agencies.

Countryline
Country reports, economic forecasts and analyses from providers including EIU, Political and Economic Risk Consultancy, Quest Economics and WEFA.

Company line
Concentrates on offering a wide base of full financial records, provided by selected leading providers worldwide.

GlobalNews Plus
A business news super-database, incorporating source files such as *World Reporter*.

The interface which characterised Profound from its comparatively recent launch is a more sophisticated version of the end-user oriented menu-based alternatives available on Dialog and DataStar in recent years. The former *DataStar Business Focus*, and the former *KR Business Base* on Dialog were business examples of subject-specific interfaces which can extract data from a limited range databases, with little more input from the user than to select a databases from several offered. A totally inexperienced searcher could make selections from a series of lists of alternatives, to be presented with a perhaps difficult choice of relevant databases, and the invitation to input terms to be matched against limited fields of records. 'Easy search' interfaces cope poorly or not at all with less common search needs and with databases with non-standard or complex structures. However, the more sophisticated options aimed at experienced searchers replicate most of the functions of the command language, though unfortunately often omitting some of the useful numerical search operators mentioned above. In DataStar web *Advanced Search* the user is *offered* most of the functions of the command-driven interface, without having to remember or input the commands or syntax. The original Dialog web interface is most appropriate for an experienced searcher because it employs a combination of Dialog commands and more typical point and click features; not surprisingly the much simpler Dialog Select was added as an alternative.

Good interfaces include information management, as well as retrieval features. Various DataStar interfaces, for instance, invite the searcher to input account codes before searching, to facilitate charging of the search to the correct client, budget head or department when the bill arrives. FT Profile's *Freeway* allows administrators to designate user categories, each with different usage limits. It can also display the cost of a display command in advance of its execution. *DataStar for Windows* can automatically adjust the user's view of available databases to those allowed by their user ID. Expenditure data for individual user IDs can be downloaded directly into spreadsheet software.

Alerting systems
Such as Dialog *Alerts*, where the subscriber is automatically notified of either any additions to specified databases or of additions matching specified search criteria.

Stored and re-executable searches, portfolio services
Systems such as Dialog's *SearchSave* allow perhaps complex search statement to be saved for ad hoc or automatic re-execution and if desired to include only records added since the last search. Although details of users' own portfolios can usually be input into financial information providers' systems, it is less common among generalist online hosts. Profound's *Portfolio* service is sophisticated enough to be used by investment research departments, and not only updates prices and values but provides links to news and reports, which can be automatically emailed to the user.

Current awareness, selective dissemination
Most hosts' and other elaborate interfaces facilitate selective dissemination through a combination of devices exemplified in other sections; including automatically re-executable searches, alert features and news services, deliverable to individuals via hosts' intranet services and/or email.

Gateways to other hosts or providers

Hosts commonly facilitate users' transfer to the computers of other collaborating and complementary hosts or publishers. A separate contract and password is sometimes necessary in order to use the second service, and the search interfaces are those of that system. Dialog offers a gateway to *Official Airlines Guide* and to several financial markets quotes services. Although *FT Profile* hosts some ICC databases, one of its gateways is to ICC's own interface and computers.

Document delivery services

As well as the choice of delivering full-text search results offline, hosts often back up their bibliographical databases with the option of acquiring the full text of a periodical article or other publication. Dialog offers *Uncover*, *KR SourceOne* and *DIALORDER* as means of obtaining the full text of patents and many other documents in the bibliographical databases, delivered digitally via the web, by fax or other methods.

Data organisation and format

Hosts' software typically eliminates duplicate records from the results of cross database searching. Other formatting, not peculiar to hosts' software, includes a choice of level of detail, so that output can be both economical (where charging is based on usage) and appropriate to purpose. Though in command-driven interfaces the generalist hosts invite the user to specify the fields to be output, their pre-defined formats are often a simplistic choice of 'short', 'medium' or 'full'. A free short format is usually available as a retrieval aid, or free table of contents for a long expensive document like a market survey. A keyword in context (KWIC) format is often also available free, and many systems allow the highlighting of search terms in retrieved textual records, as in Dialog's 'Hilight' feature. Devices like 'Profile' in Dialog's *Classic* interface allow these and many other display preferences to be set on or off. A more elaborate choice of reports of different levels of detail and cost is usually available via information providers' own direct interfaces – such as the ten options in one of ICC's services. Profound has 'Briefings' search level, within which single page or more detailed briefing versions of Market, Company, Country reports are obtained, as well as 'Stock reports' from Standard & Poor's.

More and more interfaces now allow retrieved data to be, for instance, organised into tables, exportable into local software. The default arrangement of the records output is usually added to the file by date, however, most software also allows the user to specifiy arrangement by a chosen data element; for example by company turnover. Profound has featured digital image format from its inception, so that documents such as newspaper articles and certain other documents are viewed in original full form. Thus, columns, graphical and even multimedia information is preserved, and reading and presentation quality equates to CD-ROMs, the web and in-house software.

A traditional attraction of online hosts is that subscribers can share a wide range of sources, on a payment for use basis. The situation has been somewhat affected by an increase among hosts in payment-in-advance and minimum usage contracts – exemplified below – and the availability of alternative deals direct with the information provider. Although charges for the same database (comparative costs are available in certain of the bibliographies listed in the later section) sometimes differ considerably between hosts, and between the hosts and the direct route, there is no obvious reason why prices should differ between direct and indirect distribution.

Charges and Charging

In 'pay-per-view' or 'transactional' payment plans, hosts sometimes still make separate charges for their main areas of expenditure: the payment to the provider for the data and the usage of the host's computer in searching; the user incurs a further charge for the use of national and international telecommunications networks. The former is usually the greatest, and is the cost which varies from database to database per 'connect hour'.

After experiments with all possible pricing options, the trend is away from payment for connection time, and towards the more realistic basis of payment for substantive data output. It is common for preliminary searching to be free or very cheap, including viewing brief output formats and using search-aid databases, with costs only attached to receiving detailed data.

In transactional deals, subscriptions are a more or less token amount to cover the administration of issuing a password and providing printed documentation such as database descriptions and manuals – most of which are also available online. Under such contracts, users have traditionally subscribed to a number of hosts, using each as little or as much as they need, for which they are typically billed monthly. However, hosts are currently moving towards the sort of flat-fee contracts favoured by the real-time financial information providers, for variable usage up to an agreed maximum. These fees are typically negotiable rather than fixed, and include not only the data but also telecoms, connect time, and facilities such as alerts. The trend is also towards minimum monthly charges for transaction-based contracts, driving organisations to make greater use of fewer hosts.

The Dialog Corporation, the result of MAID's (Profound host) acquisition of Dialog and DataStar from Knight Ridder in 1997, is the largest international player and inevitably a trendsetter for services, interfaces and charging methods. The firm now commands both wide North American and European content. Although common indexing and telecommunications are leading to convergence of the databases available through each of the three hosts, they have initially kept separate physical locations, interfaces and charging structures. Dialog's charging basis is moving towards Profound's pattern of flat-fee agreements for negotiable usage at a negotiable cost. To their surprise, since 1998 transaction-based contract customers have been charged according to usage of Dialog Interactive Language Units (DialUnits) which 'represent the usage of system resources necessary to execute search commands', plus a display charge per record. This harks back to charging not by data received, but by connect time – what was called CPU (Computer Performance Unit) pricing. Since both DialUnit and display charges vary from database to database, as the following pricing examples show, costs still relate to a large extent to the provider's charge to the host. A free or very low-cost 'KWIC' format is also available for each database, that is a view of the search term/s withing a limited amount of surrounding data.

Dialog transaction charges examples (as at 1998)

	Per DialUnit	Display (per record)
– Search aid databases		
Bluesheets (database descriptions)	free	free
DIALINDEX (Cross databases index)	$1.75	free
Company Name Finder	$1.75	free
– Substantive databases		
Investext (brokers' research reports)	$5.75	$7.60 per page
Dun's Electronic Business Directory	$6.50	$0.50 – full, $0.25 per element
Dun's Financial records Plus	$9.00	$25.00 – partial, $102.00 – full
Datamonitor Market Research	$5.50	$19.50
Experian Business Credit Profiles	$5.00	$32.00 – full, $0.45 per element
ICC British Company Financial Datasheets	$5.25	$41.00 – full, $0.55 per element

The minimum monthly usage fee, shown below, was introduced for Dialog soon after merger, but was said late in 1998 not to be imminent for DataStar.

In the expectation of increasing usage, direct information providers and hosts alike now appeal directly to end-users, with interfaces which are more user-friendly than the traditional command language approach favoured by professional searchers. As can be seen below, business information databases today figure strongly on the largest conventional online hosts, most of which are now in the hands of business and financial media owners. Most have recently marketed end-user oriented packages, with distinctive names, simpler interfaces and often also fixed payment terms. Most are also capitalising on business' take-up of the web, intranets, knowledge management and e-commerce, by developing software which integrates internal and external information – such as Dialog's *@Site*.

Although ever-increasing use of the Internet is certainly adding to the business of information providers and perhaps also to the traditional hosts, the greatest benefit may be to firms which are a natural or necessary gateway to the Internet for end-users. The first point of contact for most users and usages is either their Internet service provider (such as Pipex, Easynet or America Online), a search service (such as AltaVista and SearchUK), or for corporate users, the providers of software to gather, distribute and/or organise information on the intranet. All these providers are in a strong position to retail business information along with their primary service, in other words to become online hosts. Search tool providers like Yahoo! are indeed developing into information aggregators, and some pioneers of intranet push-technology and/or news redistribution are moving into broader scope information hosting – IBM for example. America Online contracts with 'preferred providers' to offer their 12 million subscribers commercial business information, on certain of their 19 'channels'.

Hosts with Major Business Information Content

(Including examples of interface and contract alternatives for several.)

Business Information Generalists

Note: At the time of writing, limited or complete convergence is underway between Dialog, DataStar and Profound. URLs are given for web-based interfaces and/or where further information can be found.

Dialog – *http://www.dialog.com/* (Dialog Corporation)

Scope

More than 450 databases, at least half of which together cover the full range of business information topics in depth. Dialog's range and combination of databases probably make it the most comprehensive business information host, and the leader for American business coverage.

Interfaces and charging

DIialog Classic

The original command-based interface, available via dial-up or web site. Charging by DialUnit and display charge, or flat-fee contract.

Dialog@Site

Intranet access to Dialog OnDisc databases (various providers' data republished on CD-ROM by Dialog) via a web browser.

DialogWeb

'Tool for intermediate and advanced online searchers'. Access to most of the databases and functions (not the menu-based databases, and gateway services) via a web browser; choice of command or guided command searching. Charged by DialUnit and display charge, or flat fee contract.

DialogSelect

Easy to use, end-user oriented version of Dialog web, includes 'industry-specific' interfaces and database collections, such as DialogBusiness, DialogChem and DialogAgro. Charging by flat-fee contract.

DialogSelect for Windows

Dial-up version of DialogSelect above. Charging by DialUnit and display charge, or flat-fee contract.

DataStar – *http://www.dialog.com/* (Dialog Corporation)

Scope

DataStar has the dual emphases of business and biomedicine. Its approximately 200 business files provide a probably unmatched breadth and depth of coverage of European business information. Many UK users also find DataStar the most useful single host for their general business information needs.

Interfaces and charging

DataStar

The original command-based product; dial-up Telnet access. In the short-term at least, transaction-based charging retained under Dialog Corporation ownership.

DataStarWeb

Access via a normal web browser. Includes Easy and Advanced Search options. Charging as DataStar, above.

KR ProBase

DataStar for Windows. Charging as DataStar, above

Profound – *http://www.dialog.com/* (Dialog Corporation)

Scope

Dedicated to business information and tending to concentrate on the 'standard', most often sought subjects and formats – that is, company financial data, market research, financial information, investment research, company information and business news. Source material appears to be as full as other major hosts' in those areas, but not as full as others in the more specialist and peripheral areas of business information. As mentioned in a section above, Profound was launched with a graphic interface aimed at end-users, linking queries with ultimate sources without the obvious intermediary of proprietary databases.

Interfaces and charging

Profound is primarily a web-based host, but a dial-up and intranet versions are also available. Charging is by flat-fee for unlimited usage up to agreed maximum, which includes unlimited use of *Briefings*, *NewsNow*, *Quotes and Custom Alert*. Alternative search interfaces include *WorldSearch* (the 'professional' GUI interface) and *QuickSearch* – as illustrated.

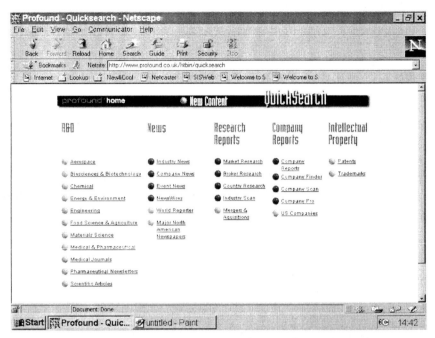

Figure 19. Contents page from Profound Quicksearch

FT Profile and FT Discovery – *http://www.ftep.ft.com/profile.htm*

Scope

FT Profile pre-dates Profound as a host specialising in business information. In keeping with its history and ownership FT Profile has unmatched holdings of British and European news titles, databases and aggregations. Its approximately 200 databases today cover at least the standard business information subjects, especially from the point of view of the British user.

Interfaces and charging

FT Profile

The standard product for professionals and others, searched via the simple Windows, or command-driven (FT Profile search language) *Infoplus* interface. Transaction-based charging; each database is allocated to one of the price bands Q1 to Q8.

FT Discovery

Web-browser interface designed for end-users, including via corporate intranets. Selected resources are presented as Country, Company, Sector, and various news categories. Charged at fixed monthly rate.

OneSource – *http://www.onesource.com/*

> A smaller American business information host with a UK office and integrated 'suites' of information available from their web site. It was formerly the LotusOne Source division of the Lotus Development Corporation, delivering data on CD-ROM with the Lotus Notes software familiar to many businesses. The following 'family of integrated company and business information suites' include complementary data from a number of UK information providers; available on separate fixed-price subscriptions:

> *Business Browser* – a general company and industry research tool; *Global, UK* and *US Business Browser* versions are also available.

> *Account Manager* – aimed at sales professionals and relationship managers.

> *Insurance Analyst* – integrated insurance industry news and trade articles, statutory filings and public company information.

>> 'Business Browser combines core business information types into a single resource.The content is not just aggregated, it's integrated – built around business applications, not merely around data. . . . OneSource integrates content from the following information partners: Comtex, Corporate Technology Information Services, Disclosure, Financial Times Information, Graham & Whiteside, Hoover's Inc., Information Access Company, infoUSA, The Investext Group, Market Guide, Marquis Who's Who, National Register Publishing, Phillips, RDS, Reuters, and Standard and Poor's.' (From product descriptions, on OneSource web site.)

Biz@dvantage – *http://www.biz.telebase.com/* (WinStar Telebase Inc.)

> As well as Dun & Bradstreet mentioned below, an impressive range of providers' databases is hosted, including from ICC, Extel, Moody's, Hoppenstedt, Kompass, Standard & Poor's, Teikoku and Thomas Register. Charging is on a pay-as-you-use basis; there are web and Windows interfaces:

>> ' . . . a comprehensive source of brand name information, featuring financial & credit data from Dun & Bradstreet, along with thousands of the world's most powerful business information sources.It's simple point and click access to thousands of the world's most powerful business information sources – private and public company profiles, international patent and trademark data, industry newsletters, worldwide research, and much more . . .'

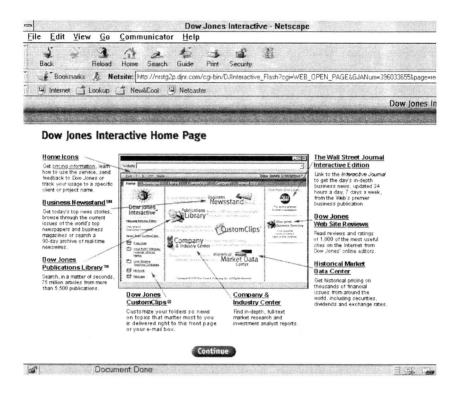

Figure 20. Dow Jones Interactive home page

Dow Jones Interactive – *http://www.bis.dowjones.com/* (Dow Jones, USA)

Scope is stated as 'business news and research'. However, Dow Jones' own news wires and financial markets data are complemented by data from selected other leading providers to create a rounded business information resource. Dial-up and web interfaces present the resources under a number of 'components', primarily:

Business Newsstand

Current newswires, full-text general and financial newspapers, and a newspapers archive.

Publications Library

Research archive of more than 3,700 US and non-US, business and non-business sources.

Custom Clips

Continuous alerts of new items on the companies industries etc. selected by editors or individual subscribers, from the many current news sources on the system.

Company & Industry Center

Includes market surveys provided by Investext's *Markintel* from 45 different publishers, Investext's own collection of reports from more than 400 financial analysts, country data from the Economist Intelligence Unit, and company reports from Dun & Bradstreet.

Historical Market Data Center

(As described in the 'Financial Information' chapter.)

Payment options include the Corporate Flat Fee Programme, and a transactional plan with separate prices for the many alternative report formats available for the different 'components'.

Specialists Within Business Information

Reuters Business Briefing – *http://www.reuters.se/informa.htm* (Reuters Holdings)

In common with Nikkei's host, Reuters Business Briefing is primarily the general user's interface to the company's own market prices and news services. However, sources from a limited number of other providers are added, not to create a complete business information service, but to satisfy the needs of investment research. Resources are presented as the following channels:

News Wires

The full range of Reuters business and non-business global news, including company and regulatory news as released by the worlds' exchanges.

News Search

Up to 10 years searchable archive of Reuters news sources, other worldwide business publications, and Reuters database of news pictures.

Company Profiles

Basic accounts data for over 22,000 of the world's major quoted companies, from Reuters own sources, disclosed company documents, and third party providers.

Quotes and Foreign Exchange

Share price, market index and foreign exchange data from the financial markets of the world; software to input own portfolio for automatic valuation.

EIU Viewswire

Business Briefing subscribers have access to *EIU Viewswire* (described in the 'Country Information' chapter), for intelligence on basic economic, political and other background factors, including alerting to changes.

Four different 'levels of service' are available to some or all of this data (from Reuters documentation):

Headline	*Target*	*Select*	*Search*
Keeps everyone aware of the top world news stories.	Provides a regular briefing for 9,000 intranet users.	Brings more in-depth news to 1000 externally facing staff.	Gives interactive access to the entire Reuters Business Briefing database to 100 'power users'.

Charging for Reuters Business Briefing is by a choice of pre-payment contracts, rather than pay-as-you-go.

Japan News and Retrieval – *http://www.nikkei.co.jp/enews/NIKKEI/pub.html#telecom* (Nikkei Telecom, Japan)

Japan News and Retrieval is primarily the English language dial-up or web interface to Nikkei's own databases oriented to Japan and the Far East. The approximately 15 databases cover news, corporate information and macro- and microeconomic indicators. Like Reuters Business Briefing, the data is aimed at the needs of the dealer and investor in the financial markets – in Nikkei's own words it is presented as:

Corporate Information

Retrieve a wealth of corporate date, unrivalled in its coverage of Japan's listed and uslisted companies. Review detailed corporate profiles, earnings estimates and over 25 years of financial statements – invaluable information for corporate analysts and fund managers.

Market Information

Access current and historical quotes covering all stocks, bonds, indices, currencies, futures and options traded on Tokyo and overseas markets. Identify important trends in the Japanese and world economies with the latest statistics, key indicators and detailed economic forecasts.

News Information

Instantly access fast-breaking news gathered by Nikkei's worldwide reporting network: real-time updates on financial, industrial and political events. Use Nikkei's vast historical article database of major Japanese and Asian newspapers.

Investext – *http://www.investext.com/* (Investext Group)

Better known as a major database of company and industry investment research reports on various hosts, Investext has increased its scope and developed as a host in its own right. Resources are the huge collection of reports from over 500 analysts, reports from 150 worldwide trade associations, and 60 providers' market surveys. 80% of the providers are said to be exclusive to Investext. The web interface is called Research Bank, which includes original image copies of the full-text reports purchasable in full or by the page. I/Plus Direct is the

Windows interface, through which the resources are presented separately as *Investext* (the analysts' reports), *Pipeline* (the latest analysts' reports), *Markintel* (the market surveys), and *Industry Insider* (the trade associations' reports).

IMR Mall – *http://www.imrmall.com* (International Market Research)

A web-based specialist market reports host. IMR Mall includes the reports of Freedonia, Beverage Marketing, Business Communications Company, Euromonitor, FIND/SVP; plus country-specific economic and related data from Quest Economics.

IBM InfoSage – *http://www.infosage.ibm.com* (IBM)

Mentioned in the 'News and Industry Information' chapter as a news redistributor, IBM is not quite yet a host in the normal sense, but were quoted as saying, 'We expect to add content and functions in the future while maintaining or even reducing prices. We see great potential to integrate the customer's internal company information into the public information provided by IBM InfoSage.' (Sara Record, 'Personalized Electronic Information service', *NetNews* – IBM's Quarterly Networking Magazine, issue 2, 1996, via *http://www.networking.ibm.com*). Although currently predominently channeling US news to intranets, IBM plans to 'expand it to additional geographies', and already adds counts Dun & Bradstreet, Information Access Company and Standard and Poor's among its content providers.

Hosts Which Include Business Information with Other Subjects

Questel Orbit – *http://www.questel.orbit.com/* (France Telecom)

Includes about 50 France and Europe oriented business databases, with many others covering science and technology, news and other subjects.

OCLC FirstSearch – *http://www.oclc.org/oclc/menu/fs.htm*

OCLC's wide-ranging and largely bibliographical service includes a minority of business information databases, including company information from Disclosure and others. Web or Telnet (i.e. dial-up) access.

LEXIS-NEXIS – *http://www.lexis.com/xchange/* (Reed Elsevier)

While LEXIS specialises in information for lawyers, NEXIS is the part of the service relevant to business people, mainly due its holdings of full-text business news sources.

'Serving customers in more than 60 countries, sales representatives are located in 50 U.S. cities and around the world, including in London, Frankfurt and Toronto. The company is a division of Reed Elsevier Inc., part of the Reed Elsevier plc group, one of the world's leading publishing and information businesses. Reed Elsevier is headquartered in London. LEXIS-NEXIS is based in Dayton, Ohio and employs 4,500 individuals worldwide. . . . an estimated 300,000 searches a day on the LEXIS service and the companion NEXIS news and information service, which began in 1979. The combined services contain more than 18,300 sources: 13,500 news and business sources, and 4,800 legal sources.' (From LEXIS-NEXIS web site.)

Identification and Selection of Sources (Bibliographical Control)

The apparent infinity of both business information needs and potential sources make a systematic means of relating one to the other absolutely essential. Even experienced researchers use bibliographic tools to ensure that if the information exists it is found, and that it is found quickly and efficiently. Lists and guides can lead to the source which not only matches the often complex parameters of the question, but which is also the most easily accessible, the most detailed and reliable, and which is the best value for money. In practice, bibliographical control is achieved through a combination of describing available sources, and arranging those descriptions for systematic access. Although the main aim of this section is to consider the range of bibliographical tools available to us, a mention is desirable of the retrieval systems which may exist within them, within collections of sources, and within sources themselves.

Controlled Vocabularies

To maximise the retrieval of relevant information and minimise the retrieval of irrelevant information, some library collections and some individual sources index business activities, place and company names, and even 'concepts' or types of information, using standardised terminology or 'controlled vocabulary'. Aspects of systems are covered where relevant in the 'Company Information' and 'Product Information' chapters, so only a brief summary follows.

Classification Schemes

The following is used to arrange documents on shelves, and to a lesser extent as the arrangement or access points in retrieval systems:

> *London Classification of Business Studies: a classification and thesaurus for business libraries* by K.D.C. Vernon and V. Lang, rev. by K.G.B. Bakewell and D. Cotton. Aslib, 1979.

Industrial Classification Systems

Although developed as methods of measuring countries' economic aciviy, certain other classification systems used to arrange entries in printed sources, to retrieve from databases, and to a lesser extent to arrange documents on shelves. Countries and even publishers have independently developed 'Standard Industrial Classifications', so the 'SIC's cited in sources are different from each other. They do have in common the fact that they break down business activity hierarchically, and allocate an alphanumeric code to each stage of division. SICs are still important in the organisation and publication of official industry statistics and many proprietary databases, though EU countries are expected to harmonise with the General Industrial Nomenclature of Economic Activities in the European Communities (NACE). Simultaneously, the USA and Canada are moving away from their own SICs in favour of the harmonised North American Industrial Classification System (NAICS), needed to facilitate the North American Free Trade Agreement. So although European and American systems will continue to differ, there should eventually be fewer industrial classification systems in use, and perhaps none sharing the name SIC.

Section of the US SIC (1987 version) showing the hierarchical structure

20	Food and kindred products
..24	Lumber and wood products
249	Miscellaneous wood products
2491	Wood preserving
2493	Reconstituted wood products

While national industrial classifications relate to activities at the level of an industry, others exist to classsify individual products. These are needed for instance for the import/export duty collection and statistics in the Harmonised Tariff System for international trade, and for the arrangement and/or retrieval system of directories and databases of product information. The information provider IAC's *Product Codes* are one such example, included below:

Examples of the industrial and product classifications used in sources

NACE (Nomenclature des Activités Economiques).

Standard Industrial Classification for the UK ('SIC'). Central Statistical Office. Harmonised with the European NACE.

Standard Industrial Classification (also known as 'SIC'; USA).

IAC Product Codes. Based on USA SIC codes; used in IAC's databases, listed in the users' manual.

McCarthy Industry Classification list. Subject codes as used in McCarthy on FT Profile.

Stock Exchange Classification Codes ('SEC', USA). To index companies by the subject of their activity.

NAICS (North American Industrial Classification System; to replace US and Canadian SICs in official data collection and dissemination).

Concept Coding

It is desirable to have a means of indexing and retrieving records by concepts which are impossible to search for by natural language text words (such as whether the treatment of a subject is *statistical*, concerning *its market*, or from a company's *annual report*); and also abstract concepts not catered for by industrial activity or product vocabularies (such as 'profits', 'disease', 'Europe'). These are prominent examples of such systems:

> *FT Type of Information codes*. Used in certain FT Profile databases, e.g. *McCarthy*; e.g. 'IND' for an industry profile.
>
> *IAC Event codes* (e.g. E33 for new products). Used in *PROMT* etc. databases, listed in the user manual.
>
> *Profound host's Scope Terms*: 'All incoming data to Profound is classified to a unique set of indexing . . . "Scope terms" in particular are unique to Profound and identify the context of the article – regardless of the words it contains.' For example, terms for the finance industry are: Company Profiles, Contracts and Orders, Corporate Funding, Corporate Performance, Joint Ventures, Legal, Management Changes, Patents and Trademarks, Regulation, Strategy and Planning, Monetary Policy, Business Failures.
>
> *Subject Category Terms* used in the SC field of the *World Reporter* news database. A large list complementing the use of US SIC codes for business activities; it includes concepts in business and commerce, documentation, political and geographical entities. The list is available to searchers in both alphabetical and hierarchical form, for example:
>
> > Company news
> >
> > > Acquisitions takeovers and mergers
> > > Bankruptcies and receiverships
> > > Buy-ins and buy-outs
> > > Results
> > > Interim results
> > > Year-end results
> > > [approximately 60 more concepts under Company news]

Standard Names

To facilitate searching for long and variable company names (and, less often, names of geographical entities), for example:

> *Textline's company codes*. Unique codes searchable on Reuters' Textline database.
>
> *Ticker symbols*. Short unique codes for American listed companies, used in some databases.
>
> *ISO Country Codes*. As used in McCarthy on FT Profile.
>
> *IAC country codes*. Used in IAC's databases, e.g. PROMT.

Bibliographical Apparatus

A bibliographical apparatus does indeed exist for systematic access to business information; however, it is so large and complex that it may be necessary for an information professional to tackle even that, let alone the sources it leads to. The solution is also imperfect because a number of bibliographic tools have to be used in combination for coverage of searcher's parameters. The tools vary in terms of scope, detail, and other parameters (which are often not made explicit), and method of access. It is an advantage when they cover *institutions* as information sources as well as documents; however, this is not usually apparent from their titles.

Tools appear in a variety of physical forms, from web search engines and gateways to printed directories; some are even published as serials. Very useful, but harder to trace systematically, bibliographical guidance often appears in periodical articles (such as in *Business Information Review*), books (like this one), and other unexpected sources. For access to many sources of relevance to business, it is necessary make use of the massive general, non-business bibliographical apparatus. Adding to this complexity, many useful business information sources are not 'controlled' by the expected bibliographies at all, or not at an adequate level of detail, especially new, changing and foreign sources. And anyway, finding a source in a bibliography is no guarantee that one has access to it.

Certain valuable guides to business information do aim to be comprehensive in terms of breadth, but they are understandably selective and sparing in coverage and treatment. The searcher may be best served by one of the many finding tools which explicitly or implicitly concentrates on one or more of the following:

- particular *systems* (such as libraries, networks, online hosts);
- specific *subject* categories – broad, narrow and overlapping – e.g. company, products, markets;
- specific *geographical* or trade areas;
- specific *forms* of, or *origins* of sources – e.g. directories, databases, statistics; free sources.

A reasonable search strategy is to enter the bibliographical apparatus at the most specific level appropriate to at least one of the important parameters of the query. For instance, if a market surveys database is definitely required, either a guide to market surveys or a guide to business databases would be appropriate, though a guide to market surveys databases would be ideal. If only Dialog were available for the same search, then the host's own catalogues and online bibliographical aids (described above) may be preferable.

Brief details of many of the relevant bibliographies and guides to sources follow, each appearing in just one category, even if like *The Instant Guide to Company Information Online – Europe*, the item not only covers a specific subject or environmental domain, but also a particular physical format.

A Bibliography of Business Information Bibliographies

1. Business information sources in general

1.1 Bibliographies of bibliographies

'Tracking British and European online business information: a guide to the guides.' H. Drenth, G. Tseng, and A. Morris. *Online Review* 15(6), December 1991, pp. 356-365.

1.2 Bibliographies and guides of broad scope

Business Information: How to Find it, How to Use it, 2nd edn. M.R. Lavin. Oryx, 1992.

A-Z of Business Information Sources. Croner. Loose-leaf printed or CD-ROM.

Business Information Basics, 1997. Pam Foster (ed). Headland, 1997. Serially published directory of sources, organisations and services, not limited geographically or by physical form.

Business Information Briefing. Croner. Monthly newsletter; free version – *http://www.croner.co.uk/*

Business Information Bulletin. Croner. Frequent issues.

Business Information Sources, 3rd edn. L.M. Daniels. University of California Press, 1993.

Directory of Business Information Resources, 6th edn. L. MacKenzie and L. Mars (eds.). Grey House, 1997.

Directory of Business Information Sources, 3rd edn. G. Tudor (ed.). MacMillan, 1992.

European Business Information Sourcebook. Bowker-Saur. Annual – also available via their web site (*http://www.bowker_saur.co.uk/*).

European Business Information Sources. Croner. Loose-leaf.

European Business Intelligence Briefing. Bowker-Saur. Approximately monthly periodical, giving news and evaluations of sources on European business information.

European Company Information. Julie Scott (ed.). Gale, 1993.

How to Find Information – Business: a Guide to Searching in Published Sources. N. Spencer. British Library SRIS, 1995.

International Business Information: how to find it, how to use it, 2nd edn. R.A. Pagell & M. Halperin. Oryx Press, 1998.

International Directory of Business Information Sources and Services, 2nd edn. Europa, 1996.

Japanese Business Information: An Introduction. R. Clough. British Library SRIS, 1995. Lists sources and aids their location.

Mind Your Local Business: Where to Find and How to Use Local Economic and Business Information. Eurofi, 1988.

Sources of European Economic and Business Information, 6th edn. Edited by the British Library Business Information research staff. Gower, 1995.

What's New in Business Information. Bowker-Saur. Newsletter issued 20 times per year; also available from online via *http://www.bowker-saur.co.uk/*

1.3 Directories of business information services and libraries

Aslib Directory of Information Sources in the United Kingdom, 10th edn. K.W. Reynard and J.M.E. Reynard (eds.). Aslib, 1998. Regularly published directory of the library and information specialisms in associations, companies, government bodies and other organisations. Alphabetical by organisation, with subject and acronym index. Print and CD-ROM versions.

Business Information from Government. L. Lampard (ed.). Headland, 1998. A-Z profiles of government departments, agencies etc., including libraries and business related divisions.

Directory of European Information Brokers and Consultants, 9th edn. M. Crawford and V. Buchanan (eds.). Effective Technology Marketing, 1997.

EIRENE Membership Directory, 1998. EIRENE, 1997. The European Information Researchers' Network.

European Directory of Business Information Libraries. Euromonitor, 1990. Brief descriptions of the scope and services of public and private collections, arranged by the organisation's name. One of the indexes allows access by subject specialism.

Guide to Government Department and Other Libraries. British Library SRIS, 1998.

2. Guides to sources in particular 'systems'

2.1 In libraries

Business Information Network Referral Database. Directory of UK's BIN, now e-BIN, members' resources.

Market Research: a Guide to British Library Collections, 8th edn. M. Leydon and L. Lee (eds.). British Library SRIS, 1994.

Trade Statistics: Principal Series Held by EMIC. London: DTI EMIC, 1987. The Department of Trade and Industry's public Export Market Information Centre.

2.2 On the Internet, including subject gateways (see section 3 for guides to subject-specific sites)

Britannica Internet Guide: Business, Economy, Employment section – http://www.ebig.com/ – *Encyclopaedia Britannica* web site which lists hypertext links, and describes and rates selected free and charged sites.

Business Information on the Internet – http://www.dis.strath.ac.uk/business/ – Web gateway maintained by Sheila Webber at Strathclyde University.

Business Information & Economic Data – http://www.yell.co.uk/yell/web/index.html – Subcategory of UK Yellow Web's Business & Industry heading; links to many sources, providers, services.

International Business Resources on the WWW – http://ciber.bus.msu.edu/busres.htm – Michigan State University Center for International Business Education and Research's free guide to international business information resources. Scope includes news services, periodicals, country-specific information, company directories, yellow pages, trade shows and events.

Sources of Business Information on the Internet – http://www.rba.co.uk/sources/index.htm – Free site maintained by the British business information broker and consultant RBA. Categorised by business information type (e.g. 'Stock market and company financial data'.)

WhoWhere? – http://www.whowhere.lycos.com/ – Free directory-type web search service, specialising in yellow pages sites, business name finding, classified ads, and Dow Jones news.

World Database of Business Information Sources on the Web. Euromonitor; documentary and non-documentary sources worldwide, printed, or web version with links to sites – http://www.euromonitor.com/srcintro.htm

Yahoo! Finance – http://finance.yahoo.co.uk/ – A major search directory with a business focus. Searches can be restricted to UK sites.

Business Information Resources Directory – http://bird-online.co.uk/frames.html – A comercially produced example of a gateway directing business to mainly free information on the web. Includes a Virtual Reference Library, and Business Bookshop.

South Wales Information gateway (SWIG) – http://www.swig-online.co.uk/index.html – A local and non-commercial example of a gateway to mainly free, internet business information sources.

3. Specific subjects (categories parallel the foregoing chapters)

3.1 Company information

European Companies: Guide to Sources of Information. CBD Research. Biennial serial.

Instant Guide to Company Information Online – Europe, 3rd edn. N. Spencer (ed.). British Library SRIS, 1999.

Yell – *http://www.yell.co.uk* – UK oriented directory of companies web sites or companies' web sites.

World Databases in Company Information (C.J. Armstrong and R.R. Fenton eds, Bowker-Saur, 1996. Very detailed descriptions of each database, often including a list of the fields present.

Corporate Information – *http://www.corporateinformation.com/* – A meta site, i.e. listing sites offering mostly free company information; organised by country.

3.1.1 Company information: specific

Business Rankings Annual. Gale. Lists of companies, products, services and activities. 10,000 rankings trawled from 1,400 periodicals.

3.2 Market information

European Directory of Marketing Information Sources. Euromonitor, 1997.

Market Research Sourcebook. D. Mort. Bowker-Saur. Annual guide to market intelligence and its sources, also available from the publisher's web site.

Research Index. Research Index Ltd. Fortnightly index to market information in periodicals; web and printed versions.

3.2.1 Market information: specific

Findex: The Worldwide Directory of Market Research Reports, 19th edn. A. Hilli and E. Reid (eds.). Cambridge Information Group, 1997. Printed, online, or on *CD-ROM* as *KR-OnDisc Market Research Locator*.

Market Research Reporter. Headland. Approximately fortnightly newsletter; articles containing findings as supplied by publishers of market research & relevant economic and other reports.

Marketsearch: International Directory of Published Market Research. K. Mann (ed.). Arlington Management Publications, 1993. Printed, or online including via DataStar as *Marketsearch*.

3.3 Financial information

Find (Financial Information Net Directory) – *http://www.find.co.uk/* – Omnium Communications Limited's free gateway to financial services companies, free sources of financial markets information, and more.

Stock Exchange Markets in the World – *http://www.qualisteam.com/eng/act.html* – Web gateway to stock exchanges' information services.

Virtual Stock Exchange – *http://www.virtualstockexchange.com/* – US-orientated web gateway to a great range of free stock market prices, statistics etc.

3.3.1 Financial information: specific

Commodities Futures Trading: A Guide to Information Sources and Computerized Services. D. Nicholas. Mansell, 1985.

3.4 Product information

> *Engineer's Guide to Product Information: Sources and Use.* R.A. Wall (ed.).
> Aslib, 1992.

3.4.1 Product information: specific

> *On Line Patents, Trademarks and Servicemarks.* J.F. Sibley (ed.). Aslib, 1992.
> *Trade Marks: An Introductory Guide and Bibliography.* D.C. Newton.
> British Library SRIS, 1991.

3.5. News

> *NISS Services, News area – http://www.niss.ac.uk/news/index.html.* Part
> of the information gateway service provided by the UK joint aca-
> demic project NISS. Links to many authoritative business news
> sources, and others.

3.6 Country information

> *Business and Economics Research Directory.* Europa, 1996. Details of busi-
> ness oriented economic and geopolitical institutions and publications
> in 150+ countries.

> 'International Economic Analysis: the Intelligence Sources.' P. Foster.
> In *Business Information Review* 8(3), 1992, pp. 3-22.

> *International Economics Gateway – http://www.altaplana.com/gate.html.*
> Created for the OECD, now owned by the Alta Plana Corporation. A
> valuable guide "resource pages and data archives" – i.e. other macro-
> economics data gateways, and many free economics web sites
> themselves.

3.6.1 Country information: specific

> 'East European Business Information Business.' In *Information Review*
> Special Report 7(2), 1990, pp. 3-32. On economic and other back-
> ground reports.

> 'Economic Forecasts: a Comparative Survey,' D. Scott. In *Business In-
> formation Review* 4(2), 1987, pp. 73-23.

4. Guides to specific forms of source, and origins of information

4.1 Online and other databases

> *Gale Directory of Online, Portable, and Internet Databases.* Database on
> Dialog; also a two volume printed version; continues the former
> Cuadra Directory of Databases.

> *Online/CD-ROM Business Information.* Bowker-Saur. Approximately
> monthly news, evaluations and in-depth 'test drives' of new sources,
> also available from the publisher's web site.

> *Online/CD-ROM Business Sourcebook 1999.* Pam Foster (ed.). Headland,
> 1999. Directory of 'the most important' UK, U.S., European and other

business databases. Databases are arranged by subject, e.g. company directories, company financial data, market data; some subdivided by country covered. Each is described.

The Online Manual: A Practical Guide to Business Databases, 6th edn. L. Amor (ed.). Learned Information, 1997. Indexes to, and descriptions of over 1000 databases and 30 hosts.

4.2 CD-ROMs

Business and Legal CD-ROMs in Print. Mecklermedia. Annual.

4.3 Government information services

Business Information from Government. Liz Lampard. Headland, 1998. Directs the user to the appropriate department etc.

4.4 Business statistics

Government Statistics: A Brief Guide to Sources. Office for National Statistics, 1996.

Guide to Official Statistics, 6th edn. HMSO, 1996. Not limited to business statistics.

Sources of Unofficial UK Statistics, 3rd edn. D. Mort. Gower, 1997. Not limited to business statistics.

Statistical Data Locators – http://www.ntu.edu.sg/library/statdata.htm. A starting point for a wide range of economic and marketing statistics on most countries, especially in the Far East.

Webstat – http://www.irnxxx.co.uk/webstat.html IRN/. Information Research Network's web gateway to electronic statistical information; available on subscription.

World Directory of Non-official Statistical Sources. Euromonitor, 2nd edn., 1998.

4.5 Organisations

Directory of British Associations and Associations in Ireland, 13th edn. S.P.A. Henderson & A.J.W. Henderson (eds.). CBD Research Ltd., 1996. Much used subject guide.

International Directory of Business Information Sources and Services. Europa, 1996. Covers only organisations.

World Directory of Trade and Business Associations, 2nd edn. Euromonitor, 1997.

4.6 In periodicals

Guide to Special Issues and Indexes of Periodicals, 4th edn. M. Uhlan and D.B. Katz (eds.). Special Libraries Association, 1994. Enables identification of 'hidden' directories, company ranking lists, etc.

4.7 Directories

> *Guide to Directories at the Science Reference and Information Service*, 3rd edn. J. Gilbert (ed.). British Library SRIS, 1991.
>
> *Current British Directories.* C.A.P. Henderson, rev. S. Murphy. CBD Research, 1993. Not limited to business directories.

4.8 Telephone directories

> *Globalyp* (*http://www.globalyp.com/world.htm*); *555-1212* (*http://www.555-1212.com/*); *Whowhere?* (*http://www.whowhere.lycos.com/*). Web gateways to business and personal telephone and other directories, and other sources.

Services

In the following sections, services primarily concerned with library and information provision appear under 'Information Services'. Those more associated with advice and other forms of business support, whether or not they are also information providers, appear under the heading 'Advice and Support Services'.

Information Services

In-house versus External Services

Many of the information management tasks identified earlier in the chapter imply the existence of an in-house service. Almost all large or information-intensive businesses do have designated knowledge or information managers and services, but there remains the option of buying-in the more day-to-day professional services. As will become apparent, many information brokers and public sector services exist for the business which either lacks its own provision or finds it more efficient to out-source anything but a core of functions. The most successful businesses, with the most impressive in-house services, make considerable use of external services of different kinds. When the streamlined in-house service is fully occupied in enquiries and monitoring involving core subjects and sources and any commercially sensitive enquiries, work on peripheral subjects or requiring less accessible sources and 'leg work' is often farmed out to brokers. Brokers are sometimes also used to independently check important information, and to contact third parties when anonymity is necessary. Some businesses, especially new and potentially short-lived franchise operations, buy in a very wide range of services; not only the bulk of ad hoc research and enquiry answering and monitoring but even a daily or weekly visit from the broker or consultant to process necessary in-house documents.

Information vis à vis Advice

A business problem cannot always be simply translated into information needs and then information solutions. Many problems can only be solved by imported *advice*, a combination of knowledge and expertise, or interpreted and applied information. Thus an information source or even an information service may provide relevant information, but not guidance on what to do with it in the context of the problem. This reveals an obvious limitation of conventional business information sources and services for some purposes. It partially explains the emphasis on analysis and interpretation in business information work, business persons' need for intermediaries who can share their own concerns, and the high fees commanded by management consultants for combining information with expertise to recommend solutions.

Small businesses short of in-house expertise and the means of buying it in are faced with a range of subsidised help which tends to be *either* of an information nature *or* of an advice nature. The information service types below may be excellent providers of specified sources, and information matching stated information needs, but cannot provide the advice element. Conversely, many of the types of advice providers listed below are not only limited in the scope of their advice, but compare poorly with the information specialists in terms of the information at their disposal. The UK Department of Trade and Industry's Business Link initiative is intended to bring together the information, advice and other components of support, at the same time as rationalising the provision for SMEs which has resulted from a diversity of funding bodies and initiatives.

Types of Information Service

Each of the following sections characterises an external provider of the sources and intermediary services identified earlier.

Information Brokers

Information brokers are assumed to be commercial intermediaries between sources and ultimate consumers. It is partly their profit motive which clearly distinguishes them, because many other services also charge for access to sources and for expertise. Information brokers are also distinguishable by their availability to any client, and still just about distinguishable by their independence from any particular set of information resources. One of their attractions is that their allegiance is to what the client is willing to pay for, rather than to their own organisational goals and limitations. As has been said in the section above, businesses have a choice between providing for their information needs in-house or through contracting out; a minority contract out the bulk of the work; however, the 'Business Information Resources Survey' cited below suggests that over 40% of in-house services farm out some work to brokers for the various reasons mentioned.

Business information brokers predominate in the 243 entries of the *Directory of European Information Brokers and Consultants, 1997* (of which 155 are British, 57 in Greater London). In the 'Subject expertise index' 69 brokers are listed under 'Company information', and 49 under 'Market information'. Among entries which are publishers or consultants rather than service providers, and public sector libraries and industry organisations which may or may not offer a fee-based information service amongst other services, less than a dozen British brokerage businesses have any significant size or national reputation. In the 'Business Information Resources Survey, 1998', other information services ranked The British Library BIS as the most used, with Disclosure First Contact second and FT Business Research Centre third (*Business Information Review* 15, March 1998, pp. 5-21).Of the top nine, four were separate businesses or at least separate units within commercial information providers; only one (SVP) was a truly independent information broker. For reasons of scale, access to shared in-house resources, as well as financial security, national reputation and authority, there are obvious advantages for brokers with accommodating parents. Organisations which can offer this range of advantages can be divided into two types: those where the relevant resources and expertise spin off publishing activities, and those where they spin off the provision of a broader library and information service.

Large information product providers (such as Disclosure, ICC and Financial Times Information) have access to diverse information resources to research their own publications, and there is little practical difference between information delivered to a number of purchasers as a publication and information delivered on demand to a single client. If the client prefers to pay for a question to be answered by the apparent expert, a provider may be happy to charge a premium for the time taken to use a combination of their own products and others to answer the question. For existing library and information services of national standing (such as the British Library's Business Information Service and the London Business School), it is a natural step to use the wide human and documentary resources to undertake paid work for a wider clientele alongside the mainstream free or subsidised services.

More numerous, but generally smaller, are the truly independent brokers: those whose main business activity is answering questions at a price. As the examples below show, these are usually one-person operations without significant information resources of their own to draw upon. They are often necessarily specialised in terms of subject expertise and client base, taking advantage of online and public collections of business information sources. They sometimes use the name *information consultant* to show their willingness to solve business problems, or to advise on information management or actually carry out professional work in the client's organisation.

A few examples of both types of brokerage related to larger parent organisations follow, as well as of independent brokers:

Brokers with private sector information provider parents

Financial Times Business Research Centre

Long-established, large wide-ranging service. Payment for work can be ad hoc or by account. The service emphasises its large human and documentary resources, and ability to undertake in-depth research on competitors, markets, products etc., to produce structured reports to clients' requirements.

Disclosure First Contact

Member of Primark Corporation which includes global company information provider Disclosure and financial information provider Datastream. Works with the worldwide network of Disclosure Information Centres to offer a comprehensive business information service, emphasising access to online resources, including Datastream, and external documentary and library and industry resources (further details below).

Brokers with library and information service parents

London Business School Information Service

A middle-sized, long-established and broad scope service ranked highly in user surveys.

Manchester Business School Business Information Service

Offering a 'fast, responsive, fexible, and confidential service' using the staff skills and internal and external resourcers of the Business School library. Typical of their kind, services include information broking, competitive monitoring consultancy, and day visits to the library by subscribers.

Business Link Hertfordshire

A broad scope fee-based information service complements the variety of services provided by individual members to their users and to the Business Link.

Independent brokers

SVP

A unique example of a multinational business information broker. Though SVP United Kingdom is quite small, it can call upon the resources of SVP International network in some 14 other countries. SVP offers subscribers consultancy, document delivery, product pick-up and monitoring, as well as research on any business topic.

Informed Business Services: Informed Research Services

Based in London, the company has separate Research, Consultancy, Recruitment and Training divisions.

Lynne Clitheroe Business Information Service

'A qualified researcher in business information and an experienced user of statistical data ...' who was an information specialist at Warwick University Business Information Service. Offers the Rapid Response Enquiry Service, training courses and additional services, 'utilising extensive hard copy collections, CD-ROMs and the Internet'. One of many one-person or small firms, offering information brokerage, consultancy, and/or on-site professional services; often without their own business premises or significant in-house resources.

Information broking has generally increased in the UK since the 1980s, although periods of economic recession have caused some very lean years. When they first became prominent, brokers were unique among services in their ability to exploit business databases and to pass the costs of doing so on to the wealthier and more aware businesses. They were also the only service providers not rooted to a finite collection of resources, and willing to devote the necessary time to research and interpret data in the way those businesses expected. As businesses themselves, most brokers knew how to promote the information use to clients, to relate to them person to person, and to respond with the flexibility, time scales and delivery methods expected in business. Public sector services have followed the brokers' lead, and partly through gaining permission to levy fees for services over and above the existing basic level, have caught up in many of these respects. Despite having to cost their services completely realistically, commercial brokers still have a niche of subject specialism, and dedication and flexibility to clients' needs and service standards. Extracts from Disclosure First Contact's promotional literature highlight business information brokers' perceived selling points:

> 'We undertake all manner of enquiries ranging from quick turnaround requests to detailed projects. Former projects have included assessing total food consumption in Europe in ECUs, calculating the average size of a bingo hall and looking at the future penetration of Teletext in the UK. We offer a flexible information service tailored to meet the needs of all clients.

> All members of the team have backgrounds in business information and are trained to identify the most efficient, effective and economic means of obtaining the relevant data. Our extensive knowledge base is complemented by a variety of hard copy directories, online sources and contacts in industry.

All research is conducted confidentially and as members of the European Information Brokers Network (EIRENE) we abide by the Code of Practice for Information brokers, supported by the EC, ensuring you receive a professional and personal service at all times.'

National Libraries

The British Library, in London, has the widest remit and collections, and the National Libraries of Scotland and Wales, in Edinburgh and Aberystwyth, more limited policies. By virtue of their legal deposit collections of British material, and their capital city locations, the British Library developed its Business Information Service (BLBIS) in 1982, followed by the National Library of Scotland's Scottish Business Information Service in 1989. The British Library wished to maximise the current information value of the comprehensive collection of British printed material, until then mainly exploited by information brokers on behalf of businesses. Hence the rather radical step for them of gathering together into an open access collection all the materials considered business information, supplementing it by purchases of foreign material, and promoting both the collection and the enquiry service which had been set up. The BLBIS soon discovered that its role was limited without access to the rapidly-expanding electronic versions of sources – not available under legal deposit – and without the human resources to undertake enquiries involving time-consuming research and analysis. Thus a fee-based service was introduced in 1988, and a pattern set which was soon followed by other public sector libraries, including the National Library of Scotland. This extract from BLBIS promotional material (on the web site – *http://portico.bl.uk/*) first shows the basic free service, then a fee-based research service compatible with commercial brokers. The self-service option and free quick enquiry services make such public sector services potentially very attractive to smaller businesses, though few can conveniently visit and very much need the quick enquiry service:

> *BLBIS services free to all*
> 'BIS holds the most comprehensive collection of business information literature in the UK. This includes market research reports and journals, directories, company annual reports; trade and business journals, house journals, trade literature and CD-ROM services.
>
> Business literature published in the UK is collected as comprehensively as possible; items published elsewhere are taken selectively. BIS aims to cover the manufacturing, wholesale trading, retailing and distribution aspects of major industries and the following service sectors: financial services, energy, environment, transport, and food and drink.

The BIS reading room is open to anyone needing access to business information. There are no formal admission procedures: readers are simply asked to sign the visitors' book to show they will abide by the conditions of entry. Assistance is available from staff to direct readers to the most appropriate sources and help them start their research.

The British Library Lloyds Bank Business Line is a "quick" enquiry telephone service which is partially funded by sponsorship from Lloyds Bank. . . .'

BLBIS fee-based Research Service
'Commercial rates are charged for more in-depth research projects. These might include market overviews, detailed company profiles, news stories, competitor tracking and compiling lists of suppliers and manufacturers. BIS has access to a broad range of UK and international databases (both online and CD-ROM) in addition to the collections of business material in the Library. Staff are also able to offer clients a business document supply service based on the BIS collections.

BIS charges an hourly rate of £82+VAT for UK customers, £88 for overseas customers. If the enquiry involves online searching, the charges are based on three elements – staff time, database connect time and output of results. Database charges vary from host to host and database to database. If the enquiry involves searching the business collections, the charges are based on two elements – staff time and the cost of supplying photocopies of relevant articles. Further information on charges is available on request.'

Public Libraries

What local authority library and information services lack in documentary resources by comparison with national libraries and information brokers is potentially compensated for by local knowledge and presence, and experience of serving businesses. 'Commercial' sections existed in cities like Glasgow, Manchester, Liverpool, Westminster and in the City of London since around the time of the First World War, and according to a survey, 65% of all UK local authorities had created formal business information services by 1990 (Diana Edmonds, 'Without the city wall.' *Refer* 6, Summer 1990, pp. 7-10, 23). In the 1980s much research on the business information role of public libraries was funded through governments' concern for small businesses, because of their role in the economy and in employment. The result is services in the pattern of the British Library, and emulating information brokers' strengths in promotion, personal contact, speed, and confidentiality. It has meant coming to terms with expensive online sources, and with the consequences of charging for time-intensive research and monitoring services. Public libraries may be recouping very little of the hoped for revenue towards providing these services, but their role in subsidising information for small local businesses is important. The viability of county services has been threatened by the creation of smaller, single tier authorities; the four successors of Clwyd in Wales have not all been able to match the former Businessline Clwyd. Public library authority services launched in the 1990s include:

> Information for Business (City of Westminster – the first public library fee-based service)
> Business Information Point (Hertfordshire County Council Libraries)
> Information Direct (Birmingham's fee-based service)
> Business Information Focus (City of London's City Business Library fee-based service)
> DataDirect (Cambridgeshire)
> Business Information Service (London Borough of Bromley)
> Business Users Service (Glasgow)
> Marketing Advice Centre (Newcastle)
> Business Information Service (West Sussex)
> Rural Business Information Service (Somerset)
> Business Key (Wiltshire)

Scope and services of Business Information Point, Hertfordshire (from the web site – http://hertslib.hertscc.gov.uk/bipindex.htm)

> 'The Business Information Point is the largest business library in Hertfordshire, England. It is an integral part of the Central Resources Library in Hatfield. We are happy to help anyone living, working or studying in Hertfordshire, England and those wanting information on Hertfordshire companies.

Uses
'The Business Information Point has information that can give you the power to:
– succeed in that interview
– start your own business
– run your business more successfully
– find information about possible suppliers
– learn about your competitors
– investigate markets
– tap into Europe - and the rest of the world'.

Resources
Principal sources of:
– market research
– financial information
– company contact details
– industry-specific information
– current awareness
– statistics
– contracts and tenders
– management practice and theory
– overseas trading information
– contacts
Periodical sources
European Information
Standards

The Library Association's 'Business Information Survey' of 1997 found these services growing in usage and appreciation by their users (*Library Association Record* 99(12), p. 665). Of the 635 clients interviewed, 19% were self-employed, and 60% workers in small businesses. Many of them described the huge tangible benefits that had resulted from use of their public library business information service, grouped in descending order as:

> Gained new clients
> Altered marketing strategy
> Introduced new product/service
> Increased turnover
> Won contract
> Changed procedures/systems
> Avioded legal action
> Increased workforce
> Gained access to grant

Nevertheless the public libraries' contribution has probably never reached its full potential. Neither their public funding nor incomes for added value services have been sufficient to do the necessary liaison with businesses, acquire or use the necessary sources, or devote the necessary professional time to in-depth research. Their actual and potential clientele is not the large, aware and successful firm familiar to information brokers, but 'reluctant' information users who need a subsidised service but who are unlikely to identify their problems with what a public library offers. The public library's contribution to business may be increased under the Business Link umbrella, discussed below.

Industry Organisations

Organisations created and supported by businesses themselves have the advantage that business are familiar with them, and naturally turn to them for services. Among a range of services to members, some national and local bodies offer sophisticated business information.

- *Local Level*
  At a local level, chambers of commerce, trade or industry typically serve members by promoting their businesses to each other and to the wider market, which may involve the creation and even publication of a local trade directory. Some larger chambers provide far more facilities and services, free, subsidised, or at full cost. Some have recently developed substantial business information services, as their adverts for information managers reveal:

  > '**Manchester Chamber of Commerce and Industry** is the largest association of businesses in the North West, and business information is seen as an important resource by

its members . . . Principal duties will include supervision of two information officers in the operation of a busy telephone enquiry service; management and development of the library and in-house databases; maintenance and development of fee-based services, using online databases and desk research; initiation and management of income generating projects.'

'Due to its rapid growth the **Tyne and Wear Chamber of Commerce** requires an Information Manager . . .'

'**CCi Thames Chiltern** is one of the most progressive chambers of commerce and industry in the UK. We have recently launched a new business information service, CCi Search and are now seeking an Information Manager to run it.'

- *National Level*
  The 'Voice of British business', the Confederation of British Industry, makes the Enquiry Desk in Centre Point, Oxford Street, London the contact point for members' enquiries, drawing on the Information Centre and other units as necessary. Members of the Institute of Directors can use its sophisticated library and information service to satisfy their own or their firm's information needs. Both the Institute of Personnel and Development and the Institute of Management (formerly BIM) offer members substantial information services. National bodies are also created to serve and represent particular industries, such as the Chartered Institute of Marketing. Those organisations include information provision among their membership services, often based on substantial physical and human information resources. Infomark is the Chartered Institute of Marketing's '. . . comprehensive library and information service created by the marketing professionals for marketing professionals. . . Whether a member of a corporate marketing team, a marketing or management consultant, or an agency account planner or handler, Infomark should be your first port of call'.

Other Types of Information Service

Although separate sections above are devoted to the larger and more obvious categories of business information service provider, several others should also be mentioned. Many academic institutions offer an information service to businesses, not only as information brokers, but more often by allowing local business people access to relevant library collections, facilities and enquiry services.

- *Government Libraries and Other Information Resources*
  Certain government libraries and government departments are equally valuable sources of business information, especially concerning legislation and regulation, trade, business statistics, and overseas conditions and marketing opportunities. The DTI's public Export Market Information Centre was referred to in the market information chapter, but there are many more sources of expert and specialist information, as described in directories such as *Business Information from Government* (L. Lampard [ed.]. Headland, 1998).

- *European Information Centres*
  The European Commission contributes another national layer of information service to business in the form of European Business Information Centres, subsequently known as Euro Info Centres or EICs. Throughout Europe approximately 200 EICs are jointly funded and operated with bodies such as local authorities and chambers of commerce; with over 20 in Britain, there are far fewer of them than there are local authorities and, sensibly, many are operated in parallel with their host's own business information service. EICs offer small firms relevant information emanating from the EC itself, and information to help them work with firms and markets in other EU states. In 1989 WYEBIC (West Yorkshire European Business Information Centre) adopted the standard brief – to open up a market of 320 million consumers to its local businesses:

  > Objectives: To ensure a two-way flow of information from the Commission towards businesses, notifying them of EC projects and decisions concerning them; and from business towards the commission in order to give the latter a better understanding of SME's concerns . . . To guide and support businesses in their efforts to participate in various EC programmes and financing schemes and in public contracts.

  > Resources: Community documents selected for their relevance to business, plus bulletins of EC news. Access to databases provided by the European Commission and other institutions. Network of EICs, via electronic mail link or direct contacts. Training provided by Brussels. Back-up project team in Brussels, including information officers.

Advice and Support Services

In drawing up the Business Information Plan for Scotland in 1993, small businesses were asked which organisations they regularly approached for information. Their response was sobering for libraries and others considering themselves the specialist information providers:

% of respondents citing each external information source

District or regional councils	54%
Banks	47%
Trade associations	47%
Local enterprise companies	47%
Professional advisers	44%
Chambers of commerce	41%
Regional enterprise agencies	31%
Public library	31%
Academic etc. library	31%
Enterprise trust	19%
National Library	10%

As well as library and information services, and professional advisers, many businesses in Britain have the following agencies locally available to them:

Training and Enterprise Councils
European Information Centres
Local authority business development departments
Enterprise zones
Small business clubs
College and university small firm units
Co-operative development agencies
Government departments and agencies
Agencies for economically disadvantaged groups

This amounts to a potentially generous, but more likely potentially confusing and piecemeal situation. In terms of quality, the Scottish respondents actually ranked the information from the libraries mentioned higher than most of the other agencies. There are unclear boundaries between information, advice and other support services; between commercial, subsidised and free services; and about which authorities are behind which services. To get the help they need, businesses are faced with splitting up their problem according to the contribution each agency might make, deal with a number of agencies, then put the results together afterwards. Moves towards co-operation, if not integration, between service providers are clearly very necessary.

Co-operation in Service Provision

Local

Information services have always engaged in co-operative efforts to share resources across organisational and geographical boundaries. Many formal local co-operatives were set up between public, academic, private sector and other libraries in counties or smaller areas, primarily to pool technical information – hence the 'T' in names like HATRICS (Hampshire), LUTIS (Luton), NANTIS (Nottinghamshire), and HERTIS (Hertfordshire). Those co-operatives still in existence are concerned as much now with business information as technical information.

Library and Information Plans (LIPS) are attempts inspired by the Office of Arts and Libraries to map and co-ordinate British regions' information resources. Although primarily involving public-sector resources, co-ordination and resource-sharing benefits inevitably extend to business information. It must be said that Business Links at a more local level, and the Business Information Network at the UK level (both discussed below), have had more impact.

Public-public or public-private joint ventures of various patterns have been initiated by public sector libraries as a means of achieving the required level of service to business. Examples include: HERTIS (Hertfordshire County Library and Hatfield Polytechnic [now University of Herfordshire]); Information in Business (Leicestershire County Library and Leicester Polytechnic [now De Montfort University]); and Suffolk County Library's contracting out of their business enquiry service to a freelance information broker.

National

It is only since the British Library took the lead in establishing the Business Information Network that there could be said to be a system of national referral and resource sharing in business information. The BIN is said to constitute a national LIP, as well as a subject or sectoral LIP. BIN was founded in 1991 with a full-time Network Manager based at BLBIS. In 1992 private sector libraries and information services were also accepted, by which time membership was over 60. BIN is supported primarily by corporate members annual subscriptions. BIN's networking role is facilitated by its *Directory of Members*, and use by members of its *Business Information Network Referral Database*. BIN has been funded by the European Commission to pilot a European version of itself, using Internet technology.

The Association of British Chambers of Commerce maintains an electronic national business information network 'Chambernet'. As well as facilitating resource sharing and communication, Chambernet effectively combines individual Chamber's member company directories into one national database.

European

The advent of the Single Market, single European currency and globalisation of business in general, has inspired correspondingly wide co-operative efforts among information services. The European Business Library and Information Network (EBLIN) links the business information services of the public libraries of around 30 major European cities. The European Information Researchers Network (EIRENE) has established common standards for the information brokers who are members, and, partly through its *Directory of Members*, serves to promote national expertise to users in other countries. The European Business School Librarians Group represents communication and cooperation between academic business information providers, some of which have very important collections, and operate fee-based services. Eurochambres is an association of more than 1,200 Chambers of Commerce and Industry, in 31 European countries plus Israel. Together they represent 14 million businesses of which 95% are SMEs. The growing European Chamber Network promises to electronically link the UK Chambernet with other similar national initiative, to create a huge and valuable information resource. Especially as in many European countries the chambers are the primary source of statutorily disclosed company data.

Integration of Information, Advice and Support: the Business Link Initiative

Figure 21. Norfolk and Waveney Business Link Home page

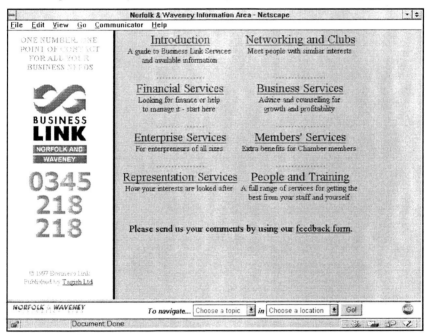

In 1992 the Business Link concept was to improve the impact of business of business information and advice available to firms by co-ordinating the efforts of at least some of the diverse national and local services. In 1994 the DTI's Business Link Prospectus was accurate in concluding for most areas of the UK: 'Firms still face a welter of advice and information of variable quality from a confusing maze of agencies whose services often appear to be in competition with each other'. 'Information and advice' was given at the top of the list of services to be co-ordinated, elements which to date had rarely been adequately provided by any single agency. The term 'one-stop shop' was much used in 1992, and continues to be cited in the Small Firms Minister's 1997 paper *Enhanced Business Links – A Vision for the 21st Century*.

Throughout England contracts have since been drawn up between government and consortia of partners led by the Training and Enterprise Councils, so that there are hundreds of separate Business Link Partnerships. Wales has gone for a rather different approach, with a country-wide 'Business Connect' system, managed in their areas by the seven TECs. Just as for TECS themselves, effectiveness in Business Links is known to be variable, and to depend partly on the quality of the local provision already available, and on which providers have become Business Link partners. Successful Business Links either already include an established business information service, and/or have appointed professionally qualified staff to create one, which is usually at the centre of the enquiry management and referral or answering system. Reviews are also showing that success relates to the degree of commitment of partners to the Business Link brand name and concept, to the creation of service agreements by partners, detailing what they will do for Business Link clients as opposed to their own, and at what cost. Effectiveness of course also depends on partners showing genuine commitment to the concept through promotion of other partner's services, and channelling of enquiries to them. More specifically, success also depends on the remit, in the supplement to the original Prospectus, of Personal Business Advisors to 'maintain regular contact with a portfolio of companies and construct an integral package of services to meet their needs'. Direct personal liaison with firms is not only an opportunity to deliver business information and diverse other services, but absolutely necessary to overcome firms' reluctance to approach the services which can help them.

Business Link Tyneside was established with the fairly typical range of partner providers listed here; surprise was expressed in the information professional press that Newcastle Public Library's established business information service appeared to have been overlooked:

> Tyneside Training and Enterprise Council (Lead partner)
> Local authorities (Gateshead, Newcastle, N. Tyneside, S. Tyneside)
> Enterprise agencies (Entrust, TEDCO, Project North East)
> Regional Technology Centre
> Tyne and Wear Development Corporation
> Northern Development Company
> Department of Trade and Industry
> Tyne and Wear Chamber of Commerce

The following is a model of the business support services typically provided in any given area of the UK, and the way they can be co-ordinated under the Business Link umbrella:

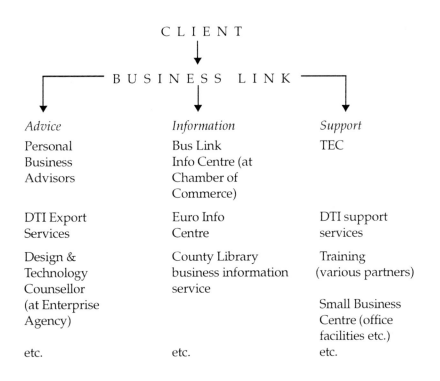

Figure 22. Business Link service model based on Thames Valley Business Link

In some of the most successful Business Links, enquiries of all kinds are channelled to a central point for analysis by staff who include information professionals. They respond from resources held by or known to them, and/or channel the enquiry to the relevant partner organisation. However, in the very well-developed Heart of England Business Link, based in Slough, all Business Link enquiries pass through a 'gateway' and a 'client management system'. They are analysed there by experienced but not information qualified staff, to be passed to the appropriate information or other specialist partner. In fact simpler enquiries are passed to a public library business information service which offers a free service, and those requiring research passed to the Thames Valley CCI business information service and European Information Centre, which contributes a fee-based service for Business Link users who are not CCI members.

Gaining 'The Knowledge': Sources of Further Information, Organisations, Education and Training

Sources of assistance on business information itself include documents which can be consulted, organisations which can be joined, and full-time or short courses. This final section provides examples of all three, in sufficient detail to be followed up.

Books

Information management

David Nicholas. *Information Management for Business.* Aslib, 1996. An edition in the Know How Guide series, on the components of information services for business people.

Information searching

Adrian Arthur Quick Guide to Online Commands, 1987. IIS for the UK Online User Group, 1987

Karen Blakeman. *Search Strategies for the Internet.* RBA Information Services, 1988. Includes: matching search tools to enquiries; how to locate company web pages; finding individuals; country specific information; PC software, intelligent agents.

Karen Blakeman. *Business Information on the Internet.* RBA Information Services, 1997.

M. Burke and H. Hall. *Navigating Business Information Sources: A Practical Guide for Library and Information Managers.* Library Association, 1998. Up to date, relevant for UK practitioners, addresses each of the standard categories of business information.

Hartley, R.J. et al. *Online Searching: Principles and Practice.* Bowker-Saur, 1990.

N. Spencer. *How to Find Information – Business: A Guide to Searching in Published Sources.* British Library SRIS, 1995. Primarily a bibliographical aid to matching standard sources to common enquiries. Each chapter concisely introduces a category (such as: company activities; company financial information; suppliers/manufacturers of products), and gives selective sources.

Services

It is difficult to cite an overview of business information services; however, the following is a practical guide to setting up in-house services:

S. P. Webb. *Creating an Information Service*, 3rd edn. Aslib, 1996.

Periodicals

Periodicals on business information are slightly more plentiful. *Business Information Review* in particular includes in-depth articles by specialist practitioners on issues such as company financial sources, or the use of information brokers. Others range from the news organ to the bibliographical service or buyer's guide, where information on new commercial sources predominates.

Business Information Review. Headland. Quarterly; printed or via the web. The most important UK source of articles and current awareness on business information.

European Business Intelligence Briefing. Headland. Monthly; printed or via the web. A newsletter which notes and evaluates new business information sources on Europe.

Free Pint. Willco (information consultancy – *http://www.freepint.com/*). Free periodical, emailed to subscribers, or accessible via web site. News and articles on web information resources and techniques, often involving business information.

Information World Review. Headland. Quarterly periodical containing substantial articles on business information sources and services; unmatched coverage for the UK business information user.

Journal of Business and Finance Librarianship. Haworth Press. Quarterly, articles on both sources and information management issues.

What's New in Business Information. Headland. 20 issues per year; printed or via the web. A newsletter reporting and analysing developments in business information sources.

Managing Information. Aslib. A practical periodical, aimed at business people as well as information professionals, so much of the content concerns business information sources and management. The large proportion of space devoted to news items includes relevant electronic product reviews.

Electronic Discussion Groups and List Servers

Not least in the area of information management, free, loosely-controlled, electronic notice boards and discussion platforms are eclipsing formal periodicals in circulation and currency. Nevertheless the only notable one dedicated to business information is the US oriented buslib-1 (email: listserv@idbsu.edu or usenet group: bit.listserv.buslib-1). Newsgroups relating to specific business or business information subjects or countries can be traced using *Reference.COM*'s searchable Directories of newsgroups and mailing lists (*http://www.reference.com*).

Professional Organisations

While membership of the Library Association is necessary to join their special interest groups, most of the more business-information-oriented organi-

sations can be joined directly. Whether or not they hold a professional qualification, information workers gain from formal and informal networking
with people with similar work interests. Many of the following bodies hold
professional and social meetings, arrange visits, courses and conferences,
and organise resource sharing benefits. It has been impossible to confirm
that all the specialised groups listed below are active:

> *General*
> Aslib Economics and Business Information Group
> Library Association Industrial and Commercial Libraries Group
> Library Association Information Services Group
>
> *Specialised*
> Accountancy Librarians Information Group
> Advisory Services for Small and Medium Sized Industry (Interna-
> tional Federation for Documentation; FID/ASSMI)
> Bank Librarians Group
> British Business School Librarians Group
> Chamber Information Specialists Group (i.e. Chambers of Commerce)
> City Information Group (CIG; Institute of Information Scientists;
> London centred))
> European Business Schools' Librarians Group
> European Information Researchers Network (EIRENE; for Informa-
> tion Brokers)
> Insurance Librarians and Information Officers Group
> Society for Competitive Intelligence Professionals in Europe
> Special Interest Group on Banking, Finance and Insurance (Interna-
> tional Federation for Documentation; FID/BFI)

Education and Training

Most of the 18 UK university departments of information and library studies offer at least an optional module as a minor component of their bachelors and first qualification masters degrees. As an example, Aberystwyth's
optional Business Information module constitutes 10 credits or one twelfth
of a typical year's study, and focusses on sources and their use. There is a
distance learning version, which is currently only available as an optional
part of the bachelors degree scheme. In several other institutions' departments business information is a larger component, and even appears in the
name of degrees. In some universities attention to business information is
facilitated by the location of ILS teaching in for instance a school of business studies. Business information has a high profile at City University, coinciding with that institution's location and particular mission.

The majority of business information posts are in the private sector, where relevant degrees and the professional qualifications which they can lead to are
rarely a prerequisite. In either sector and whether ILS graduates or not, few of
those joining the expanding business information workforce in the last dec-

ade, have studied even a module in the subject. This fact, together with the ever-changing nature of the subject, explains the wealth of short courses available from a wide variety of providers. One-day and sometimes longer packages are commonly used by commercial employers, as a conversion course to business information for new staff, particularly to the subjects, source types, and techniques prevalent in that institution. Training courses tend to deal with the sources appropriate to particular subjects (market information, company information and so on), to complex individual sources and retrieval systems (for example searching DataStar or exploiting the web), or relating information skills to business and business needs (for example the interpretation of company accounts). As the examples below also illustrate, some providers have a profit motive and others, such as the British Library Business Information Service, a promotion and training responsibility. Although the courses of professsional associations, such as the Library Association's Industrial Group, and Career Development Group, are less advertised and cheaper, the more commercial trainers typically charge £200 per day.

Examples of short courses (fees are as quoted for non-members in 1998):

> *On groups of sources*
> EU business information sources you may have missed (British Library SRIS; 1 day; £175).
> Business information: Russia and Eastern Europe (Aslib; 1 day; £275).
> Business databases on the Web (UK Online User Group; 1 day; £120.
> Company and business information on the Internet (British Library SRIS; 1 day; £160).
> News information: online, CD-ROM and Internet resources (British Library; 1 day; £175).
> Internet for business information (TFPL; 1/2 day; £125).
> Internet for insurance (TFPL; 1/2 day; £125).
>
> *On individual sources or systems*
> Searching DataStar on the Web (Dialog Corporation; series of half-day workshops, priced).
> Searching Dialog: The Basics(Dialog Corporation; one day priced course).
> Profound for Windows – Introduction and General Level (Dialog Corporation; 3 hour module, priced).
>
> *On information management and business*
> Doing business on the Internet (Informed Business Services; 1 day; £245).
> Competitor intelligence (TFPL; 1 day; £245).
> Intelligent agents: today's SDI (TFPL; 1/2 day; £125).
> Statistics for business (Aslib; 1 day; £290).

Appendix

Examples of Business Information Prices

The intention here is to give the full price, as advertised in at least one source. Please see the relevant sections in the final chapter for examples of costs of data from online hosts, and of training courses.

Information Sources

Market Information

Directory of Consumer Brands and Their Owners: Europe. Euromonitor, 1998.
  2 vols; £495.

IIS Tearsheets. Mintel Group.
  'Off the page' advertising tear sheet service; £300 per market category (e.g. alcoholic drinks), for Europe or USA.

Marketstat. Information Research Network.
  Ongoing syndicated market research on the online business information market. Standard service £5,800 per annum, Gold service £9,400 per annum.

Retail Opportunities in Turkey. Corporate Intelligence on Retailing, 1997.
  220 pages; £950.

World Database of Consumer Brands and Their Owners. Euromonitor, annual.
  CD-ROM; £995 to purchase, plus £150 per 1,000 addresses printed as mailing labels.

World Marketing Data and Statistics. Euromonitor, 1997 etc.
  CD-ROM; £556 single user, up to £1,388 for up to 50 users.

Company Information

Companies House Services Directory.
  CD-ROM updated monthly. £300 per annum. Microfiche copy of a company documents ('standard search') £5.00 by post, £3.50 in person.

FAME: Financial Analysis Made Easy. Bureau van Dijk. CD-ROM subscription including 12 updates; 1st installation £10,000 per annum, 2nd - 5th installation £7,500, additional to 5 installations £1,800.

Infocheck's *Global Scan* international company reports service (ordering and delivery by Internet or mail etc.). £36 per full report, or £5,000 per annum, plus £26 per report.

Jordanwatch company database. £9 per company credit report.

Key British Enterprises 1997. Dun & Bradstreet, 1997.

6 vols printed	£438
Above when purchased with CD	£295
CD *KBE50* read only	£495
CD *KBE50* print & view	£995
CD *KBE50* open access	£2,195
CD *KBE200* open access	£3,250

RM Online. aRMadillo.

Web-based UK company documents images service. Latest and up to 3 years £14 + VAT per company.

UK Quoted. Onesource.

CD-ROM of circa 2,200 quoted companies; subscription £8,500 per annum.

Financial Information

Financial Times on CD-ROM; monthly updates.

1998 subscription £1,425; archival disks £195 per year.

FT Prices on CD-ROM. Financial Times Electronic Publishing.

13 years of financial markets price and index data. Annual subscription including monthly updates £1350; single disk (private investors) £395.

News – Databases

FT McCarthy on CD-ROM. Financial Times Electronic Publishing.

Annual subscription, including monthly updates, £2,850.

News – Redistribution services

IBM's *InfoSage* (*http://www.infosage.ibm.com*).

News items redistributed from major business information providers, via web or email and corporate intranet if required, according to user profiles. $24.95 per month for up to 30 stories twice daily. September 1996 figures.

Industry Sources

East European Monitoring Service series. Business International.

Seven printed periodicals covering different chemical industry sectors, and 13 covering other industrial sectors. Subscription: £830 per monitor per year.

Country Information

EIU Viewswire.

> Online access to the Economist Intelligence Unit's country-specific data, via Reuters Business Briefing. US$4,800 per year, allowing access to up to 300 articles per month; unused credits carry over.

Summary of World Broadcasts. BBC Worldwide Ltd.

> Printed version posted to subscribers.Daily political reports: subscription £470 per year for each of 5 world regions. Weekly economic reports: £335 per region. Combined: £600 per region.

Bibliographical Tools

World Database of Business Information Sources on the Web. Euromonitor
> *http://www.euromonitor.com/srcintro.htm*
> £995/US$1,990 per year to subscribe to the web version.

Information Services

Brokers and fee-based services

British Library Business Information Service – subscription service.

> UK customers: £82 + VAT per research hour.

Index